Swift, the Book, and the
Irish Financial Revolution

Swift, the Book, and the Irish Financial Revolution

Satire and Sovereignty in Colonial Ireland

SEAN D. MOORE

The Johns Hopkins University Press

Baltimore

© 2010 The Johns Hopkins University Press
All rights reserved. Published 2010
Printed in the United States of America on acid-free paper
9 8 7 6 5 4 3 2 1

The Johns Hopkins University Press
2715 North Charles Street
Baltimore, Maryland 21218-4363
www.press.jhu.edu

Library of Congress Cataloging-in-Publication Data

Moore, Sean D.
    Swift, the book, and the Irish financial revolution : satire and sovereignty in Colonial Ireland /
Sean Moore.
        p.   cm.
    Includes bibliographical references and index.
    ISBN-13: 978-0-8018-9507-4 (hardcover : alk. paper)
    ISBN-10: 0-8018-9507-3 (hardcover : alk. paper)
    1. Swift, Jonathan, 1667–1745—Criticism and interpretation. 2. Satire, English—History and
criticism. 3. English literature—Irish authors—History and criticism. 4. National characteristics, Irish.
5. Ireland—History—Autonomy and independence movements. 6. Ireland—Economic conditions.
7. Book industries and trade—Ireland—History. I. Title.
    PR3728.S2M66 2010
    828'.509—dc22   2009052388

A catalog record for this book is available from the British Library.

*Special discounts are available for bulk purchases of this book. For more information, please contact
Special Sales at 410-516-6936 or specialsales@press.jhu.edu.*

The Johns Hopkins University Press uses environmentally friendly book materials, including recycled
text paper that is composed of at least 30 percent post-consumer waste, whenever possible. All of our
book papers are acid-free, and our jackets and covers are printed on paper with recycled content.

In memory of my mother, Joanne M. Moore

CONTENTS

It is a pleasure to acknowledge my indebtedness to a great many people and institutions who have helped me with this book directly or indirectly. The patience and dedication of Srinivas Aravamudan, who supervised it as a dissertation, were crucial to its completion. Neil DeMarchi, Michael Moses, Thomas Pfau, James Thompson, and Jennifer Thorn provided help with it when it was in its infancy. The comments of Janet Aikins Yount, Sarah Sherman, and Katherine Gillen helped transform it into a book, and the members of the University of New Hampshire Eighteenth-Century Interdisciplinary Seminar, especially Nadine Bérenguier, Burt Feintuch, Jan Golinski, Ed Larkin, Michael Ferber, and David Watters, furnished a friendly forum in which to rehearse its argument. I am grateful to Brigitte Bailey, Jane Bellamy, Dennis Britton, Tom Carnicelli, Monica Chiu, Walter Eggers, Burt Feintuch, Diane Freedman, Robin Hackett, Betty Hageman, Delia Konzett, James Krasner, Doug Lanier, Lisa MacFarlane, Courtney Marshall, Martin McKinsey, Petar Ramadanovic, Siobhán Senier, Sandhya Shetty, Rachel Trubowitz, Cord Whitaker, Reginald Wilburn, and many other members of the UNH English literature faculty for their collegial support. I also received much encouragement from my colleagues in creative writing, journalism, linguistics, and composition: Cristy Beemer, Mary Clark, Jessica Enoch, John Ernest, Sue Hertz, Shelly Lieber, John Lofty, Paul and Aya Matsuda, Mekeel McBride, Andrew Merton, Lisa Miller, Thomas Newkirk, Christina Ortmeier-Hooper, Alex Parsons, Thomas Payne, David Rivard, and Charles Simic. This book would not have been possible without the daily assistance of the staff of the UNH English department: Janine Auger, Roxanne Brown, Carla Cannizzaro, Jennifer Dubé, Susan Dumais, Dawn Haines, Tory Poulin, and Joy Winston.

For inspiring this project, I thank the conveners of two Folger Institute seminars on Irish political thought, Jane Ohlmeyer and Sean Connolly, and the following seminar participants: Frank Boyle, Clare Carroll, Scott Cummings, Christopher Fox, Edward Furgol, David Green, Jacqueline

Hill, James Kelly, Patrick Kelly, Catriona Logan, Charles Ludington, Robert Mahony, Ian McBride, George O'Brien, Leigh Tillman Partington, James Patterson, Linda Levy Peck, John Pocock, Lahney Preston, Eileen Reilly, Jim Smyth, and Iain Valentine. Folger seminars convened by Bruce Smith, David Kastan, David Armitage, and Luke Gibbons also helped develop this work. Carol Brobeck, Richard Kuhta, Kathleen Lynch, Barbara Mowat, Sarah Werner, and Owen Williams of the Folger Institute facilitated my participation in these seminars.

In Dublin, the University of Notre Dame's Keough Centre for Irish Studies provided offices, books, and contacts that enabled my primary documentary research. There, Seamus Deane, Luke Gibbons, Dáire Keogh, Katie Keogh, Helen O'Connell, and Kevin Whelan gave me invaluable support. Máire Kennedy of the Dublin Corporation Library at Pearse Street and the staffs of the National Library of Ireland, the Royal Irish Academy, the Marsh Library at St. Patrick's Cathedral, and the Manuscripts Room and Early Printed Books Room at Trinity College were very helpful in pointing me to items in their holdings. Louis Cullen and David Dickson gave me the opportunity to present my research at a seminar in Modern Irish History at Trinity College. Michael Brown, Charles Ivar McGrath, and many other Irish historians helped me track down eighteenth-century Irish primary sources.

This project has also been shaped by several international seminars and colloquia. The Fifth Münster Symposium on Jonathan Swift, convened by Hermann Real of the University of Münster in 2006, provided me with the opportunity to present my work to leading Swift scholars too numerous to name here. Robert Mahony, who organizes the Dublin Symposium on Jonathan Swift at St. Patrick's Cathedral, invited me to vet my work there in 2004. I am grateful to the organizers of the Money, Power, and Print colloquium series, Rick Kleer, Christopher Fauske, and Charles Ivar McGrath, for providing a forum for a discussion of the British Financial Revolution. I also thank the participants in those colloquia: John Bergin, Arne Bialuschewski, Jill Bradbury, Michael Brown, Linda Bomstad, Noel Chevalier, Dwight Codr, Chrysta Collins, Christine Desan, J. A. Downie, Catherine Eagleton, Christopher Finlay, Natasha Glaiyser, Joyce Goggin, Hugh Goodacre, Farley Grubb, Neil Guthrie, James Hartley, Charles Larkin, Anne Laurence, Eoin Magennis, Anthony Malcomson, Anne Murphy, Steven Pincus, Helen Julia Paul, Martyn Powell, Stephen Timmons, Paul Tonks, Carl Wennerlind, and Patrick Walsh.

The Duke University English Department and Graduate School of Arts and Sciences underwrote this project from the outset, and I thank the staff and faculty for this critical contribution. The Fulbright Scholarship board awarded me a grant to perform my research in Ireland, and for that I am eternally grateful. For funding to attend scholarly meetings and otherwise complete this book, I thank the University of New Hampshire's English Department, College of Liberal Arts, Graduate School of Arts and Sciences, Center for International Education, Center for the Humanities, Office of the Provost, and Cambridge Summer Program. I am also grateful for a fellowship at the John Carter Brown Library at Brown University which provided me with the time and resources to write. Librarians Ted Widmer and Susan Danforth, as well as fellowships coordinator Valerie Andrews, were especially helpful. The staff of Georgetown University's Lauinger Library and the University of New Hampshire's Dimond Library have unceasingly provided support for my research. In addition, I am grateful to the editorial boards of *Eighteenth-Century Ireland*, *Atlantic Studies*, and *PMLA* for publishing portions of Chapters 2, 4, and 5, respectively. I also thank Lynn Festa and Dan Carey for reading part of the third chapter. The members of C18-L, a listserve in eighteenth-century studies moderated by Kevin Berland, answered innumerable queries related to this project.

I am most grateful to the Johns Hopkins University Press for undertaking publication of this book. Michael Lonegro had faith in it from the beginning, and Trevor Lipscombe, Matthew McAdam, Greg Nicholl, Anne Whitmore, Robin Rennison, and other staff have seen it through to completion. To Jack and Lea Angell, as well as Trish, Mary, Michael, Tom, Helen, Frank, F. Eugene, and Terry Moore, and many other friends, I owe a debt of gratitude for both tangible and intangible support. Special thanks are due to my friend Brad Reich. The encouragement of my wife, Jessica, and my son, James, has been fundamental to the completion of this book.

NOTE TO READER

Most passages of Swift's prose works quoted in the text of this book are taken from *The Prose Works of Jonathan Swift*, fourteen volumes edited by Herbert Davis and published by Blackwell between 1939 and 1968. Citations are given by volume and page numbers in this edition.

Many dates in this book are given in "old style," the Julian calendar in which the new year began on 25 March, because the Gregorian calendar was not adopted in the English-speaking world until 1752, seven years after Jonathan Swift's death.

Swift, the Book, and the
Irish Financial Revolution

Introduction

Ireland, the Fiscal-Military State, and the Colonial Print Media

Eighteenth-century Ireland was locked in a struggle with the British "fiscal-military state," an imperialist political system in which the government provided military support to joint stock companies seeking to expand their trading networks.[1] Wars were waged to open colonial markets, which not only enhanced the private profits of these companies but also, by bringing ever-increasing portions of the globe, including Ireland, under the control of the British Empire, raised the tax revenues that financed the government's civil and military operations.[2] The fiscal-military state was a consequence of the English financial revolution of the early eighteenth century, a "synthesis of sovereignty and capital" made politically possible by the Glorious Revolution of 1688.[3] The financial revolution consisted of the founding of the Bank of England in 1694, its dissemination of its banknotes as currency, and its management of a national debt by which a permanent standing army and navy could be financed. Jonathan Swift was among the first to comment on the political implications of these developments, articulating how paper credit—a term for the stock certificates, public bonds, and paper currency that began to be circulated at this time—fueled the emerging imperial war machine. These new paper forms of money, many of which were debt obligations that the government owed to joint stock companies, became his "favourite topic" for political polemic because, in his view, these creditors were taking advantage of the state's indebtedness to influence public policy.[4] The debt enabled them to own large portions of the taxes levied on the British and Irish people in perpetuity, effectively forcing the government to act on their behalf and not for all taxpayers. Swift was especially conscious of the deleterious effects of these developments on the sovereignty of government over commercial interests because he was from Ireland. His country had witnessed the erosion of the rights of its political institutions as it was asked to pay for British wars and the debts that financed them. Much of Swift's writing on Irish affairs attempted to make Ireland's populace aware of this problem and to manipulate public opinion in favor of preserving the sovereignty and effectiveness of Ireland's institutions.

In Swift's view, the defense of Ireland's constitutional rights and an effective critique of British imperialism required the creation of national print media. He sought to mobilize Irish writers, booksellers, and printers in the creation of a patriotic public sphere that would both facilitate political objectives and encourage the development of a domestic publishing industry. An account of Swift's engagement with the problems of Ireland, accordingly, is also a history of the emergence of the Irish book as a vehicle by which an Irish nation was formed and a means by which Irish identity came to exert political, commercial, and cultural influence. Anglo-Irish literature, which Swift helped to found, was the central transformative category of the Irish book in this period. It contributed to the establishment of Dublin as the "second city" in English-language publishing, after London.[5]

Approaching the emergence of modern Irish identity and literature as the effect of resistance to the fiscal-military aspect of the British Empire requires examining problems of cultural imperialism and literary nationalism alongside the material foundations of English colonial rule over the British Isles as a whole. By the time Swift was writing, Ireland's status in this empire had been contested for centuries, largely due to disputes over its wealth. As a kingdom constitutionally equal to England that was nonetheless treated as a colony, Ireland had long served as a revenue farm, paying for the armies and other expenses of English monarchs; indeed, that was the reason for its conquest by various forces from the twelfth century onward.[6] Further, when English control of Ireland was threatened by wars and rebellions associated with the Protestant Reformation in the seventeenth century, the soldiers who put down these disturbances and the creditors who financed their expeditions were paid with lands seized from rebels. During the Civil Wars of the 1640s and 1650s, for example, the English Parliament had passed the "Adventurer's

Act," which authorized granting captured Irish lands to those who contributed to the war effort. After the conflicts of the 1690s, King William III gave property seized from Ireland's Catholic gentry—the Jacobites—to his most loyal Protestant soldiers.[7]

These conflicts reestablished Anglicanism as the official religion of the territories controlled by England. Seeding Ireland with loyalists to that religion and the government that it served helped guarantee that Irish tax revenues would be available to the fiscal-military state that King William was fostering. Apportioning the property taken from the Jacobites required land surveys and a rationale for dividing the land among various grantees. As Mary Poovey has pointed out, William Petty, who had served in the English army in Ireland in the mid-seventeenth century, had already invented modern statistical economics—what he called "political arithmetick"—to legitimate previous property seizures, and his maps and methods were used in this latest allocation.[8] The practice of land seizure brought into being the first pillar of England's domination of Ireland throughout the long eighteenth century: the monopolization of land ownership and the rents that went with it, building an economic base. The second pillar was an ideological superstructure, in the form of religious discrimination: the Penal Laws designed to prevent Catholics from owning land, serving in government or education, and practicing their religion. This form of sectarian privilege thereby established the identity of the Anglicans as the "Anglo-Irish," a "curious hybrid, . . . conscious of themselves as a minority within a minority threatened almost as much by the growing strength of Presbyterianism as by the Catholic majority."[9] The economic dominance and ideological hegemony generated by these first two pillars—rendering Irish life in the colonial period as the product of a "gigantic experiment in primitive accumulation"—made possible the third pillar: state finance capitalism in the form of an Irish financial revolution.[10]

The Irish financial revolution began in 1716, when a group of prominent Anglo-Irishmen, who came to call themselves the "Protestant Interest," made a national security loan to the Irish Treasury to raise troops to fight an expected re-invasion by Jacobite exiles living in France. This public loan formed a political and economic community, what amounted to an informal republic based on the shared risk of mutual investment, in which each lender depended on the others for protection of existing property and future interest payments. That loan established Ireland's national debt—referred to by contemporaries as "the Debt of the Nation"—as a "funded" obligation, meaning that the Irish Parliament promised to repay the creditors from money that the Irish Treasury received in taxes.[11] Because the Irish Parliament, like the subscribers to this fund, were composed of Anglo-Irishmen only, this revenue legislation was a particularly colonialist instance of self-interested economic behavior. Many of the members of Parliament who were voting for these measures were the lenders themselves, and they were using their positions to appropriate the tax payments of the whole population.[12] As a long-term mortgaging of revenues, the "Debt of the Nation" established the temporal basis for this group's national identity as the Anglo-Irish "Protestant Interest"; the circularity of their status as both creditors and debtors to Ireland bound them together into a very small clique that would continue to dominate the kingdom of Ireland until 1829. That they excluded Catholics from this circle of investors reflects their fear that "papists" would reassert Jacobite control over the country, not only by profiting from investment in taxation, but also by influencing policy to make it possible for them to again become landed gentry and members of Parliament.[13] Those members of the Protestant Interest who controlled almost all private property and enterprise, through this mechanism, were enabled to claim a portion of the country's public revenues indefinitely. When, in 1720, the British Parliament passed the Declaratory Act, a measure establishing Parliament's right to legislate for Ireland in matters of taxation, the Protestant Interest sensed a threat to their prerogative in public revenue matters and to their private investment in those revenues.

The Debt of the Nation thus came to be the material basis for eighteenth-century Anglo-Irish political thought, which, like British political theory in this period, drew from Continental discourse on republicanism and other forms of government. Although politicians and investors did not know the technical terms for describing what they were doing when they formed the funded debt in 1716, George Berkeley, an eminent Anglo-Irish philosopher, was able to give a name to it. In response to the sovereignty crisis provoked by the Declaratory Act, an exploding debt resolution experiment called the South Sea Bubble, and a project to form an Irish national bank like the Bank of England, Berkeley was hired by the future Earl of Egmont in 1720 to do a study of different forms of banking in Europe and their impact on political systems. Berkeley rejected the banks of Amsterdam, Rotterdam, Hamburg, Stockholm, and Venice as examples of what had been constituted in Ireland in 1716, because they were banks of deposit. The Anglo-Irish system, on the other hand, could be called a *Monti*, like those of Rome, Bologna, and Milan because it was not a bank where deposits were held but one established for income from future tax funds.

> The Banks of the Second kind, call'd in Italian Monti, which are for the benefit of the Income only, are the Banks of Rome, Bolognia, & Milan. These Banks are made up of numbers of persons who in time of War or other exigencies of State advanc'd Sums of Money upon Funds granted in perpetuum, but redeemable. Those concern'd therein content themselves with the Interest, or Sell their Stock when they want the principal: but these Banks keep no Cash, nor ever have any Stock of money. They are under the direction of Some few Overseers, who take care to divide the Revenue to the Proprietors. These *Monti* are properly Funds of perpetual Interest transferable and redeemable.[14]

The Anglo-Irish community and fiscal system fit this definition because the Debt of the Nation had been established for both war financing and investment in perpetual interest paid by taxes. There is evidence that contemporaries knew that the debt constituted a *Monti* in all but name and that only the interest, not the principal of the loan, was to be repaid. Archbishop William King of Dublin, for example, wrote in 1725 that this "bank," which was really an imaginary entity holding stock in the Irish Treasury's revenue intake, was founded with £50,000 that "was a Debt contracted by a loan in 1715 and was not designed to be paid, only payment of the Interest provided for."[15] Because this form of loan had no scheduled repayment date nor a limit on the number of years that interest would be awarded, the interest returned would dwarf the principal more and more into perpetuity. Though there were attempts to pay off the principal, including during a 1753 dispute between the English and Irish Parliaments over who controlled that fund, outcomes of earlier debates over taking such a measure suggest that the majority of the subscribers and of Irish MPs opposed eradicating the national debt. The members of the *Monti*—the investors—were thus holding stock in the nation and the permanence of its future and would defend that exclusive benefit against all internal and external political, legal, financial, and cultural challenges to it.

The British Parliament attempted to take control of these funds, arguing that it had a constitutional right to them, and the members of the *Monti* responded by using the Dublin press to cultivate popular support for their legal claims. Though their primary motivation was private profit, they partook of a traditional public rhetoric in arguing the rights of the Irish Parliament to make laws for and to determine the taxation of Ireland. They were defending their own property and their status as elites, but that struggle also incorporated many in the subaltern majority who identified with Anglo-Irish emotional appeals to economic resentment. The specific exigency that prompted Swift's recruitment and participation in this media campaign was the threat posed to Anglo-Ireland's fiscal control by the bursting of the South Sea Bubble investment scheme and the British government's related inroads into Ireland's revenues in the 1720s, such as the Declaratory Act.[16] If the Anglo-Irish Swift can be credited with helping to cultivate a new nationalism in the following two decades, it was only because a distinct national identity, an "Irishness," underwrote the colonial appropriation of the traditional rights of sovereignty. A newly patriotic Irish press held the potential to protect leading citizens' investments in their national security in the form of the Debt of the Nation. If the Irish popular imagination had to be mobilized to defend the *Monti*, friendly domestic print media organs were necessary for that task, and their production of works on Irish themes planted the seeds for a new market in Anglo-Irish literature. This book tracks the management of the *Monti* during Swift's lifetime and details how concerns about Ireland's public finances were expressed in sovereignty discourse, public opinion, and cultural production in the medium of books and other printed matter.

The first arena of argument chosen for the *Monti*'s publicity campaign was political economy, a discipline of study and genre of print that not only had broad appeal to a variety of people but also had the ability to foster the patriotic public it hailed as a national entity.[17] Because of Ireland's dire financial and commercial situation, there was a vast increase in the volume of pamphlets on economic matters published in the 1720s, "a corpus of writing," as L. M. Cullen points out, "due mainly to the controversies of that decade and the nascent economic nationalism and constitutional resentment that they fed on and in turn fed."[18] The hortatory force and ideology that united a range of genres in this economic pamphlet culture reflects a problem in the construction of Ireland as an entity: how to represent a community lacking the independent institutions that supply the standards of value necessary to produce a sovereign identity. If "in the eyes of contemporaries . . . economic development was subsidiary to political issues; not only subsidiary, but its achievement or negation a product of policy," then the problem of the loss of money to Britain due to trade restrictions and taxes, the subtext of this economic and constitutional debate, had to be resolved first in the realm of politics and public opinion.[19]

The issue of public opinion and its relationship to the public sphere in Irish studies has always been considered alongside economic problems, suggesting that Ireland provides an important case study of the connections between print culture, public opinion, and political economy. W. E. H. Lecky, in 1883, first observed that various Anglo-Irish interests in Ireland had been invested in "the proper directing of public opinion" through interventions in press controversies when economic difficulties generated "strong local political feeling" threatening to those interests. Lecky called Swift the "creator of public opinion in Ireland" because his publications succeeded in redirecting popular resentment of the Anglo-Irish landed class towards the British government, effectively forging a unified national Irish identity out of economic crises.[20] As R. B. McDowell argued, it was the Anglo-Irish elite like Swift who shaped the opinions of the whole country: "everybody in Ireland was bound to be affected by the opinions, prejudices and principles with which the ruling and educated classes approached economic issues."[21]

Manuscripts and printed matter from early-eighteenth-century Ireland, deploying terms such as "public spirit," document how economic discourse hailed readers, teaching them to believe that they were part of a larger patriotic community of shared financial interest and political sentiment. One writer, the Earl of Abercorn, linked the creation of public opinion to the maintenance of the interests of the *Monti* when he asked a correspondent to support a scheme to found a central bank that would manage the Debt of the Nation, by appealing to his "publick Spirited Zeale."[22] Abercorn suggested that if his friend participated in a project to found a national bank, he would become part of an elite public. Abercorn referred only to the Anglo-Irish "public," which, if not restricted to government creditors and subscribers to the debt, was at least limited to the gentlemen of estates who had the largest stake in finance.[23] Similarly, printed works invoked the existence and sentiments of an imagined Irish public. One pamphlet of 1738, *Reflections and Resolutions for the Gentlemen of Ireland*, thanks Anglo-Irish economic writers in general for their patriotism: "It is true indeed, the Spirit you have shewn, and the Pains you have taken, this way, must seem needless and unnecessary" from the point of view of other countries, such as Britain. The pamphleteer suggested that "Some Gentlemen . . . were convinc'd, nothing but a good Degree of Public Spirit could preserve this Island from Destruction," a statement that indicates how central public opinion was to the defense of Ireland's right to govern its own economy.[24] The print campaign generated by the *Monti* in the years following the bursting of the South Sea Bubble defended Anglo-Irish political and economic interests largely by using the local press to generate a form of nationalist opinion helpful in the assertion of Ireland's constitutional rights in public finance.

This commingling of political economy, public opinion, and print culture in eighteenth-century Ireland provides a colonial example of how writing and printing influenced the conceptualization of nations and the boundaries of fields of knowledge. According to Clifford Siskin, the rapid increase in the amount and variety of texts being published in eighteenth-century Britain had created a crisis in classification of works by genre and discipline. Because political economy had arisen as the "branch of philosophy which concerned itself explicitly with the regulation of growth," its concepts were uniquely suited to governing this burgeoning textuality.[25] This juncture in the history of the English-language book was "dedisciplinary," in the sense that old categories of and approaches to knowledge were no longer of use.[26] Political economy helped rediscipline the administration of published writing by the criteria of productivity, which required the invention of specialization: "disciplines made narrow could become deep and thus serve to induce and control the proliferation of writing and knowledge."[27] This led, for example, to the formation of academic subjects such as literary studies, which governed a distinct category of printed works and led to specialization in the study of that branch of knowledge.[28] Political economy's role in shaping new disciplines also contributed to the study of British national identity as a species of narrow, yet deep, textual history.[29] As Siskin has suggested, these political consequences can be viewed as the result of competition among national book markets: "The stage was also set for the entry of the printers and booksellers of Ireland and Scotland into a print world that had been dominated by London; print both proliferated and performed a new role in nation building."[30] Ireland's employment of political economic practice, because of its ability to form book markets and nations, formed the basis upon which its domestic printing industry could begin producing the idea of the Irish nation.

Because these cross-disciplinary features of market development and nation formation were inherent to the growth and management of a national print culture, the Anglo-Irish challenge to Britain's hegemony in works of political economy was simultaneously an interrogation of British cultural production in general. British books imported into Ireland, regardless of whether they were nonfiction or literary titles, were not only affecting the political opinions of Irish readers but also influencing their tastes and values. By the eighteenth century, "print capitalism"—Benedict Anderson's term for the relationship among the rise of vernacular print cultures in Europe, the emergence of printing as a commercial force, and its nation-building effects—had created "Britishness" as a commodity that helped sell British books and a variety of other products and imperial policies. British identity, the product of print capitalism's formation of the "imagined community" of the British nation-state, threatened Irish political and economic interests by undermining the taste for the products of the Irish print industry, which were crucial to the dissemination of Irish nationalist public opinion.[31] Further, the British book trade had brought about a new, modern form of sovereignty, in that it had replaced an aesthetic focused on the overthrown divine-right monarchs, James II and his predecessors, with one that celebrated the nation-state as a broader, more diffuse and diverse community in which power was more evenly distributed. The nation-state, "limited" because it has "finite, if elastic, boundaries, beyond which lie other nations," is "imagined as *sovereign* because the concept was born in an age in which Enlightenment and Revolution were destroying the legitimacy of the divinely-ordained, hierarchical dynastic realm."[32] The literary and publishing histories of Britain, in Anderson's view, were central in shaping the secular identity of the modern nation, constituting patriotic history, taste, and subjectivity within a national canon. In short, what the British book trade had formed was a "culture industry" that both produced nationalist ideology and advertised its books and other products, commodifying culture and art.[33] The culture industry was selling the "Britishness" expressed in English literature as a commodity, the possession and performance of which was an index of one's cultural capital, or literacy, in the hierarchical scheme of national taste that the British book was creating.[34]

The study of print culture alone, however, cannot explain the relationship between publishing and finance explored in Swift's writings, a connection rendered more visible in recent new economic criticism by Patrick Brantlinger, James Thompson, Diedre Lynch, Sandra Sherman, Catherine Ingrassia, and Colin Nicholson. According to these critics, the culture industry helped maintain "public credit"—the contemporary term for confidence in the national debt obligations represented by government bonds—by cultivating readers' desires for the lifestyles and scenarios depicted in works of fiction. These desires encouraged the forms of speculative investment necessary to persuade the marketplace of the state's solvency and ability to repay debt profitably. Aesthetic products, particularly works that imagined the nation as the object of this desire, were necessary, explains Brantlinger, because "patriotism and nationalism underwrite public credit (and vice-versa) but also the nation-state's own facilitation of . . . the economy."[35] The fiscal-military state required both overt and subtle forms of propaganda to model itself as the force overseeing the market and guaranteeing its exchanges. British cultural capital in the form of literature supported state-sponsored finance capital and, by doing so, helped insure public credit and the state itself.

These new economic critics have contended that paper credit and national debt were as important in forging a British public sphere as literature and other species of printed materials. Brantlinger, for example, contends that national debts are "even more fundamental to the fictional or ideological creation and maintenance of the imagined communities of modern nation-states than . . . literary canons," but it is not likely that the fiscal-military state could have achieved hegemony without the simultaneous rise of a national aesthetic.[36] New economic studies of the rise of the novel, in particular, stress how that genre's invention of the domestic space of the home as the interior conscience of the nation helped to establish faith in the reproductivity of the family as the security on British Treasury bonds. In Thompson's view, the novel resolved doubts about such investment by serving "as an ideological regrounding of intrinsic value" in its depiction of "the home and companionate marriage" as instantiations of "real" worth, creating confidence that new generations of taxpayers would be available to pay off those bonds.[37] For Sherman, however, novels were important because they accustomed readers to the idea that such a payoff might never occur. Investment in "undifferentiated tokens of epistemological opacity," such as books and paper credit, helped create faith in a society in which the purely nominal essences of cultural capital and financial equity were replacing ontological value and in which the success of individuals required highly chameleonlike self-fashioning.[38] Similarly, Lynch suggests that paper money and the characters of some of these novels were "flat" or "faceless" fictional entities that circulated throughout eighteenth-century Britain, generating a transparent zone of credit and an affective nation of sympathy, respectively. Yet, these economic and emotional effects are not heuristically separable, for they build community through the same process of circulation and appropriation, and "collect the characters of experience" for the reader of both credit texts and fiction.[39] What Lynch refers to as the "double character of money" as both "material" and "abstractly representative" applies to wealth and emotions in the same way, as both capital and affect must shed their particular properties—their materiality—in order to become transferable and communicable forms.[40] Ingrassia, however, has taken a different stance, arguing that the proliferating textuality of money and literature provokes a search for a limiting principle such as authorship to determine meaning and assign value. The novelist Eliza Haywood, for example, benefited from having a "distinct authorial persona," demonstrating that a woman could not only succeed in print culture but could also design plots portraying female characters who advanced in the world of finance.[41] For Ingrassia, the English financial revolution was beneficial, providing new opportunities for the empowerment of women, the middle classes, and others who did not possess land or hereditary titles to it.[42]

Colin Nicholson is one of the few new economic critics to address the English financial revolution's impact on Swift's writing, and then only in regards to his English works. Nicholson says that the defense of "real" property, meaning land, and its proprietors by Swift was predicated on his knowledge that the "real" had already been mobilized and made "imaginary" and discursive by the market forces of public credit and the print culture supporting them. He proves this point by establishing that Swift, traditionally regarded as a reactionary for his public statements against public credit and the professional writers who created a culture amenable to it, was privately investing in those very Bank of England stocks and funds while personally owning no land himself. Nicholson contends that, as paper credit was helping Britain develop an imagined community in the early eighteenth century, Swift was becoming aware that British subjectivity was being formed by print; he was developing a recognition "that writing does not simply translate systems of domination, but becomes itself a location of power and of resistance to it."[43] Swift's satires were a way of manipulating that highly abstract and formal culture of writing in order to undermine the transparency of the British public sphere and to make readers think more skeptically about that writing. Nicholson says that these satires were meant to suggest that value did not inhere in written discourse alone but also in immanent, nonrepresentational presences that were elsewhere. Given the discrepancy between Swift's public statements against public credit and his private investments in it, the ideology of real property that he promoted in satire can be taken as precisely that—an ideological and nostalgic gesture as opposed to a practical conviction in a material reality. This nostalgia, expressed in satire that worked to underwrite confidence in the marketplace, aesthetically effected the impression that a reserve of "real" property and of being existed for which the paper notes of exchange linked to public credit were ultimately redeemable. Public credit seemed to require a presence beyond discourse—an identity—to substantiate its "imaginary" value. In short, Nicholson suggests that the British identity being generated in English print culture became a target of Swift's critique because it was that identity that was ideologically supporting the fiscal-military state. Paradoxically, however, Swift contributed to the reification of that culture, by publishing in London and participating in it, though as a publicist for the Tory opposition. Swift's denigration of the English book, for Nicholson, is therefore problematic. By producing skepticism about the cultural production of the fiscal-military state, Swift intimated that there was an alternative British identity—one espoused by his Tory allies—that was nonetheless complicit in that ideological support. Though his strategy of using satire to underwrite that alternative and its financial function is also central to an understanding of his later writings, Nicholson has not examined how that strategy worked in the Irish colonial context in which Swift spent the second half of his life.

The study of the eighteenth-century Anglo-Irish critique of the British culture industry, I argue, presents the opportunity to expand the new economic criticism expressed by Nicholson and others, by lending it a postcolonial dimension that accounts for how the financial needs of the fiscal-military state affected colonial discourse. Simultaneously, it opens a path to interventions in theory, by revealing that the problems of race, gender, and nation that postcolonial studies explores are deeply entangled with the financial objectives of empire and the cultural production that helped achieve those objectives. This book should also inform Irish studies by linking the rise of a national Irish print culture to the fiscal consequences of colonialism, locating the beginnings of modern Anglo-Irish literature in Swift's resistance to the fiscal-military state. Swift hated war, conquest, and colonial oppression, as Edward Said has written, and he transformed himself from an English traditional intellectual into an Irish organic intellectual via this very discourse on Ireland's status within the empire, using the press to articulate this resistance.[44] By investigating the relationship of cultural distinction to political independence, I hope not only to contribute to the scholarship on literary nationalism but also to intervene in a *topos* of central importance to postcolonial critics: the meaning of sovereignty. As Robert Phiddian has written, when reading Swift's Irish satires it is hard not to see that national debt and the financiers to whom it is owed still compel nation-states to sponsor wars and make economic policies not in their best interests, a problem that has tempted some postcolonialists to reclassify their work as "World Bank literature."[45] Unlike postcolonial nation-states, however, eighteenth-century Ireland had domestic, not foreign, creditors, and the real obstacles to its fiscal control were British political institutions that were attempting to claim its revenues. Ireland's leaders were in an enviable position to check such coercion, and Swift took it upon himself to remind them of the sovereignty implications of their decisions about taxation, revenue, and debt repayment.

This book, accordingly, intervenes in the new economic criticism by extending its critique to the problem of empire, asking how British cultural production was underwritten by colonials and imitated by them for their own nationalist projects. In doing so, this book models the new economic criticism's potential to step beyond postcolonial and Marxist criticism and imagines how political and cultural concerns may be linked to economic analysis. It makes this claim on the basis of early modern political philosophy, some of which established that language and money were considered homologous representations of state authority.[46] As Jean-Joseph Goux has explained, in the early modern period, precious metals had come to serve as the "general equivalent" for all values, and this development required an ideology of political thought in which monarchy would guarantee this homology.[47] The person of the king or queen organized the "isomorphic" unity of the state's responsibilities in the arenas of law enforcement, fiscal control, regulation of public opinion, and the biological reproduction of the guarantor of the social contract in the form of a legitimate heir.[48] Jean Bodin, a sixteenth-century French philosopher, consolidated this theory in *Six Books of the Commonwealth*, which established the importance of censorship in regulating that isomorphism and that, in Jotham Parsons' words, "money was the embodiment as much as the creation of the law" given and executed by the monarch.[49] The early modern sovereign had a moral obligation and political incentive to maintain a sound currency: "Successfully causing a coin to circulate at a fixed value was therefore the success of the state, and a failure to do so was a threat to the state. . . . If the money was defaced or devalued, so was the prince himself."[50] In this formulation, the linguistic sign, as expressed in the media, censorship, and publicity, secured the value of currency by promoting the reputation of the state and the legitimacy of its constitutional functions. Controlling signification was a necessity if the state was to guarantee the transparency of all contracts, public and private, with a sound legal tender. The indivisibility of these aspects of sovereignty was highly rarified in the eyes of dispossessed colonials like Swift, who saw how the British fiscal-military state substituted an abstract commodity—national identity circulated in literature—for the material resources it needed for its wars.

A postcolonial new economic criticism renders visible that the Irish financial revolution was like the English one in that it, too, gave rise to a national print culture, one that, in Ireland's case, sought to secure confidence in the fiscal and political potential of the *Monti*. Ireland's debt was the economic foundation of the ideology of Anglo-Irish Protestant nationalism. The Anglo-Irish colonial caste, a hybrid entity caught between the natives it governed and the metropolis to which it was subject, soon learned to adopt the empire's homologies of finance, language, and law to protect its investments and claim its parliament's right to regulate Ireland's economy. The *Monti* encouraged the Dublin press to produce domestic cultural capital that would sow the seeds for regional fiscal independence. I argue that Swift, though he continued to publish some of his works with London presses, attempted to motivate Irish printers and booksellers to disseminate the idea of "Irishness" in domestic fiction and nonfiction. By doing so, he hoped to encourage Irish readers to consume the work of Irish writers and thereby value their regional culture in a way that would support the *Monti* and, by extension, the independence and health of the whole domestic economy.

Ireland's use of the press to provide an imaginative foundation for the economy resolved a problem of value then being debated: whether money was intrinsically valuable (having a material value rooted in its gold or silver metallic content) or nominally valuable (having an abstract value agreed upon by habit and convention). As Thompson has argued, the eighteenth century, because it witnessed an increasing use of paper money, was the moment when the nominalist argument eclipsed the intrinsic argument. "The cultural work of this period revolves around the transition from real to nominal value in semiology and in economics; Horkeimer and Adorno characterize the Enlightenment as 'a nominalist movement.' Indeed, economics could be described as the theorization of nominal value—its essential stock in trade."[51] Accordingly, print culture, in the genres of both political economy and literature, was harnessed to create models of value that could populate this immaterial universe of absent ontology with fictional presences, and these models and fictions became what was real. Symbolizing the value of a unit of currency by the stamp of the sovereign—a representation of the political consensus and social contract required to standardize measurement in the new nominalist era—may have been more important than the materials out of which that unit was made. "Rethinking the materiality of currency is, of course, related to changing attitudes toward paper and the question of the authorizing stamp. The importance of the authorizing stamp grows as materiality diminishes in importance."[52] The sovereignty represented by the stamp, accordingly, was what supplied currency with value. Imagining that sovereignty through print—stamping pieces of paper with symbols indicating that they were money or literature—became crucial to sustaining that value. The formation of a national imagined community through print capitalism was of great political and economic necessity, therefore, not only because it generated ideological support for the fiscal-military state but because it gave meaning to the medium of exchange in which that state's income was measured.

Swift knew that he was living in a new monetary era and had believed for some time that even silver and gold coins were only nominally valuable. As a clergyman, he saw how the value of his church's land had depreciated over the years. His "ancient fear of inflation" is articulated in *Some Arguments Against Enlarging the Power of Bishops, In Letting of Leases*, published in 1723 in response to the Irish Parliament's Act for the Preservation of the Inheritance, Rights, and Profits of Lands belonging to the Church and Persons Ecclesiastical.[53] To combat inflation, Swift's pamphlet made the case that the church's leases should be shorter so that rents could be raised as money depreciates: "He showed how unfair it was to fix ecclesiastical incomes in terms of money, seeing that the purchasing power of gold and silver fell unceasingly."[54] The Anglo-Irish intelligentsia, many of whom were landlords also suffering from devaluation of their rents, seemed to share this view that the age of silver and gold's inherent value had passed, especially after the bursting of the South Sea investment bubble had drained both Britain and Ireland of coin. Although Swift's pamphlet was a reaction against the attempts of lay landlords to transfer the costs of inflation to the church, it does reflect the sense, which he shared with them, that the reality of value now lay in the imagination, suggesting that contemporaries were beginning to understand the relationship of imaginative literature to sovereignty and currency.

This Enlightenment epiphany, also taking place in Britain and other European countries, is particularly visible in the early-eighteenth-century Irish context due to the decolonizing threat that it posed; severing the Irish culture industry from the British one for reasons of currency control had political and economic ramifications for the integrity of the empire. The third and fourth decades of the eighteenth century are the period when a modern national literature rose in Ireland, because the bursting of the South Sea investment scheme in 1720 marks the moment of transition to an era of nominally valuable money in British society. Ireland's investors, even before the crash, had become accustomed to regarding money thus because the currency circulating in their country was an odd assortment of mostly French, Spanish, and Portuguese coins of uncertain value. Therefore, they were in a unique position to understand the relationship of culture to money. As Dipesh Chakrabarty has written, it is precisely this colonial species of monetary practice that forms the economic basis for alternatives to historical constructions of culture in more developed nations, and Ireland's traditional linkage of currency's value to the imagination enabled it to react to the crash with a publication-based recovery plan.[55] Only a patriotic press could effectively bail out Ireland's national economy, so members of the *Monti* risked both public and private funds to sponsor the writers and publishers who helped create a new Irish culture industry.[56]

The history of political and economic developments in Swift's era must consequently be understood through the study of this nationalist appropriation of the printing press. Media critique of this kind, as Leah Price has argued, has evolved into "a discipline that owns up to a raft of aliases: book history, print culture, media studies, textual scholarship," all of which have been fueled by a renewed interest in historical bibliography and the materiality of texts.[57] This methodology, now generally known as "the history of the book," has been pioneered by Robert Darnton. His research has shown that eighteenth-century readers regarded books not just as conveyers of information but as physical objects possessing value in their own right due to their very raw materials: "the material quality of the book mattered as much as its intellectual content." Readers "paid attention to the stuff of literature as well as its message," taking an interest in the quality of the paper, type, spacing, layout, binding, and cost.[58] As Adrian Johns and Lisa Maruca have written, the history of the book attempts to defamiliarize us from our current approach to printed texts as transparent mediators of meaning and to recover this earlier appreciation of how such material details worked to construct faith in books' messages.[59] The early modern period witnessed the attempt to legitimate the printed book through standardized reproduction leading to the fixity of a text—the construction of a book that is typographically identical in every copy—and its dissemination in a manner that created confidence in its contents.[60] By seeking to know "how publishers drew up contracts, editors handled copy, printers recruited workers, and booksellers pitched sales talk," the history of the book demonstrates that "the business of book historians is business history."[61] In short, this methodology focuses on authorship, reading, and publishing in order to establish how books were packaged to influence public opinion, a task that Darnton deems a necessary prerequisite for any theoretical assessment of the politics of the text in its contexts.[62]

This book, however, focuses less on the materiality of texts and more on what Roger Chartier has called the "cultural uses" of the book trade, taking a more theoretically synthetic approach that links culture to political and economic concerns via the study of "systems of representation and the acts the systems generate."[63] In doing so, it echoes Swift's own skepticism of the truth claims of the British print media of his period, a skepticism that challenges literalism with allegory. As Everett Zimmerman writes, for Swift, "literalization, in its ultimate 'lettoral' sense, is returning the book to its status as a physical object, and allegorization ultimately implies replacing the book with a meaning."[64] Allegories such as *A Tale of a Tub*, *The Battle of the Books*, and *Gulliver's Travels*, as well as many of Swift's Irish-published works, continually ask their readers not to take books at face value but to supply meaning in a manner that questions the fixity of the text. Indeed, as I argue in Chapter 3, Swift's Irish scatological satires sought the "reduction of books to the materials of which they are made" in order to highlight their disposability, an act that simultaneously privileges the activity of the reader.[65] Consequently, his advocacy for and participation in the Dublin publishing industry, though effective in producing a national forum for the assertion of Irish public opinion, were ambivalent. Even as he critiqued British books and encouraged the production of Irish ones, he called attention to how the value of both, as modern texts in the age of the rise of nationalism, could be reduced to their literal components in a manner that makes us rethink the history of the book's focus on the materiality of the text. In short, Swift encouraged the productions of Ireland's book craftsmen not because he attributed great value to nationalist books as physical commodities but because he regarded them as necessary in an era when Irish public opinion needed to be won over.

This book argues that Dublin printers in Swift's period were encouraged to cultivate a supply of patriotic, Irish-made books and, by extension, a distinctly Anglo-Irish standard of taste. It adopts and extends Mary Pollard's argument that the largest portion of books produced in Ireland were targeted at and sold to Irish readers.[66] Though a great deal of what was consumed by those readers consisted of reissues of London publications, this very profitable reprint trade supported the production of plenty of original domestic works for national political purposes. This is not to say that Ireland's most talented writers were always publishing at home; Britain provided many of the works, including ones by those authors that the Dublin book trade reprinted.[67] Rather, it is to assert that Ireland had many advantages in the business, including the absence of a copyright law, lower taxes on paper for printing and leather for binding, and lower wages for printing house employees—advantages that helped Irish publishers rival London in sales and in the battle of ideas and opinions.[68]

In this work I consider political satire as the foundational means of literary expression by which domestic imagined communities such as Ireland's were formed. Political satire can inhabit ideologies and their generic conventions like a virus, and it infers the existence of opposing normative, nationalist assumptions to which its audience should subscribe.[69] Particularly in its parodic mode, satire clears space in the book market, creating room for sometimes explicit, and sometimes immanent, alternatives to the authority inscribed in the host texts. It thereby attempts to incorporate readers into a single body, a strategy crucial both for the propagation of fictions of national unity and for the circulation of the reputations of the writer, the publisher, and the category of literature itself. Because of this universalism, satire, like currency, is a text without a particularity or an identity of its own and cannot properly be classified as a genre. Nonetheless, this lack of qualities makes it the genre of genres. Like money, the fetish form of capital that bears no trace of the origins of its value, satire is the fetish form of textuality, creating space for literature to enter as its own species of print. As Swift's writing attests, satire thereby served as the prerequisite for the rise of anticolonial national literary canons, carving textual and political territory out of hegemonic cultural and administrative imperial apparatuses.

The traditional view of Swift's satire is that irony is its main formal effect, forcing readers to see the gap between the satire's text and its subtext. John Bullitt, for example, argued that Swift's central strategy was one of "*dissimulation*: the ironist appears to say or to be one thing while making it apparent to his audience that he means or is something quite different." Often, this effect is generated by the interplay of two voices, that of the narrator, which is received first in the literal reading of the text, and that of the "detached" author, who can be seen to be using the narrator's voice as a mask, parodying it and, by extension, the attitudes expressed in the literal text.[70] According to Wayne Booth, the contrast between these voices is usually perfect enough to be classified as "stable irony." This form has four qualities: it is intentional and not unconscious; it is in possession of a covert meaning that the reader can unveil; this meaning is fixed or limited in that no further exegesis is necessary after its realization; and the form is finite in that this closure confines interpretation to the narrow issue at hand and not "broad subjects." Swift's *A Modest Proposal*, the best-known of his Irish satires and therefore often the one taken to represent them all, has been dubbed the "finest of all ironic satires" and the preeminent example of stable irony in the English language because it so well fits this definition. The stability is generated by the balanced interplay between its two speakers—the motion between "the true, angry but rational voice describing Ireland's woes" (Swift) and "the mad, almost cheerfully 'rational' voice describing the remedy" (the narrator). This effect enables the reader to unveil the message—that Swift is registering his rage about the exploitation of the Irish and the way they are spoken about—in a manner that "makes a kind of finished sense as a whole," closing off other interpretive possibilities and limiting the subject to the state of the Irish poor.[71] *A Modest Proposal* is therefore an example of how Swift savagely attacked complacency by mimicking its modes of expression. As F. R. Leavis wrote, Swift's "ironic detachment is of such a kind as to reassure us that this savage exhibition is mainly a game," in which the author demonstrates the constructedness of the texts and attitudes being satirized.[72]

I depart from tradition by contending that the irony of Swift's Irish writings sits within a larger allegorical framework that, while defying definitive interpretation by some audiences, enables other readers to receive them as ironic. By arguing that most of these works make use of metaphors for the print trade—what Michael Treadwell has called the "book trade jokes" in which Swift had been engaged since his early work with publishers and printers in London—I suggest that these metaphors are continuous enough to be regarded as an allegory for national cultural production.[73] This book also reclassifies many works as ironic that hitherto have been regarded as straightforward patriotic pamphlets about Ireland's economic grievances. Swift's Irish works, in this view, give rise to a "national allegory," a particularly colonial and postcolonial mode of writing and reception within which irony is made available as an interpretive option. If, as Booth claimed, there is a "reciprocal effect of irony on its context and context on perception of irony," the historical situation of colonialism in Ireland and the censorship associated with it provided the conditions for a form of allegorical communication that made irony perceivable. *A Modest Proposal*, for example, cannot be taken as an ironic text without at least a minimal knowledge of the contexts that supply it with the covert allegorical meaning in which that irony is at play: "without the assumption . . . that conditions were in fact intolerable in Ireland, the essay will lose much of its meaning and power."[74]

Swift's Dublin corpus, I argue, can be taken as both a literal advocacy on behalf of Ireland's trade in wool and other commodities and an allegorical commentary on the necessity of cultivating a domestic culture industry. Particular narratives within developing nations' material cultures, I contend, must be understood as "conscious and overt" attempts to construct more general narratives of history and identity for the nation.[75] They are received as such, however, primarily by other participants in the business of cultural production in those developing nations, the readers most capable of understanding the metaphors. Understanding the covert narrative is a prerequisite to appreciating the irony within the satiric metatextual printed work. Dublin's writers, printers, and booksellers, for example, would be a target audience for this supplemental meaning, for they could process a political tract on the bad state of Ireland's textile industry, as I argue in Chapter 1, as a discourse on the difficult working conditions for colonial publishers under British rule. There is evidence to suggest that a work like *A Proposal for the Universal Use of Irish Manufacture* was read by Dublin cultural workers both literally, as an essay advocating the easing of trade restrictions against Irish wool, and as an allegorical text promoting the Irish book trade, which is apparent in documents that note its discourse on "weaving" to be a metaphor for "writing." Because "the concept of *national allegory* introduces a model for a properly materialist approach to postcolonial texts and contexts," and what it "names are the conditions of possibility of metacommentary," "national allegory" is an appropriate term for understanding Swift's metaphors for the material culture of the Irish book.[76] The process of reading these works, accordingly, is one in which "the preceding satiric text is itself retroactively transformed" into national allegory by the reader, who understands that the ironic gap between what it says and what it means is itself a reference to the absence of the national narrative that it is asking him or her to help create.[77]

Existing scholarship viewing some of Swift's satires as "satiric allegory" supports this postcolonial reading, not least because colonialism rendered allegory available as a genre and mode of reception in Ireland after it declined as a dominant form in Britain in the late seventeenth century.[78] As Maureen Quilligan has contended, "allegory always presupposes at least a potential sacralizing power in language, and it is possible to write and read allegory intelligently only in those cultural contexts which grant to language a significance beyond that belonging to a merely arbitrary system of signs."[79] Because Ireland, as reflected in the colonialism and agrarian capitalism governed by the *Monti*, remained more medieval in economy and social structure than Britain, it had not yet detached language from its allegorical symbolic system. If Swift, in a work like *Gulliver's Travels*, was capable of satirizing the literal-mindedness of its central character as symptomatic of the scientific revolution and other forces of modernization in Britain, it may have been because he was composing it in Ireland, which was suffering the consequences of Britain's modernization in the form of the fiscal-military state. *Gulliver's Travels* is obviously allegorical from the point of view of the reader, though the narrator, himself an allegorical figure for modernity who is being satirized by Swift, cannot see it: "Gulliver suppresses the obviously allegorical (and even allusive) tendencies of his narrative in the interest of truth, which he believes is expressible only as the literal and univocal."[80] When we approach Swift's Irish works without being aware of their potential for satiric allegory, we fall into the same modern literal-mindedness for which Gulliver stands as the ridiculous example.

Given that *Gulliver's Travels* was written in the same period as the most significant of Swift's Dublin publications, it is not likely that Swift was averse to his works' being read as allegories of print nationalism. As Irvin Ehrenpreis observed of Swift's political satires in this period, they follow a formula that begins with a "large allegorical image" incorporating ironic contrasts between virtue and vice in character and policy.[81] For example, M. B. Drapier, the narrator of the *Drapier's Letters*, is an allegorical figure for the typical Dublin textile merchant, and it is through his voice that we are presented with irony: "The drapier is biographically distinguished from Swift, but he controls the ironies of the letters, and he shows his awareness of the evils that he describes rather than his implication in, or obfuscation of, them."[82] As I discuss in Chapter 4, because textiles had been used by Swift and others as metaphors for texts at least since the printing of *A Proposal for the Universal Use of Irish Manufacture*, M. B. Drapier can further be seen not only as a textile merchant, but also as an allegorical figure for a bookseller or printer. The irony of Swift's Irish satires, in this view, is produced via this continuous metacommentary on Ireland's economy, which refocuses attention away from issues of trade and currency and towards the potentiality of the national print culture that could facilitate that economy and resolve those issues.

Works like the *Drapier's Letters* subsume the arguments of various Anglo-Irish political economists into one sovereign national opinion and, by doing so, make the case that the creation of a more universal "Irishness" through a rising colonial literary sphere was crucial to the formation of a distinct Irish economy. These works ideologically underwrote Ireland's "Debt of the Nation" and the taxation of the poor that serviced its creditors, the *Monti*. Swift recognized that only the new secular discourse of political economy had the potential to universalize the interests of these investors with those of the recently conquered Catholics, Dissenting Protestants, and other constituencies. His advocacy on issues concerning trade and currency hailed the country's diverse demographic groups as a unified colonial public that should oppose any obstacles compromising payments to these lenders. These acts of ventriloquism, even as they forged a modern political nation, also gave rise to a sphere of Anglo-Irish literature that has been profitable to printers ever since. The broader implications of this study are that markets in national and ethnic literatures, like satire itself, may be parasitical on serious political controversy. Swift may have invented a political public sphere in his works of the 1720s, but in the 1730s and beyond that sphere's "Irishness" was a platform for Anglo-Irish writers, who imitated his style, but not necessarily his political seriousness, in more strictly literary works. If "Anglo-Irish writing does not begin with Swift, but Anglo-Irish literature does," as Seamus Deane declares, it is because Swift's manipulation of "the Irish art of controversy" led to sales that supported the growth of Dublin's printing industry and the birth of a national canon of which he is the founding figure.[83]

This book's thesis—that Swift was advocating on behalf of the Dublin book trade both to increase its prosperity and to achieve political goals—is not without its problems. The fact is that even after publishing his collected works with the Dublin printer George Faulkner, he continued to publish some of his writings with London booksellers. Also, Faulkner and others continued to partner with London printers, like William Bowyer, after Swift's death. Swift's continuing, though diminishing, role in the London book market nonetheless coexisted with his helping to form a book market in Dublin, partly by critiquing London print culture from within. It must be acknowledged that the patriot discourse that Swift seeded mobilized domestic printers for the production of the distinct "Irish" identity necessary for securing a provincial symbolic order of value.[84] Value, from Swift's provincial point of view, had to be modeled in Ireland's arts before it could be lived as political agency and economic prosperity, and encouraging Dublin's publishers to cultivate local talent was fundamental to this process. An Irish republic of letters and Irish decorum were necessary to produce domestic control of law and the flow of capital. I therefore suspect that the objective envisioned by the creators of modern Anglo-Irish literature was the support of the *Monti*. Eighteenth-century Ireland thus serves as a location for the emergence of an alternative modernity, one forged out of provincial resistance to the economics and culture of the fiscal-military state. Swift, by resisting the colonial consequences of the English financial revolution in the name of an Irish one, asserted a provincial modernity specifically focused against the development of the British empire and culture industry. The transformation in the history of the Irish book and its modernization during his lifetime, accordingly, was largely owing to his advocacy of fiscal control and cultural autonomy in his Irish works.

CHAPTER 1

"God knows how we wretches came by that fashionable thing a national debt"

The Dublin Book Trade and
the Irish Financial Revolution

Jonathan Swift's *A Proposal for the Universal Use of Irish Manufac-ture* (1720) was the first major Irish-published political work he had composed since returning from England to Ireland in 1714.[1] Like Daniel Defoe's writings of the same years concerning calicos imported into England by the East India Company, this pamphlet spoke in defense of the domestic producers of cloth made from native materials; but unlike Defoe, Swift directed his animus towards British textiles, not Indian ones.[2] Consequently, the work can be taken as an anticolonial text. Its discourse on cloth, however, also critiques Ireland's appetite for British commodities in general, objecting to such imports both because they threatened the Irish economy and because they represented an imperial cultural identity that had ramifications for Ireland's political sovereignty. On the literal level, *A Proposal* was certainly advocating a boycott of cloth, fashions, and other English products that were impoverishing Ireland's weavers by depriving them of their share of the market. As this chapter will explain, however, this advocacy was also addressing the imbalance of trade in books, between "domestic" Irish and "foreign" English ones—a problem that compromised not only the health of Ireland's publishing industry but that trade's ability to mobilize anticolonial public opinion.

Weaving, as Clive Probyn has contended, had become a traditional metaphor for writing by Swift's time, to the extent that the figure of the textile tradesman was often a "doubled sign" signifying both cloth and books of domestic manufacture.[3] Swift's repetition in other writings and his explanation of this dual meaning of *A Proposal*'s textile advocacy, together with evidence of the reception of this and other pamphlets on commerce, suggest that some Irish readers understood this metaphor. Dublin's book craftsmen may have been the target audience for the interpretation of this covert message, because the jargon of their trade closely resembled that of weavers. A contemporary handbook on the craft of bookmaking, *Mechanick Exercises on the Whole Art of Printing* by Joseph Moxon, a member of the London weaver's guild, documents this shared terminology. It is known that Swift acquired a copy of this book during the years that he was living full-time in Ireland (1714–1745), so it is possible that *A Proposal* was exploiting this jargon as well as Moxon's weaver-as-author and author-as-weaver status to make a case for the development of the Irish publishing industry and a national culture.[4] The trades of bookmaking and weaving were allied so closely that the Dublin Company of Booksellers, established with the help of Swift's Dublin printer, George Faulkner, required its members to buy a new suit of "native manufacture" every year.[5]

A Proposal's metadiscursive pairing of the cloth and book trades, accordingly, implies that textiles served colonial nationalists as both commodities representative of British political domination and as metaphors for the cultural imperialism of British texts.[6] The consumption of imported cloth and books from the metropolis, anticolonial intellectuals argued, constructed schemes of cultural capital and identity that perpetuated imperial ideology and attenuated colonies' claims for political autonomy. From early modern Scotland, where "clothing was an especially public sign of one's Englishness or Scottishness," to twentieth-century India's homespun movement, textiles provided colonial figures for national texts and narratives, signifying allegiance to one set of cultural norms or another.[7] By urging their readers to wear locally made fabrics, writers on the periphery of empire were not only supporting their domestic textile workers but also encouraging the production and consumption of colonial books and the alternative standards of taste that they represented. The economic threat that boycotts of the empire's fashions posed, consequently, may have been primarily not to sales of finished and unfinished cloth but to the symbolic power of English identity as an advertisement for the benefits of membership in the empire.[8] The aesthetic representation of this identity, manifest in the marketing of apparel, soap, and other products, linked colonial subjects into the administrative, legal, and financial components of empire.[9] English literature was the exemplary commodity in this scheme because it was a material import and a vehicle of ideology—a type of writing and an academic subject that originated in cultural imperialism.[10]

Fashion served British nationalism "not simply to regulate costume but to institute modes of social relations as well," and the study of mid-eighteenth-century discourse on textiles shows how the problem of taste stood at the center of the period's "several related revolutions—sociopolitical, financial, commercial, and literary-cultural."[11] From its beginnings in the wake of seventeenth-century civil wars, British imperialists recognized that the empire's power "could appear *symbolically legitimate*" through the arts.[12] The proper functioning of the fiscal-military state—its ability to obtain war funding from taxpayers—depended on favorable representations of its actions.[13] British philosophers theorizing about the relationship of public communication, emotion, and nation building realized that the English financial revolution could be furthered through cultural hegemony abroad, "the extension of the imagined community of the nation into the unimagined community of the empire."[14] This extension was done in a manner that guaranteed that "Englishmen, as the true currency or standard of value in the empire, would and must always be able to control political and economic exchange, to their own benefit."[15] The "Englishness" of fashionable taste, in short, served as a "universal equivalent" that standardized the value of all commodities, identities, and behaviors in the empire.[16]

Movements for decolonization from the eighteenth into the twentieth centuries therefore advocated not only challenges to Britain's political power but also the dismantling of that standard of taste and the dissemination of new national symbolisms that could mobilize the population. Consequently, the critique of "Britishness" that emerged from England's early modern dependent kingdoms, particularly from Ireland, may have served as a precedent for the critical ethics of postcolonialism.[17] Anglo-Irish literature, a field of print culture emerging in the eighteenth century, provides an important example of this contrapuntal critique. It not only questioned political domination through art but also forged a distinct culture industry that produced the marketable fictions of "Irishness" necessary to secure colonial sovereignty.

Swift, already a major author in England before returning to live in Ireland in 1714, was the key literary figure who helped Ireland make this transition. His satires appropriated weaving as a metaphor for how the colonial book trade could spin Ireland's sovereignty out of whole cloth, seizing the empire's ideological machinery—the printing press—and reversing its trajectory. To steal the means of information control was to cut into what early modern political thought regarded as a part of the sovereign's body politic—its rights of publication and censorship—and therefore to do violence to that body as a whole.[18] The Anglo-Irish colonials risked punishment for this breach of executive privilege to defend their own, provincial financial revolution, an action that was bred of their desire to enhance, yet regulate, their contribution to the British fiscal-military state and empire. The members of the *Monti*, which formed as a consequence of this Irish financial revolution, were worried that they might lose their investment in Ireland's future tax funds.[19] *A Proposal*, published in 1720 at the moment the Declaratory Act threatened to give the British Parliament control over these taxes, can be interpreted as the opening salvo of a patriotic press campaign defending the *Monti*. It literally would advocate for the Irish Parliament's right to initiate and administer revenue matters and would metaphorically call for the production of the patriotic public opinion necessary to this political campaign, doing so through a newly nationalist press. Its publication was a "media event" that shaped public opinion and historical action and provides an important example of how colonial and postcolonial societies used cultural production to claim sovereignty.[20]

I

When *A Proposal for the Universal Use of Irish Manufacture* is read from a postcolonial perspective that contextualizes its metaphors, then its discourse on textiles, trade restrictions, and boycotting can be seen as an allegorical call to literary arms. The pamphlet makes no clear separation between the economic remedies it prescribes and its anti-British political polemic, so the term "universal" in its title should be understood as a reference mainly to the Irish Protestant national community that Swift was trying to call into existence. It begins with the observation that Irish "Commodities, or Productions, lie under the greatest Discouragements from *England*"—a reference to the protectionist Wool Act of 1699, which prohibited Irish weavers to weave, allowing them to export to England only and only in the form of raw wool, not spun and finished cloth (9:15). This situation, Swift suggests, was causing Britain to have a monopoly over the market for Irish wool, bringing down its price and forcing Irish landlords to produce more of it in order to compete, either legitimately or by smuggling (9:15, 9:18). Accordingly, Irish landlords reserve more land for grazing, leaving less for tenants to grow crops: "the politick Gentlemen of *Ireland* have depopulated vast Tracts of the best Land, for the feeding of Sheep" (9:15). The supply of domestic foodstuffs being thus diminished, there was a "prodigious Dearness of Corn," which caused Ireland to import much food from England. Consequently, the supply of currency—that which was traded for food in lieu of commodities—was drained, causing a shortage of a medium of exchange with which to pay workers and do domestic business (9:15).

The pamphlet first recommends an Irish parliamentary sumptuary law, then proposes an extraparliamentary boycott that amounts to economic patriotism: "Upon the whole, and to crown all the rest, let a firm Resolution be taken, by *Male* and *Female*, never to appear with one single *Shred* that comes from *England; and let all the People say, AMEN*" (9:16). Its yet more subversive comment along these lines is to complain about English appointees to positions in Irish government and the church, who exacerbate the currency problem by drawing Irish government pay out of the country (9:19).

This call for a boycott was not novel in Irish history. For example, as early as 1682, *The Interest of Ireland in its Trade and Wealth Stated*, by Richard Lawrence, had recommended boycotts to remedy the loss of currency due to the unfavorable balance of trade.[21] Lawrence responded to the issue of imports exceeding exports by advising sumptuary laws against foreign textiles, and he referred to an earlier proposal—"A general Subscription proposed against wearing foreign Manufactures"—that had been inserted into the minutes of an Irish Privy Council meeting that took place in 1664. In short, *A Proposal* was revisiting a long-standing problem in trade and currency flows.

In addition to reviving a much older Irish moral economic discourse on the role of consumption in the constitution of the Irish body politic, *A Proposal* echoed trends in economic thought in British Atlantic colonies that were coping with the monetary problems associated with trade deficits. The anonymous Massachusetts pamphlet, *The Present Melancholy Circumstances of the Province Consider'd, and Methods for Redress Humbly Proposed, in a Letter from One in the Country to One in Boston* (1718/19), for instance, complains about the loss of silver coin from Massachusetts due to the colony's consumption of foreign—particularly British—goods. It advocates a boycott of British imports, the encouragement of domestic industry, and popular consumption of Massachusetts-produced goods. The anonymous author was skeptical about paper credit, believing that only silver and gold constituted real money, and was dismissive of paper money practices current in Massachusetts. Given the similarity of these essays, it is important to characterize Swift's economic argumentation as primarily monetary inasmuch as its recommendations are meant to resolve the outflow of precious metal currency from Ireland due to the unfavorable balance of trade. Yet this task could only be accomplished by promoting a favorable image of Ireland and its products, and that could only be done with the printing press, itself an industrial machine for manufacturing commodities: books.

The term "Irish Manufacture" in *A Proposal*'s title, consequently, may refer not only to products like textiles but also to texts. There is evidence that contemporaries had used the term "Manufactures" before to describe both cloth and books. For example, in 1719 Bishop William Nicolson of Londonderry, in a letter to Swift's friend Charles Ford, called Bibles imported from London "English Manufactures." So, before *A Proposal* was published, "Manufacture" may have been common parlance for products of the printing industry and for cloth.[22] This dual usage was not unique to Ireland. As Lisa Maruca has documented, printing was referred to as a "branch of manufacture" in European economic discourse in general in this period.[23] Swift's use of the term "manufacture" may have been a deliberate attempt to blur the line between textiles and texts and convey the idea that the production and consumption of both of these commodities was necessary for the development of the Irish economy.

Similarly, when the pamphlet begins to discuss incinerating English commodities (9:17), it may be comparing the advancement of the wool trade to the production of public opinion through the printing press, suggesting that Swift is recommending burning not only imported clothes but also imported books. He blames Dublin's shopkeepers for not petitioning Parliament to "improve the *Cloaths and Stuffs of the Nation*" and intimates that the publication of such appeals will set into motion a patriotic press that will serve as the means of achieving the weaving industry's goals. He signals this metadiscourse on printing by arguing that the merchant class, if it seeks to advocate for itself through the Dublin press, should "first be sure to get some Body who can write Sense, to put it into Form" (9:17). Over the course of a close reading of *A Proposal* and analysis of its reception, however, this metadiscourse comes to seem more central to the pamphlet's effectiveness than its literal signification. As Mairead Dunlevy has contended, eighteenth-century Ireland did not witness a whole-scale embrace of domestically produced clothing, though the aristocracy would wear it at formal occasions to signal, however disingenuously, their allegiance to the Irish economy. There was no national dress as such until the late-nineteenth-century cultural revival, which suggests that Swift's call to boycott foreign textiles and consume domestic ones was not pragmatically effective as an economic strategy in his era.[24] Consequently, as Helen Burke has argued, *A Proposal*'s terms, like "stuffs of the nation," should be taken to signify domestic cultural production, including paper itself. "Stuff," according to the *Oxford English Dictionary*, is a term used in papermaking to describe pulp made from rags (*OED* "Stuff, n.1." def. 4c). Burke writes, "this kind of Irish 'stuff' trope takes its meaning from the discourse and practice of Irish Protestant nationalism. . . . this figure, as it was reiterated in performance and discourse, represented a widening of the Irish imagined community that had sprung into existence in reaction to English oppression in the first decades of the century."[25] In Burke's view, this community was more the product of print, drama, and other domestic cultural media than one brought into being by an economic expansion of the woolen industry.

The pamphlet's reference to Ovid's tale of the contest between Arachne and the goddess Pallas Athena further complicates readings that seek to limit its scope to the realm of textiles. By choosing to write about the character Arachne, a figure for a spider that is also a weaver, Swift revisits his use of Aesop's fable of the spider and the bee in *The Battle of the Books* (1704). In using this image, as I argue in Chapter 3, he established that these spiders are to be taken as spinners of both threads and words, indicating that he was revisiting a figuration with which his readers would have been familiar. In *A Proposal*, Swift employs Ovid's fable to allegorize the plight of Dublin's Protestant weavers, who were his neighbors in the Liberties around St. Patrick's Cathedral.[26] It describes the economic relationship of Ireland to England, suggesting that England (Athena), another weaver, has struck down Ireland (Arachne), and has passed an unjust sentence on her by turning her into a spider: Swift writes,

> I confess, that from a Boy, I always pitied poor *Arachne*, and could never heartily love the Goddess, on Account of so *cruel and unjust a Sentence*; which, however, is *fully executed* upon *Us* by *England*, with further Additions of *Rigor* and *Severity*. For the greatest Part *of our Bowels and Vitals* is extracted, without allowing us the Liberty of *spinning* and *weaving* them. (9:18)

On a first reading, it would appear that Swift is arguing that in the case of Ireland, the Wool Act of 1699 actually prevented the spinning and weaving of wool—the "bowels" of Ireland's portable wealth or commodities. In this context, however, a third signification attaches to spiders and weaving; they also should be understood metaphorically as writers and texts, because spiders were a well-developed figure for the writer by Swift's era. The "emphasis upon Arachne's skill both as maker of the finest thread and upon her skill in weaving narratives of the gods" had been manifest in English literature since the early modern period; Swift's use of Ovid's fable to discuss writing was therefore a fairly canonical gesture.[27]

Swift's use of this text/textile homology may have been inspired by his reading of Moxon's work on bookmaking. Though Moxon was a member of the Stationer's Company of London, a guild in which members were bound to conceal how their craft was practiced, his status as a freeman of the city and mapmaker to the King gave him the ability to "freely give away 'secrets'" of the print trade.[28] Moxon, a weaver by profession, describes the parts and operations of the printing press as if it were a loom, arguing that there was a "*Printers* Dialect" used in the printing house by which the tools, materials, and processes of bookmaking were made to resemble other handicrafts such as weaving.[29] He writes that the press is like a body, "a Machine consisting of many Members" such as "Hooks," the "Spindle," and the "Carriage"—all parts that one would also find in machines for spinning thread and yarn.[30] The "Composister" and the "Pressman," craftsmen who, respectively, set metal type into a "Form" according to the author's edited manuscript and print pages, are also shown to be textile workers.[31] The "Pressman" uses "Pelts" or "Sheepskins" stuffed with "wool" to make "Ball Leathers," by which ink is applied to the type. When he is "[d]rawing the Tympans and Frisket," he is preparing "Vellom, Forrells, or Parchment" to take the ink, cleaning it "as women wash Cloaths."[32] Paper runs like cloth through the press.

The link between textiles and texts in Joseph Moxon's work may best be examined by comparing *Mechanick Exercises* to *Minerva, or, the Art of Weaving*, a book printed by his son James Moxon. The title page suggests that it was printed for the elder Moxon and that it was therefore his intellectual property, though the author is listed as "R.C.," a person who has not yet been identified. Because Minerva is the Roman name for the goddess Athena, this book, written in verse, is an appropriate one to use in establishing that weaving is a metaphor for writing and printing in Swift's *Proposal*.

The narrator of *Minerva* argues that the goddess invented the weaving of wool but that she learned her trade from silk weavers in China, a country where printing had been in use for "no man knows how long."[33] He sets out to establish how all other crafts and trades depend upon the weaver, noting that the mercer, draper, silkmaker, haberdasher, and upholsterer would have no work without the weaver. Printers and stationers were listed among these dealers in textiles because paper was made from cloth. He writes:

> Nor let the Printer o're the Weaver vapour,
> For without Cloath, what would he do for paper?
> The Stationer too would get but slender fees,
> If men did write on bark, or leaves of Trees
> As they have done: for if weaving were gone,
> Could skins be spar'd to write or Print upon?[34]

This passage establishes that the production of texts is dependent upon textiles, again connecting the printing trade to the weaving trade, placing them in the same family of arts. Because linen weaving is said by the narrator to be the invention of Arachne, and because Swift was largely focused on promoting Ireland's linen weavers, this connection is particularly relevant to the metaphorical meaning of his *Proposal*.[35]

Swift reiterated the weaving/writing homology in further works. Perhaps feeling the need to explain *A Proposal*'s metadiscourse, he signaled this connection in an epilogue that he wrote for a performance of *Hamlet* in 1721, staged as a charity event for Dublin's textile workers. It explicitly links weavers to writers:

> Perhaps, you wonder whence this Friendship Springs
> Between the *Weavers*, and Us Play-house Kings.
> But Wit and Weaving had the same Beginning,
> *Pallas* first taught us Poetry and Spinning;
> And next Observe how this Alliance fits,
> For *Weavers* now are just as poor as Wits,
> Their Brother Quill-Men Workers for the Stage,
> For sorry *Stuff*, can get a Crown a Page.[36]

By identifying Pallas Athena as the goddess of both "Poetry and Spinning" and comparing weavers to "Their Brother Quill-Men Workers for the Stage," Swift makes explicit what had been implicit in *A Proposal*—the link between Dublin book production and the overall success of Ireland's economy.

This metaphor is extended in *A Letter of Advice to a Young Poet; Together with a Proposal for the Encouragement of Poetry in this Kingdom*, a book sometimes attributed to Swift that was also published in 1721. If by Swift, the book can be taken as another signal to his readers to interpret *A Proposal* as advocating on behalf of domestic textiles and domestic texts. If not by Swift, clearly other Dublin writers, booksellers, and printers received that dual meaning and felt strongly enough about it to render the metaphor literal. A key passage provides evidence that *A Proposal* was taken to be an essay on behalf of both general Irish industry and the specific trades of writing and printing:

> Add to this, the Expediency of furnishing out your Shelves with a choice Collection . . . above all, those of our own Growth, printed by Subscription, in which Article of *Irish Manufacture*, I readily agree to the late Proposal, and am altogether for *rejecting and renouncing every Thing that comes from* England: To what Purpose should we go thither, either for *Coals* or *Poetry*, when we have a *Vein* within ourselves equally Good, and more Convenient. (9:337)

The author is asking readers to line their bookshelves with Irish-made books, telling them to interpret *A Proposal*—the "Article of *Irish Manufacture*" in question that exemplifies Irish printing—as a call for the encouragement of domestic textual commodities.

In addition, *A Letter*, following the logic of *Minerva*, links Ireland's linen production to its publishing production, saying, "it is plain our *Linnen-Manufacture* is advanced by the great-Waste of *Paper* made by our present set of *Poets*." Because paper was made from linen, Irish poets, by producing what the writer called "*Bum-Fodder*" or subpar literature, were retailers of cloth and therefore in the same industry as weavers. An edition of William Congreve's comedy *Love for Love* that was published in Dublin the following year developed this link further, speaking of a writer "carrying her Linnen to the Paper-Mill, to be converted into Folio Books of Warning to all Young Maids."[37] It is apparent, then, that *Minerva* and *A Letter* establish links between weaving and printing that Irish authors would continue to exploit in their efforts to encourage their country's publishing industry.

When Swift appropriates Ovid's fable, then, he is not only allegorizing textual production by reference to textiles but also calling for the "creation of social memory" crucial for reminding Ireland of the basis for its historical claims to its parliament's legal sovereignty.[38] As J. G. A. Pocock has written, "spinning" also was used during this period in discussing political legitimacy and its basis in history. Sir John Davies, a seventeenth-century English administrator in Ireland, complained that the natives insisted that their rights were based in "custom," which was "recorded and registered nowhere but in the memory of the people." Custom stressed the role of memory in the institutionalization of rights. This discourse was imagined in the ideology of the "ancient constitution," the belief that the legitimacy of jurisprudence was "founded upon the individual's ability to recall and summarize his own experience and to presume its continuity with the experience transmitted to him as that of his ancestors."[39] When Davies wrote that this plea of customary title to possession resembled that by which "the silkworm spinneth all her web out of herself only," he was rehearsing the long-standing allegory of weaving that saw society as a seamless web in time and space.[40] This version of legal historicism united particular circumstance with precedent and formulated the origins of law and claims to sovereignty on its foundation. The desire to ground such claims—and the transparency of linguistic signification that accompanies them—is always a proprietary search for a "*nomos* of the earth" that abolishes the play of doubt and skepticism about their legitimacy. The justificatory process expressed in the term "*nomos*," according to Bruno Bosteels, is the product of an act of memory that establishes "land appropriation as the originary event of all human history."[41] The ideology of the "ancient constitution" was an attempt to come to terms with the questionable legitimacy of the modern age by reconstructing an authorizing *nomos* in which "common law, and the constitution as it now stood, had been essentially the same . . . since time immemorial, or at least since an unrecorded beginning in the woods of Germany."[42] What Swift's pamphlet was "weaving," accordingly, was a traditional, rather than new, claim of ownership in Ireland's land and the products it yielded.

Swift's defense of Ireland's textile workers, in this legal and administrative context, provided abundant opportunities to deploy this ideology of customary constitutional rights. His reference to Athena's turning Arachne into a spider for besting her in a weaving competition encapsulated how England had used the Wool Act to punish Ireland for its success in the textile trade. But Ireland could not spin the interlocking web of sovereign prerogative—accomplished economically by giving birth to products and reproducing capital—because it had been eviscerated by having to sell raw wool instead. The story that Swift was spinning was a simulacrum of that work, one that does not materially reproduce capital, but rather "custom"—the key to provenance over the process of accumulation. The outflow of coin was the issue at the heart of the debate over the Irish Parliament's sovereignty in economic matters, and Swift was exploiting the period's homology between coining and signification to suggest that regardless of whether language or capital is the base or superstructure of society, the situation at hand is a rhetorical one. Ireland had to make legal claims before wealth could be created; its print culture had to develop a patriotic readership to realize those claims.

His discussion of the modes of print circulating in Dublin affirms that textiles are figures for texts and that the disposal of revenue for the Debt of the Nation is what is at issue in his resistance to the Declaratory Act. He ironizes the alienation of the country's revenue to England in a paragraph on political patronage, ventriloquizing "a Person" with "a great Estate in this Kingdom" who complains that governing Ireland "*costs the Lord Lieutenant three Thousand six Hundred Pounds a Year, so much* net *Loss to POOR* England" (9:19). This *genus iudiciale* attacks the claim that "the Revenues of the Post-Office here, so righteously belonging to the English Treasury . . . should be remitted to London" (9:19). He is also outraged at the "Pensions paid out of the Irish Revenues to English Favourites" and the appointments of English Bishops, Judges, and Revenue Commissioners to Ireland, who lament that the exchange rate diminishes their Irish salaries and that they should get yet more out of Ireland's taxes (9:19).

The narrator of *A Proposal* further encourages the Dublin publishing industry by discussing the Anglo-Irish community's aesthetic tastes. In a note of irony, he attacks their preference for English cultural production: "It is wonderful to observe the Biass among our People in favour of *Things, Persons*, and *Wares* of all Kinds that come from *England*. The *Printer* tells his *Hawkers*, that *he has got an excellent new Song just brought from* London" (9:19). He caricatures several figures in the English printing industry who had come to Ireland, two of whom are identifiable as Martin Bladen and William Luckyn Grimston. Of the former, he writes:

> I remember a *Person* who, by his Style and Literature, seems
> to have been *Corrector* of a Hedge-Press, in some *Blind-Alley*
> about *Little-Britain*, proceed *gradually* to be an *Author*, at least
> a *Translator* of a lower Rate, although somewhat of a larger
> Bulk, than any that now *flourishes* in *Grub-street*; and, upon the
> Strength of this Foundation, came over *here; erect* himself up into
> an *Orator* and *Politician*, and lead a *Kingdom* after him. (9:20)

Because the translation has been identified as *Caesar's Commentaries*, published in London, this figure seems to be a relative of the William Bladen who had held the king's license to monopolize printing in Ireland from 1641 to 1660. Swift is suggesting that there is a relationship between spinning public opinion for the state and elevation to political office, considering that Martin Bladen had become an important figure in the Irish government.[43] Similarly, Grimston, already a gentleman, had started in the literary, rather than political, world and was elevated to the Irish peerage: "This, I am told, was the *very Motive* that prevailed on the *Author* of a Play called, *Love in a Hollow-Tree*, to do us the *Honour* of a Visit; presuming, with very good Reason, *that he was a Writer of a superior Class*" (*Dictionary of National Biography*, 9:20). As a younger man, the author had written this play, admitting his pursuit of patronage by stating in the preface, "He that writes Faction is certain of obliging a Party, and hopes Preferment."[44] Taking this accusation of the mercenary motives of Bladen and Grimston's writing further, Swift claimed that, in addition to their printed work, their speeches were "contemptuous" and in "high Style." He argued that this style suggested that they "look[ed] *down* upon this Kingdom, as if it had been one of their *Colonies* of *Outcasts* in *America*" (9:21). This divisive rhetoric about language, power, and opinion, by linking the success of England's writing to its government's appropriation of Ireland's wealth through revenue and patronage, calls for the Dublin press to counterattack. It also implicitly promises similar patronage rewards to those domestic writers who spin opinion well.

The question over which register took precedence in establishing provincial sovereignty—*A Proposal*'s metaphorical inculcation of patriotic opinion or its literal advocacy for an economic boycott—was not so important: one would lead to the other interchangeably. People responded by dressing in clothing produced in Ireland, but the economic impact of such consumption of domestic woolens might not have been as significant as its aesthetic gesture of national solidarity among classes. Textiles, as such, became a symbol of cultural production to the extent that one poet referred to the domestic writers emerging in Dublin's print industry as "*Wool gathering* Sonneteers" and "*Home-spun Witlings*."[45] A major reason that Swift was more successful in this effort than William Molyneux in the 1690s was the development of the book trade after 1699. Another was that the advent of the Debt of the Nation had raised the stakes of constitutional debate. Important figures in Irish politics were not only threatened by their country's loss of public revenue in this constitutional crisis, as they had been in 1699 when the Wool Act was introduced, but also worried that they would lose their personal investments in Ireland's future taxes.

A Proposal's linkage of Ireland's printing presses to the conjoined problems of its political sovereignty and fiscal control, however, was derived from Swift's experience as what Victoria Glendinning has called a "spin doctor" in England for the Tory political administration of 1710–1714.[46] His writings from that period, particularly his contributions to the *Examiner* newspaper and his pamphlet *The Conduct of the Allies*, reflect his views of the financial revolution and its impact on political decision making. He was concerned about how the evolution of the fiscal-military state was affecting English liberties. He believed that private financial institutions and foreign governments were making increasingly expensive claims upon English public funds. After the Glorious Revolution, the Bank of England was founded for the express purpose of lending money to the government in a time of foreign wars and domestic instability, and the English Treasury began to issue promissory notes to it and its investors that promised scheduled repayment. That contracted debt was secured not only by current government revenues but by anticipated taxes. Because of these developments, Swift began to imply that Britain had become a colony of finance capitalists—the "moneyed interest." He suggested that the revenues of the Treasury, funds largely raised in small amounts from common people, but increasingly on the "landed interest" (agrarian capitalists), were being spent to pay a debt contracted from a domestic and international community of financiers. These were "men with no stake in the land but what they could take away," as one contemporary pamphlet complained, and they were said to be controlling public policy.[47] Their commercial ventures required the support of Britain's military forces, which were directly paid by taxation and indirectly funded by such loans. As a partisan pamphleteer, Swift claimed that Whig publishers were enabling these sovereignty-eroding developments and that it was actually the Tory press that was more capable of constructing a public that could make economic policy in the interest of the nation. As in his later observations about Ireland, he saw the press as an integral part of maintaining political sovereignty and fiscal control and represented his position as that of an English patriot. This position is inextricable from his views, however problematic, of the political economy of the Glorious Revolution of 1688.

Swift's political biographers have attempted to ascertain his attitude towards the revolution and its significance to his writings. F. P. Lock contends that early in his life, Swift accepted "the commonplace idea of a necessary 'balance of power' within the state and a 'mixed government . . . combining monarchic, aristocratic, and popular elements.'" Marginal notations in his copies of works of philosophy suggest that in theory, he opposed the absolute monarchism outlined in Jean Bodin's *The Six Books of the Commonwealth*, which would not be unusual for a supporter of the revolution that overthrew James II. Because of this evidence, Lock argues that Swift might have preferred, in keeping with John Locke's views, that ultimate power be in the legislature. Lock, however, admits that this assumption is dubious because Swift "makes absolute submission to constituted authority the rule," which places him "much closer to Hobbes than . . . to Locke." Swift is said to have been very conservative in exceptional circumstances such as national security crises, for he believed in loyalty to existing institutions and in granting the king or queen, not Parliament, sweeping authority.[48] Because of the powers Swift thought the executive branch should have in such states of exception, Ian Higgins contends, he most likely was a "'naturalized' Tory of the Queen Anne and Hanoverian period," who had "political and ecclesiastical attitudes with identifiable Tory party-political positions."[49] Notations that Swift made late in life to a copy of Gilbert Burnet's *History of His Own Time* suggest that the author sometimes supported a compromise between the contractualist position of Locke and the absolutist argument of Bodin, by regarding the monarch as custodian of a multigenerational sacred trust leading back to the *nomos* of the English nation. He had become disaffected with some Whigs' dismissal of arguments for the necessity of preserving the continuity of this responsibility: "Against Burnet's account of a 'party . . . made up of those who thought that there was an original contract between the kings and the people of England', Swift wrote: 'I am of this party, and yet I would have been for a regency'" at the time of the crisis in the reign of James II.[50] In short, he accepted part of the spirit of arguments concerning the importance of the doctrine of divine right yet recognized that political circumstances often required changes in leadership incompatible with that doctrine. J. A. Downie has stressed that this position—his acceptance of the Revolution Settlement—politically identified him as an "Old Whig," even when he worked for the Tories, whom

Swift considered "Old Whigs" as well.[51] That ideology, for David Oakleaf, meant that Swift opposed absolutism in politics while remaining authoritarian regarding the relationship of church and state, believing in the mixed, balanced government expressed in the idea of the crown-in-Parliament.[52] Oakleaf, concurring with observations that I made in an earlier essay, has gone so far as to suggest that Swift's most consistent political concern was with how war and the rise of the fiscal-military state were compromising that settlement.[53]

These political biographers, however, have not accounted for how his growing awareness of the role of finance in war and government affected his political thought. As Steven Pincus has contended, the 1688 revolution was partly a transformation in economic theory and policy that had partisan overtones. There was "a fierce debate between a land-based Tory political economy and a labor-centered Whig one" both before and after 1688.[54] Though the revolution was, as W. A. Speck has suggested, more the product of religious controversies, such as the Exclusion Crisis and James II's appointment of Catholic military officers and professors, this debate also played a role.[55] Though the emergence of the fiscal-military state certainly was not among the initial plans of the revolutionaries, 1688 "produced, and by many was intended to produce, a revolution in political economy."[56] Before the Glorious Revolution, James II had consolidated the monopolies of the East India Company and Royal Africa Company, alienating many merchants, financiers, and manufacturers who sought to compete with those monopolies and who labored under a tax system favoring the landed interest. After the revolution, the tax structure became more favorable to the moneyed interest, and financial policy became amenable to the material and ideological concerns of the Whigs.[57] As John Brewer has noted, this moneyed interest was "overwhelmingly whig in politics and disproportionately Dissenting in religion," and it was clearly gaining the upper hand in politics and economics.[58] Following this line of argument, Pincus contends that "the Bank of England was a Whig creation against Tory resistance" when it was originally formed in 1694 and that Tories were constantly defending the East India Company against it.[59] In short, there is substantial historical evidence that the political conflict between Whigs and Tories in the twenty years after the revolution was an economic one—one largely waged over the Bank's role in the financial revolution and the formation of the fiscal-military state.

It is in this context that Swift's publicity work for the Tory government of the Earl of Oxford (Robert Harley, first lord of the Treasury) and Viscount Bolingbroke (Henry St. John, secretary of state) should be understood. He argued that the War of the Spanish Succession, the national debt, and taxation to pay interest on it not only impoverished the British people but also impinged upon their sovereignty. By the time he was writing *The Examiner* in 1710, it seemed to him that the country was hopelessly bound down, like Gulliver by the Lilliputians: treaties, loans, foreign wars, and colonial expeditions had forever eliminated the revolution's promise for a restoration of good government with the return of a Protestant monarchy. As a clergyman, he had envisioned the revolution as an instrument in the reestablishment of the Church of England, and his career stood to benefit from the confiscation of lands as well as government and ecclesiastical posts from James's followers. But the income of those patronage positions, and the growth of the church, was being undermined. As an institution dependent upon property, the church's fate was tied to that of the landed interest, which was suffering under the weight of the fiscal-military state's tax structure.

Given these conditions, his critique of the corruption of the previous Whig regime was more than what Isaac Kramnick called the "politics of nostalgia"; it was propaganda for a specific economic program for the landed class and the established church.[60] When he wrote, in his first contribution to the *Examiner*, that "the Country Gentleman is in the Condition of a young Heir, out of whose Estate a Scrivener receives half the Rents for Interest, and hath a Mortgage on the Whole," he was citing the new taxes that had been placed upon land (3:5). These taxes had been established in 1689, replacing the hearth tax of the pre-1688 era, as a means of paying for war and accounted for as much as 52 percent of England's revenues during the reigns of King William and Queen Anne.[61] Some of these revenues had been earmarked to pay interest on the national debt, which, in his view, was really paying the moneyed interest at the expense of the landed interest, "So that if the War continue some Years longer, a landed Man will be little better than a Farmer at a rack Rent, to the Army, and to the public Funds" (3:5). Consequently, political authority followed the transfer of money from the agrarian capitalists to the commercial capitalists, "So that *Power*, which, according to the old Maxim, was used to follow *Land*, is now gone over to *Money*" (3:5). This argument was not new, as it had been articulated by John Briscoe and others when the founding of the Bank of England was debated in 1694.[62] Thus, the *Examiner* may be said to have been participating in a Tory polemic reaching back to the earliest years after the revolution.

The problem for Swift, the clergy, and the landed interest was one of lost agency—how could a government that had beholden itself so heavily to domestic and foreign creditors, their trade interests, and the consequent military alliances and expeditions be considered sovereign? This question was explored most thoroughly in Swift's pamphlet *The Conduct of the Allies*. It was published in 1711 to help the Tories bring about the Treaty of Utrecht, an arrangement that not only ceded North American and other territories to Britain but also advanced the interests of the South Sea Company by awarding it the "Asiento," the right to trade slaves from Africa to Spanish colonies in the Americas. The pamphlet made the dangerous, nearly Jacobite assertion that before 1688 England's wars had not required the kingdom to carry permanent debt and perpetual taxation. The War of the League of Augsburg (1688–1697) and the War of the Spanish Succession (1702–1713), on the other hand, had involved Britain in its allies' conflicts to the extent that it bore far more than its share of the military and financial burden. The pamphlet claimed that Holland, against whom Britain had been fighting only a few years earlier but was now supporting, was the cause of this international engagement. The Dutch Republic was having trouble with French incursions into its own political sovereignty and physical territory, and through the Partition Treaty (1698) and Barrier Treaty (1709) had obliged its allies to defend its frontier. Swift contended that England had joined the Grand Alliance of the League of Augsburg (a group composed of the Holy Roman Empire, the Netherlands, Sweden, Spain, Bavaria, Saxony, and the Palatinate) only because England's King William III (William of Orange) "was a Native of Holland" and to "make *France* acknowledge" William's right to the English throne (6:11). The pamphlet details how loans for the costs of the wars had undermined Britain's autonomy and protests about "what Opinion Foreigners have of our Easiness, and how much they reckon themselves Masters of our Mony, whenever they think fit to call for it"—a claim repeated in his later pamphlet *Some Remarks on the Barrier Treaty* (6:33, 6:97). His point is both prudent and xenophobic, as he blamed the sale of the government on both domestic and international factors. He saw greed in the Duke of Marlborough, (commander of British forces), Sidney Godolphin (Queen Anne's lord high treasurer), the Duke of Sunderland (secretary of state for the Southern Department), and other Whigs as perpetuating this corruption. The pressure applied by allies, creditors, and corrupt officials, he wrote, had so restrained the power of the queen that she could not rid herself of these men (6:33–34). This seeming conspiracy, Swift implied, had effectively made Britain's monarch and ministry puppets of the moneyed interest and external governments. The history of the first twenty postrevolutionary years, which Swift outlined in these pamphlets, proved to the Tories that the country had indeed become a colony of domestic and foreign commercial capitalism.

The Whig press, in Swift's view, was partly to blame. Contrary to our current idea, promoted by Jürgen Habermas, that the rise of coffeehouse culture and journalism in eighteenth-century Britain was bringing about a disinterested public sphere, Swift contended that this arena for debate was partisan and complicit in exacerbating England's fiscal problems.[63] He was not alone; some contemporaries regarded even *The Tatler* and *Spectator* of Joseph Addison and Richard Steele, generally remembered for developing an apolitical concept of British civility, as organs of Whig propaganda.[64] *The Conduct of the Allies* linked this Whig coffeehouse public sphere to the moneyed interest: "It is the Folly of too many, to mistake the Eccho of a *London* Coffee-house for the Voice of the Kingdom. The City Coffee-houses have been for some years filled with People, whose Fortunes depend upon the *Bank, East-India,* or some other Stock: Every new Fund to these, is like a new Mortgage to an Usurer" (6:53). As he did later in his Irish writings on behalf of the *Monti* (itself representative of the Irish landed interest), Swift envisioned an alternative public sphere that would produce public opinion that would help protect British sovereignty and, consequently, the British public funds. His contribution to the history of the English book, accordingly, was to link the importance of a sovereign, national print media to the problem of public finance and political agency.

Analysis of Swift's mobilization of the Irish print industry for a similar project of producing patriot opinion clarifies connections between the history of the Irish book and contemporary legal and fiscal matters—links that are less obvious in studies of British print culture. Colonialism, and various documented acts of censorship related to it, seems to account for this relative visibility of the relationship of Ireland's press to the country's problems of authority, law, and economics. Ireland's political agency and cultural identity were affected by the fact that the Irish publishing industry had from its origins been a governmental exercise in the production of a favorable image of England through the spread of Protestantism, the dissemination of the English language, and the licensing of printers and other specialists, who also stood to gain from the development of literacy and sales. Ireland's print culture thereby partook of the early modern period's absolutist concept, articulated in Bodin's vision of a commonwealth, of the sovereign's responsibility to standardize all aspects of society. Raymond Gillespie has argued that England was trying to apply this concept in its colonization efforts in Ireland: "The early modern Irish 'political experiment' was principally concerned with creating a uniform commonwealth within the country with one king, one religion, and one set of cultural attributes."[65] The very introduction of printing technology in Ireland may be regarded as the first English attempt at what Edward Said has called cultural imperialism, propaganda that follows upon a colonizing power's military acquisitions in an effort to consolidate them. Mary Pollard says that the English were even using Irish-language Bibles and other texts to convert the Irish to following English culture: "In the sixteenth century the press was introduced into Ireland specifically as an instrument of propaganda to win the natives over to Protestantism through the Irish language."[66] Ireland served as a model for later acts of cultural imperialism elsewhere because it reflects how the new technology was used to recolonize the country for a new regime and religion. In many European kingdoms, as Benedict Anderson has argued, "the coalition between Protestantism and print-capitalism . . . quickly created large new reading publics . . . and simultaneously mobilized them for politico-religious purposes."[67] This effort failed, however, in Ireland, and the publishing trade began to focus mainly on works written in the English language, though there was a significant increase in French titles published in Ireland and imported from France, the latter being mainly literary and scholarly journals, classic drama, and religious works.[68] Universities were the principal means by which readers were produced, books sold, and ideology disseminated; and with the chartering of Trinity College Dublin by Queen Elizabeth I in 1592, the foundation was established for a regional English-language literary market.[69] The first regular newspaper, Robert Thornton's *The News-letter*, ran from 1685 to 1688, and more papers soon followed; a "proliferation" of them began in Dublin in 1700.[70] Many were retailed in coffeehouses and spread the genre to the extent that there was a thriving provincial journalism by the middle of the eighteenth century.[71] When Swift began to publish in Ireland in earnest after 1720, then, domestic print culture was able to sustain his intervention in public opinion, although it was clear that the majority of printed materials were for, by, and about the ruling Anglo-Irish Protestant minority.

Swift's defense of Ireland's constitutional rights via the transformation of the Irish press into an anti-British publicity machine was necessary. The century had begun with a convergence of problems in each major aspect of Ireland's sovereignty. The Irish parliamentary session of 1698–99 found itself constitutionally undercut legislatively by its English counterpart, and Dublin's publishing industry was attempting to assert hegemony in publication of opposition opinion. The bills in question concerned trade, especially the market in wool. The Wool Act was intended to bolster England's wool trade, so as to increase its inland tax receipts as well as its income from exports to other colonies in the empire and to Europe. The crown needed to raise additional revenues for the salaries of the standing army of twelve thousand men that had been sent to Ireland, but it also owed back pay to the disbanded regiments from King William's War. Anticipating the wool legislation, William Molyneux had protested these measures in *The Case for Ireland's Being Bound by Acts of Parliament in England, Stated* (1698). He claimed that by five hundred years of custom, the king of England had defended Ireland's "*Rights* and *Liberties*" and he argued that Ireland was a kingdom of its own, established as such by the elevation of King John to the lordship of Ireland in 1192, and that therefore the Irish Parliament was answerable to the English crown only, not to the English Parliament.[72] In a further complication, a legal case about the rights over the fisheries in the Diocese of Derry had posed questions as to the location and jurisdiction of the final court of appeals for Irish cases. After a stand-off between the Irish and English Houses of Lords on this issue, a bill was passed in 1704 to resolve the case and defer the question of appellate jurisdiction. Meanwhile, because the British government's currency problems jeopardized its ability to provide security within the empire, there being no funds with which to pay the army, England sent soldiers to be barracked in Ireland and asked the Irish legislature to pay for them.[73] One way the Irish Parliament contended with these inroads into its political rights and revenues was to supply its government with only one year's revenue, an approach initiated in 1699.[74] This arrangement was altered in 1703 to provide two years' revenue, a system that was to endure until the abolishment of the Irish Parliament with the Act of Union in 1800.[75] This incremental budgeting gave Ireland a check against English interests.

This legislative dueling suggests that, while the Anglo-Irish Protestant community may have finally consolidated its dominance in Ireland in the 1690s, it had begun to face an issue that had confronted previous regimes: the relationship of the Irish legislature to the crown. The traditional reason for the Irish Parliament's existence was to discover and approve ways and means of providing the crown's Treasury with revenue. The revenue systems that emerged in both England and Ireland during the eighteenth century were more advantageous to the legislatures than they had ever been, because both parliaments no longer met only at the king's pleasure (before the Triennial Act of 1694, English kings had often ruled without holding parliaments at all). Nonetheless, the Anglo-Irish Protestant leadership found itself facing the same issue that had vexed Ireland's relationship with England for centuries: the English crown's and English Parliament's encroachments upon their economic rights. The Irish legislature had consistently asserted loyalty to the crown, insisting that it was constitutionally dependent upon it but also claiming that it had equal rights with the English Parliament. With the destruction of personal monarchy at the end of the Restoration, however, the emergent Whig parliamentary ministerial apparatus proved less favorable to Ireland; the Irish were no longer appealing to a personal monarch but to a crown more heavily controlled by the ministers derived from the legislature. The ever-increasing funding required for imperial wars heated the conventional debate over revenue control, and the beginnings of the *Monti* complicated the situation further. In these circumstances, the identity and status of Ireland within the empire was receiving scrutiny from all sides—scrutiny that recent historians have revisited.

There has been much historiographical debate as to whether Ireland, administratively an English-style kingdom, can be considered to have been a colony in this period, the difference primarily being whether the polity was governed by civil legal code or by a more martial law recommended for territories in a "state of nature." Historians such as T. B. Barry, V. G. Kiernan, Roy Foster, Aidan Clarke, Jane Ohlmeyer, Patrick Kelly, and Nicholas Canny have been willing to use terms such as "established Protestant colony" or "Anglo-Irish colonists"; some of them have contended that English colonial administrators such as Edmund Spenser wrote tracts that were "a blueprint for the continued colonisation of Ireland." For the most part, however, these scholars have been careful to distinguish their own current consideration of Ireland as a colony from the contemporary discourse used by those living in Ireland in the period. From the point of view of administrative history, Swift and others in authority in Ireland, in the words of Joseph McMinn, "resented and rejected any suggestion that Ireland was a colony."[76] They claimed that they were indeed subjects of the same crown as Englishmen but that their parliament was autonomous. They felt that no legislation enacted in the English Parliament was binding on them without their consent. Such arguments had been formulated by "Old English," Catholic descendants of twelfth-century Anglo-Norman settlers since the passage of "Poynings Law" (an English law asserting authority over the Irish legislature) in the later fifteenth century and the establishment of Ireland as a kingdom in 1541. When "New English," Protestant settlers of the late sixteenth century and beyond found themselves in authority and thought of as "Irish" by the English government, they appropriated those older, Catholic claims of legislative autonomy and kingdom status in self-defense. New settlers in Ireland and the Americas occasionally shared the vocabulary of colonization, as Canny has written, though local authorities in Ireland claimed the rights of subjects of an independent kingdom. Irish residents feared that, if their country were indeed a colony like those English settlements in the Americas, they would have less control of their lives, property, and rights. In reality, because of the difficulty of travel and communication, American legislative assemblies were far more autonomous than the Irish Parliament.[77] Ireland's situation might be considered to have been similar to that of Scotland, another kingdom under control of the English crown, but for the fact, which Swift wryly allegorized in *The Story of an Injured Lady*, that Scotland formed a union with England in 1707 that made its partnership in the empire superior to Ireland's (9:1–12).

The question of whether Ireland was a kingdom, like England and Scotland, or a colony, like Massachusetts, ultimately depends on point of view. That perspective depends on whether the commentator had appropriated territory and authority, lost it, or was promoting or contesting the term "colonisation" for political gain; to use or oppose the term was to "take sides in a long and bitter intellectual conflict, which has accompanied, derived from and also itself shaped the recurrent political violence of modern Irish history."[78] The identity of Ireland and the Irish, as an old saying goes, is determined by whether one has been mauled by the Irish situation.

By the eighteenth century, however, "New English Protestants," who have been continuously renamed—the "Anglo-Irish," the "Ascendancy," or more recently the "Anglo-Irish kleptocracy"—could claim to have finally consolidated military and bureaucratic control over the whole of the country.[79] S. J. Connolly, citing Molyneux's *Case for Ireland's Being Bound*, has written that "Irish Protestants of the late seventeenth and early eighteenth centuries indignantly rejected the suggestion that they lived in a colony," for the reasons mentioned above.[80] Yet there had been some augmentation to Ireland's authority because the Irish Parliament began to meet on a regular two-year cycle to approve a supply of revenue to the crown. "For the first time . . . the Irish parliament . . . became a regular and essential part of the machinery of government."[81] The vocabulary of the period spoke of the governing community as the "Protestant Nation" or "protestant Interest."[82] This community, in the works of Molyneux and Swift in particular, began to display "colonial nationalism," a term J. G. Simms borrowed from American history to describe the rise of notions of sovereignty in the discourse of political economy.[83] Indeed, Neil Longley York has shifted the conversation back towards notions of sovereignty to problematize comparisons with other Atlantic settlements: "Eighteenth-century Ireland was distinct from the American colonies in the sense that it was called a 'kingdom' rather than a colony, with a parliament theoretically more powerful than any legislative body in the colonies. Kingdom or not, Ireland was, like the American colonies, still caught up in a dispute over sovereignty that plagued the empire."[84] David Lloyd has developed this question into a broader epistemological conundrum, arguing that the kingdom/colony debate is "immaterial" and that "the function of the modern state" in creating the definitions of sovereignty and colonialism is part and parcel of the process of cultural imperialism. Because "colonialism is . . . always a forged concept," its meaning is "predicated on materially embedded political and cultural struggles."[85] The rules of engagement and conduct in those conflicts, accordingly, seem central to Ireland's claim to have "a shared solidarity and history of oppression" with other postcolonial nations.[86]

The Irish book trade was central to this dispute because the desire to influence public opinion through the press, especially in the wake of the changes in the government of the British Isles in the 1690s, was deeply connected to the questions of fiscal control over Ireland's revenues that had provoked the political arguments of Molyneux and others. As Andrew Carpenter has discussed in his edition of John Dunton's *The Dublin Scuffle* (1699), a narrative of an English bookseller's tour in Ireland and his confrontation with his competitors, Ireland's print industry was emerging as a threat to its English rival in the year of Molyneux's publication.[87] Dublin's book trade had certain advantages because it was more loosely organized and made no fine distinctions between its branches: "Many of the booksellers were also printers and binders, most of the printers published and sold books, and there were not many specialist binders."[88] This lack of regulation led not only to significant reprinting and pirating of London titles but also to less control over public opinion than one would expect in a colony.

From the time of the first printing of a book in Ireland in 1551, the first publishers in Dublin, Humphrey Powell and William Kearney, were considered official printers to the crown and were given government loans to start their business.[89] In 1604, John Franckton was given a monopoly on all printing and selling of books to such an extent that he was allowed to seize and levy a 10 shilling fine on any book owned by anyone, a right that existed in law until 1732, though not always in practice.[90] The Stationer's Company of London, which had invested in a project for the colonization of northern Ireland sponsored by the Company for the Plantation of Ireland in 1611, hoped that the Scots-Irish Presbyterian settlers would create "a rapidly growing market" for publications there. They took over the book publishing monopoly from Franckton in 1618 and held it until 1641. William Bladen was granted the patent as the "King's printer," with a license for government printing only, from 1641 to 1660, an uncertain business during the Civil War era due to the collapse of central authority and the rival propaganda presses of various factions. This limited monopoly was transferred to John Crooke by King Charles II when he was restored in 1660. He was challenged by rivals and "made a clear and plain statement of the state's reasons for granting a monopoly to one person, and in a politic fashion underlined the fact that the King's Printer, as licenser, was responsible to the government for preventing the publication of seditious matter."[91] Like Charles II's advocates in London, Crooke and the viceregal administrative branch of government considered censorship an important component of royal sovereignty in that it suppressed "false doctrines" threatening to the state. By the eighteenth century it was well known that "the single greatest beneficiary of that culture of print was the Dublin Administration."[92]

Meanwhile, Dublin's Guild of St. Luke, a strangely mixed fraternity of stationers, cutlers, and painter-stainers that had incorporated in 1670, began to seek the right to print. Due to the lapsing of the Irish version of the Licensing Act in 1695, as well as the admission of the King's Printer (then Crooke) into the guild, the guild took effective control of the patent. The guild asserted their ownership of the patent in a prosecution of the printer of some illegally printed "popish" Bibles, but they had less success controlling booksellers. Though in law they technically had a monopoly on printing, in practice it seems to have applied only to official printing of Bibles and to acts, statutes, proclamations, and other government publications. There was "little or no restraint on the printing of such privileged books as almanacs, primers, and school books," so rival printers and booksellers had, in all practical senses, the right to compete with the guild until 1732, when a new patent officially liberated them by giving only a very restricted monopoly to its holder.[93]

The 1709 Copyright Act was enacted in England but not in Ireland. The corresponding lack of an Irish intellectual property law was in many ways profitable for Dublin's industry because it meant that it could reprint English editions without any fees. That legal advantage was enhanced by the fact that the 1712 Stamp Act did not apply in Ireland until 1774, which meant that there was no tax on printed matter in Ireland. The lack of copyright and taxes on printing or paper, and lower cost of living and lower production costs made Ireland's printing industry much more profitable than England's over time. Though Dublin continued to import from London more books than it exported there, it nonetheless engaged in piracy and reimportation to England. This activity led to the English Parliament's protectionist Importation Act of 1739, which provided for fines on sellers of pirated books and destruction of Irish reprints arriving on its shores.[94]

The lack of intellectual property rights for Irish authors deprived the domestic industry of homegrown writers. They were not only unprotected from piracy if they published in Dublin, but they could not sell their copyright to a bookseller for a fair price. Irish booksellers "could not afford to outbid London in tempting Irish writers," though they did, as with the compositions of English writers, reprint English editions of Irish writers' works for sale at much lower prices. Most of the Anglo-Irish readership considered London the center of culture, so "even before the passing of the Copyright Act most writers preferred to publish in London—for the sake of reputation and the better circulation of their work amongst the discerning."[95] Consequently, they wrote for English tastes, an economic decision that also bonded Ireland's readership too tightly to the values of Englishness, at least in the eyes of Swift and others who were attempting to attenuate that connection for political and economic reasons.

One major advantage Ireland had in weakening Irish people's loyalty to English booksellers and encouraging the Irish values being disseminated by Dublin booksellers, at least by the eighteenth century, was censorship conditions more favorable to the liberty of the press. By Swift's era, Andrew Crooke II had been dubbed King's Printer, and the Guild of St. Luke's was rarely exercising its right to censor works that violated its monopoly, so censorship was less a matter of private license than public law. In these circumstances, the government relied on libel and sedition prosecutions in Parliament and in law courts. Consequently, Irish trials for libel and sedition, unlike those in England, were governed mostly by common law, meaning that they were often jury trials. This practice favored Swift's printers; most of the prosecutions in the period involved Tory printers, and though various branches of the government could arrest and detain the accused in prison for limited amounts of time, many juries refused to convict them. These conditions were favorable to the production of patriotic Irish public opinion and the formation of nationalistic attitudes, and Irish writers like Swift and printers like John Harding exploited them.[96]

IV

The emergent eighteenth-century Anglo-Irish Protestant identity that these writers and printers articulated was derived from their leadership's expectations of returns on their investment in national security—expectations that shaped contemporary Irish political thought. The *Monti* banking system differed from the Bank of England, a more bourgeois institution of financiers who were not necessarily land owners; the Debt of the Nation structured Irish finance in such a way as to make a more broadly "public" form of government borrowing impossible, or at least unfavorable, for interested lenders. Instead, the Debt of the Nation arose as a form of "private" national debt, or more specifically, private governmental debt. This arrangement ensured that only established Anglo-Irishmen would hold a financial interest in the policies of the Irish executive and the Irish Parliament. It also created a public sphere, but one of a particularly "private" Anglican kind. Because the Irish Parliament controlled the crown's supply of revenue, the Debt of the Nation may be seen as a crucial pillar of Anglo-Irish identity in the eighteenth century.[97] The founding of the *Monti* established legal bonds between subjects, conforming them to its law and oversight under the sign of economic interest—the components most often associated with the signing of a national constitution.

The history of the Irish national debt begins with the Hanoverian ascension in 1715–1716. At that time, both a nonfunded debt and a funded debt were established. The nonfunded debt initially consisted of £16,107 of military pay arrears. The funded debt consisted of a £50,000 emergency loan that the Treasury was permitted to take out by private subscription in 1716 in order to pay for the military costs of combatting the Jacobite uprising in Scotland in those years. In this way, Irish money contributed to the British fiscal-military state, supporting armies all over the empire, a situation which persisted well into the twentieth century. The loan, initially, strengthened British regiments already supported by Irish revenues and barracked in Ireland and shipped them over the Irish Sea for the defense of Scotland. It also paid for the formation of several new regiments for this purpose. It is significant that the subscribers to this initial loan, which promised eight percent interest in return, were members of the Anglo-Irish Protestant establishment.[98] These well-established Anglican people, I argue, were the founding members of the *Monti*, making a private subscription to fund the government that both sustained their positions and provided for the general security of the Protestant interest in Ireland. Their pressing concern, however, was not only for the maintenance of security but also for the preservation of the legal regime that had established their fortunes at the "Glorious Revolution."[99]

The use of Ireland as a barracks for a large portion of the British army controlled rebellion in that country and established that army pay would come from Irish revenues and borrowing by the Irish Treasury. When these regiments were deployed abroad in Britain's military ventures, Irish revenues played a role in the growth of the British Empire. Anglo-Irishmen's loans to the Irish Treasury—the establishment of a national debt separate from Britain's—were thus crucial to the maintenance of empire both in Ireland and across the world. The Debt of the Nation not only founded Anglo-Irish identity as that of a proto-republican cartel committed to the future of Anglican hegemony on Ireland's domestic front, but also provided for the hidden costs of Britain's empire, costs that thus did not register on Britain's own Treasury.

V

Swift's call, in *A Proposal for the Universal Use of Irish Manufacture*, for a general boycott of British commodities, in this context, is more figural; the Anglo-Irish *Monti* needed to divide itself from Britain by censoring English-made texts and the opinions advocated in them. The consequence of publishing this pamphlet—the prosecution of its printer, Edward Waters—suggests how threatening this mobilization of colonial opinion for the retention of revenue control was to the empire's military expansion. The pamphlet's message about the loss of coinage due to an imbalance in trade was clear. For the country to possess legislative authority over its own revenues and economic policy, it had to exploit and amplify economic resentment of Britain. If England had dominance but not hegemony over the country in the eighteenth century, it was because the Irish press waged a constant culture war defending Irish authority and Ireland's distinction as an autonomous society.[100] The pamphlet can be read as a literary text that brings together the history of the book in Ireland and Irish economic history, an unexpected convergence rendered visible in the study of Dublin's print culture in the decades following the founding of the *Monti*. As I discuss in the final chapter of this book, a distinct literary sphere parasitical on colonial politics—one that nonetheless underwrote political activity—was emerging from this process. The discourse on Irish political thought provoked by the crisis in political sovereignty, fiscal control, and public opinion in 1720, consequently, was an interdisciplinary one.

Despite the publishing campaign's inclusive rhetoric and the enthusiasm of a diverse group of readers, the limitation of membership in the *Monti* to the ranks of established Anglo-Irishmen came to define what truly constituted the "public" in Ireland. The willingness of established Anglo-Irishmen to contribute to the maintenance of the Irish government was born of self-preservation: defense of their property and their profit from investment in government futures and ensurance that the Irish executive, and its policy, would remain under the influence of Anglo-Irishmen. The private nature of borrowing by Ireland's Treasury thus kept the Irish economy in a primitive state, yet one that pleased Swift because it put control over the system of public finance in the hands of the landed class, rather than professional financiers as in England. The threat that the Declaratory Act posed, however, derived not only from its assertion of control over their revenues but from the fact that it was passed within weeks of the South Sea Act, which attempted to convert shares in England's national debt into shares in the South Sea Company. In short, the Declaratory Act was assuring investors that those shares would be backed by Irish revenues. This arrangement was something that Swift understood, as is reflected in a letter that he wrote in the weeks following the passage of both acts.[101]

A Proposal's brief discourse on political thought reacts to the Declaratory Act not with the complex legal historicism that characterized Molyneux's *Case* but with a less intellectual approach that eschews theory in favor of pragmatism. S. J. Connolly has argued that such pragmatism characterized Anglo-Irishmen's political thought throughout this period. This pragmatic attitude may have reflected what David Berman has identified as the antitheoretical orientation of the Church of Ireland's particular brand of Anglican theology.[102] *A Proposal* first indulges academic questions about whether the Declaratory Act is consistent with existing philosophy of sovereignty, then says that those questions are not so relevant as matters of common sense (9:19). By dismissing theoretical assertions about whether men can in good conscience follow laws made without their consent, the pamphlet reflects the era's idea that public opinion often trumped academic legal discourse. In the Declaratory Act, the English Parliament had produced a legislative fiat—its opinion was the only significant one—yet members of the Irish Parliament were able to harness the local press to rally domestic opinion and help nullify the statute as a practical reality. The legislative sessions of 1721, 1723, and 1725, all of which roused furious controversy over who had final authority over the Irish economy, forced the British crown and Parliament to retreat, in practical terms, from their formal legal claims of 1720. "English ministers took care to avoid giving unnecessary offence to Irish opinion," writes Connolly; "proposals for legislation coming from the [Irish] House of Commons were treated with respect, and sparing use was made of London's extensive powers to veto Irish bills or to impose legislation on Ireland from Westminster."[103]

A Proposal's interior economic argumentation envisions a self-sufficient Ireland consuming its own products and boycotting imports. Its political polemic—particularly that against the Declaratory Act—thus generated an "exterior" force and created the "Other" that defined the Anglo-Irish political subject. Given the epistolary evidence of Swift's understanding of the British courtly causes of the Declaratory Act, we must regard his handling of the act in this pamphlet as calculated purely for rhetorical effect, to inculcate a political Anglo-Irish Protestant identity in his readers. This identity was coming to be organized along newly economic lines. It was reiterated in later works of his, like *A Short View of the State of Ireland* and *Maxims Controlled in Ireland*, both of which complain of trade restrictions and recommend boycotting to resolve Ireland's problems (12:8, 12:132). The dearth of coin in Ireland in this period was attenuating the link between Ireland and Britain; the "coin of the realm" was in short supply, so its practical ideological effects in innumerable acts of exchange no longer fostered a practical loyalty. The very development of an Irish printed discourse on this problem, regardless of the positions taken in it, functioned to constitute a distinct Irishness that was of economic and cultural value.

A few Anglo-Irishmen, observing their peers' rush to buy South Sea Company stocks in 1720, were concerned that members of their caste might move their money, divesting from the *Monti* and investing instead in the South Sea Company. Because Ireland did not have its own central provincial finance company, this group began a project for a national bank of Ireland, to pull investment towards an institution that would be connected to the *Monti*. Swift's rhetorical division of an "Irish" economic body politic distinct from the British one cannot be separated from the bank project, because he closes *A Proposal* with a reflection upon it. The last paragraph of the pamphlet derides the national bank idea, especially for its proposals to circulate what Swift described as "altogether imaginary" money, or paper currency (9:21–22). By insisting on a firm division between "real" and "imaginary" money in the context of this pamphlet, he not only constructed a heuristic device that lends a putative materiality to coin—a materiality of value about which he personally had doubts—but links the Irish national interest to a belief in the intrinsic value of gold and silver money. If the goal of mobilizing the press was to manufacture an Irish imagined community from which claims to sovereignty would issue, however, Swift's skepticism of "imaginary" money— the paper currency promised by the bank—is perplexing. It suggests that part of his agenda was the direction of that "real" money to only some members of that nation—the vested interests of the *Monti*. By revising the history of the Irish book and that of the Irish financial revolution, this reading of Swift's Irish pamphlets reflects the "tendency of recent research . . . to emphasize the extent to which patriot rhetoric could mask vested interests and the pursuit of political power."[104] Nonetheless, Swift's encouragement of the Irish printing industry to support the *Monti* had broader significance in Irish history in that it may be taken as the founding moment of a distinctly modern form of nationalism created first in the discourse of political economy.

CHAPTER 2

Banking on Print

The Bank of Ireland, the South Sea Bubble,
and the Bailout

The 1720–21 project to create the Bank of Ireland is significant to the study of Irish economic history, the history of the Irish book, and Swift's Irish writings in several ways. First, it marks a moment when the political basis of the *Monti*'s investment in Irish revenues was challenged by the Declaratory Act and by schemes to manage the Debt of the Nation through a central bank in a way that might eliminate the need for the Irish Parliament. If, as some contemporaries thought, confidence in the South Sea investment bubble of those years was supported, in part, by the act's implication that the British Parliament would take over Irish taxation, the bank would pose a further risk by placing the majority of Ireland's cash in one place. Though there were many other reasons for opposition to the bank, the uncertainty about who had legal control over the bank's deposits, especially in the wake of much-publicized incidents of South Sea Company executives' absconding to the Continent with investors' funds, may have been central to the *Monti*'s fears and to its members' eventual rejection of the bank project. Second, Anglo-Irish investors such as members of the *Monti* who had lost money because of the bursting of the bubble stood to gain from a planned bailout of the company's shareholders by the Bank of England, and they feared that creating an Irish national bank, by drawing investors away from the Bank of England, would jeopardize that bailout. Third, the pamphlet controversy that emerged during parliamentary considerations of the bank may have been more important than the project itself, inasmuch as they initiated a modern Irish identity based on the concept of shared risk in a national venture. These pamphlets and books were written in a variety of genres and styles and printed and priced at a range of costs. They addressed landowning, commercial, and common constituencies to sway opinion in favor of or against the bank idea and functioned to unify a diverse population around the question of Ireland's economic interests. Fourth, Swift's participation in the bank controversy may be taken as an extension of his engagement with Irish political economy that began with *A Proposal for the Universal Use of Irish Manufacture*. He may have exploited the occasion of the bank project to deliver on *A Proposal*'s call for Dublin printers to begin to produce "Irish" works.

The Bank of Ireland project was first proposed during the South Sea Company stock boom of the spring of 1720—a fact of some importance, as opponents of the bank would later use that origin to suggest that it was merely another "bubble company" and as such should be damned as a chimera that would lead to a similar financial disaster. John Irwin's *To the Nobility, Gentry and Commonality of this Kingdom of Ireland*, published sometime in April or early May of that year, argued that investment in the South Sea and Mississippi companies had drained Ireland of cash and that a new bank would remedy that problem by introducing an Irish paper currency. The pamphlet formally announced the initial public offering of stock, saying that subscriptions would be accepted beginning 19 May to capitalize the bank with £500,000.[1] A petition for a royal charter for the bank, pleading that "the extreme Scarcity of Coin in this kingdom has already occasioned a General decay of Trade" in Ireland, was submitted to the viceroy on 28 May.[2] By September, another bank proposal emerged, but this one proposed a capitalization of one million pounds and linked the establishment of a bank with paying off £50,000 of Ireland's national debt. A third proposal failed to attract interest, and the first two were eventually merged, and a charter dated 29 July 1721 linked the bank to paying off that £50,000.[3] When the Irish Parliament opened in September 1721, it initially considered a bill for the certifying of the charter favorably but then appeared to turn against it in a vote in the House of Commons in October. Meanwhile, the House of Lords in early November voted against the bill. The pamphlet controversy erupted during a three-week recess, and the bill was soundly defeated by the House of Commons when it reconvened in December. Because the 1721 session of Parliament was the first to meet after the passage of the Declaratory Act, it is likely that concerns about that act weighed heavily in the consideration of the bank legislation.

Most historiography on the bank episode has focused on the sovereignty dimensions of the debate. As Philip O'Regan has written, for leading Members of the Irish House of Commons and House of Lords, "the question of a national bank had become embroiled in the larger constitutional issue."[4] Isolde Victory says that the debate was over who had control over the bank's capital and how that control would affect Ireland's economy and political sovereignty: "Without ultimate legislative control the [Anglo-Irish] colonists could not guarantee that the bank would work in the national, that is to say Ireland's, interest."[5] This argument followed in the tradition of F. G. Hall, who has suggested that "agitation against the bank project was aroused and conducted by the Anglo-Irish patriotic movement, usually associated with the names of Molyneux and Swift."[6] Dismissing these claims, Michael Ryder contends that "the discussion of the merits of the bank was conducted in terms which fall outside the tradition of legal controversy" and that there has been a tendency to overestimate the importance of Swift's contribution to the bank controversy.[7] Ryder maintains, "It seems impossible to treat the bank controversy as a simple antithesis between Irish liberty and English control"; he prefers to see in the defeat of the bank the triumph of a Locke-and-Molyneux-inflected Irish version of English "country" ideology. This ideology of real property saw the moneyed interest—financiers who were not gentry or nobility—as a threat to the country's landed interest—agrarian capitalists with a stake in the material geography of the country that made them capable of practicing more virtuous and disinterested politics on behalf of the nation. English country ideology's defense of these principles was usually couched as a retrenchment of what was labeled the "Constitution in Church and State," as documents from Swift's earlier career—in England—such as the *Examiner* papers, make clear (3:3–5, 3:124, 3:169). In Ireland, this defense was usually couched in the principle of the "Protestant interest," by which was meant not the entirety of the Protestant or even specifically the Anglican community but proprietors of large amounts of land.

This chapter contributes to Ryder's argument by contending that what lay behind this Anglo-Irish country rhetoric was the defense of the *Monti* as a form of banking in which the landed interest was its own moneyed interest, opposing the bank because it would give financiers greater control over Irish affairs. The Protestant interest did not need a central bank, because it used the Irish Treasury as one and, by doing so, linked its economic interests to its political control over Ireland's taxes. In this view, a national bank was perceived as a danger to the *Monti*, not only because it threatened to eliminate Britain's dependence on the Irish Parliament for revenue, but also because its plan to pay off the £50,000 principal on the national debt would undermine the much more valuable perpetual interest payments to which the Protestant interest was entitled.

Primarily, however, this chapter intervenes in the historiography of the bank episode from a literary perspective, arguing that the pamphlet controversy over the bank was itself a means of constituting an imagined economic community for Ireland. The pamphlet writers' opinions created the political public sphere that, in turn, enabled the conditions in which many perspectives could be freely debated, and those opinions themselves formed a consensus that a distinctly Irish stake was on the table. The Declaratory Act had already rendered Ireland Britain's "other" by symbolically denying it equal legislative rights, and the pamphlets mirrored that division by cultivating a contrast between the political and economic interests of these kingdoms. The various rhetorical strategies and points of argumentation of the pamphlets, in this reading, were not as important as the development of the Irish printing industry, book trade, and domestic readership that were made possible by them. As one pamphleteer noted, the pamphlets and books about the bank themselves constituted a form of "bank" to which many authors and readers "subscribed" as if they were depositors and investors, and many hands— including those of the practitioners of the various crafts of the stationer's guild—went into making them.[8] Swift, as Ryder argues, may not have been a significant figure in the controversy because he did not alter specific opinions about the bank project, but the debate itself may have been his first opportunity to actualize the publishing agenda recommended in *A Proposal for the Universal Use of Irish Manufacture*. His contribution mostly consisted of poetry, which, as another book contended in the year of the controversy, could be considered "a Fund as real" as the subscription for the bank (9:344). Print, in the view of the writer of this book, had the potential to serve as the cultural capital through which a standard of taste—and the scales of valuation accompanying it—could be imagined and reified as Ireland's medium of finance capital. *A Letter of Advice to a Young Poet, The Run Upon the Bankers, The Bubble*, and other short pieces may have been literary works parasitical on the controversy's more serious pamphlets, but their discourses on value may have been more significant because they constructed the "nation" as the location of redemption in the wake of the South Sea Bubble.

I

A Letter of Advice to a Young Poet; Together with a Proposal for the Encouragement of Poetry in this Kingdom, which some attribute to Swift, was not the first pamphlet in the controversy nor one that made the bank project its main topic.[9] It is central to an understanding of the debate, however, because it argues that the development of a national print culture could help Ireland remedy its problems as much, if not more, than the bank could. Though its last page declares that it was written "*December* 1, 1720," its title page says it was published in 1721 by John Hyde, the Dublin reprinter of many of Swift's London publications, including *Gulliver's Travels*. Herbert Davis argued that *A Letter of Advice* was printed during the Parliamentary session of the fall of 1721 because it mentions *Swearer's Bank*, a satirical pamphlet that he says was published in November 1721 (9:345, 9:xix–xxi). Internal evidence indicates that the charter for the Bank of Ireland had not yet been obtained, suggesting that *A Letter of Advice* was either printed between 1 December 1720 and 29 July 1721 or that its language about the charter had not been changed in the process of converting the manuscript into print sometime after 29 July (9:344). Regardless of the exact timing of its appearance, the pamphlet's recommendations about the necessity of a domestic book trade anticipate and comment upon the way in which the bank debate was contributing to the formation of an Irish imagined community. As an essay structured like a proposal for a business or investment project, it closely mirrors the form of pamphlets proposing the bank and other companies. This format, however, was not unusual, as booksellers engaged in projecting ideas for a book before hiring an author to bring those ideas to fruition. In this fashion, the bookseller and his backers were like investors speculating on the success of a book in the marketplace.[10] *A Letter of Advice* compares the Irish book trade to the bank in a manner that indicates that both are potential sources of wealth for the country. Its discourse on the learning, rhetorical strategies, and poetic devices that a writer must have at his or her disposal, consequently, reads as an inventory of the capital and assets necessary for the success of the individual artist and the advancement of Ireland's poetry in general. This format, considered as both an accommodation of the debate's style and its parody, enables a metacommentary on the bank controversy as a national media event and a critique of making all genres and disciplines conform to the language of political economy to prove their utility. Nonetheless, this parody of the Anglo-Irish economic pamphlet, most notably perfected in Swift's *A Modest Proposal*, also may be taken as a serious project for a national literature that would render other improvements to the economy possible. A literary public did not emerge in Ireland until the 1730s, however, so this pamphlet may be taken as planting the seeds for a form of literary production that would take root in the economic discourse that was generating a more strictly political public in the 1720s.

The jargon of accounting used in *A Letter of Advice* competes with its jargon of book production, dissolving the distinction between them into a general, though subtle, discourse on the relationship of money, credit, and literature. It approaches writing and publishing as both a business and a means of disseminating the idea of nation. The work of the individual artist, as described in advice from an older poet to a younger one, is linked to recommendations for the growth of the Irish book trade. Some passages compare literary talent to domestic "stock" that does not need foreign investment (London book titles) to mature into profit, but may, like a garden, be fertilized by it. One passage suggests that the poet's "stock" is comparable to the Dublin book trade's—a connection signaled by the seemingly misplaced terms "foreign assistance" and "abroad"— making the case for the domestic production and consumption of Irish-made texts. Swift is arguing, in the modernist sense, for the autonomy of the author, but also for the autonomy of Irish art. Ireland's literature should spring, "root and stem," from domestic soil and should be "a Fountain that feeds it self." Like "dry pumps that will not play till Water is thrown into them," however, duller Irish wits may need to consult the "Authors of Antiquity" (9:333).

Accordingly, *A Letter* recommends that the young poet imitate notable authors; it does so using language that compares the poet's commonplace book to a merchant's accounting book. "Wit," or fine literature, is like money because both are media of exchange by which the buyer and seller, or reader and writer, establish a contract (9:337). The young poet who reads and records the words of a notable author in his commonplace book lends that author credit that will be repaid when the young poet imitates him in his own work, much as a merchant expects a customer to eventually pay the debt that he has incurred by purchasing on store credit. This neat encapsulation of the harmonious relationship of literary lenders and creditors, however, is undercut by Swift's previous satire of poets as "*Readers*, who only read to *borrow*, i.e. to *steal*" (9:334). This poet is a book thief, and if the merchant may be taken as the bookseller from whom the book was stolen, the poet is not listed in the credit book and attempts to lead a life in which he does not owe anything to anyone. He is a pirate, and if *A Letter of Advice* is linking the individual poet's career to "the encouragement of poetry in this kingdom," it may be recommending one means—reprinting and pirating London titles—by which the Dublin publishing industry may prepare itself for more original productions.

This accounting and printing language is extended to consider books as assets to the poet, and by continuing to compare the individual artist's needs to those of the Dublin book trade, Swift discusses the relative merits of original versus pirated material in the capitalization of that industry. The Bible, for example, may be a resource for the poet and may legally be reprinted in Dublin: "the Scriptures are undoubtedly a Fund *of* Wit. . . . Shut up the Sacred Books, and I would be bound our Wit would run down like an Alarm, or fall as the Stocks did, and ruin half the Poets in these Kingdoms. And if that were the Case, how would most of that Tribe . . . rejoice that they had drawn out in time, and left the present Generation of Poets to be the BUBBLES" (9:330). The Bible is compared to the subscriber's list or accountant's book for a ponzi investment scheme in which new investors in the material must continually be allowed to participate if the older ones want to profit. Yet they may be "bubbled"—duped—by the older generation of poets if appropriating and/or reprinting the Bible is banned. The South Sea Bubble, the author implies, was inflated as much by the production of texts, including sacred ones, as it was by the rising influx of money. The lesson to politicians and the Dublin book trade, consequently, was that if Ireland was to have a rising economy, it too must produce texts creating confidence in the country's ability to survive on its "own Materials" (9:333).

The development of Irish poetry and the Dublin publishing industry is explicitly linked in *A Letter of Advice* to the bank scheme, which had not yet received a charter from the king. Its author suggested that literature was as important as the proposed bank as a potential resource for improving the nation's economy.

> If any further Application shall be made on t'other Side to obtain a Charter for a *Bank* here, I presume to make a Request, that *Poetry* may be a Sharer in that Privilege, being a Fund as real, and to the full as well grounded as our Stocks; but I fear our Neighbours, who envy our *Wit* as much as they do our *Wealth* or *Trade*, will give no Encouragement to either. (9:344)

Poetry itself, the author contends, could function as a national bank because it is not only real value within itself but also that which may influence what the imagination *regards* as real and valuable. The term "Fund" has a dual meaning here—one for banking, the other for printing; as Moxon's *Mechanick Exercises* explains, a printing house's supply of fonts of type was often referred to as a "fund."[11] These fonts, because they print on paper, are like a source of capital, a fund. Because wit or literature is money in this pamphlet's lexicon, Britain may be taken to be jealous of Ireland's trade in it as well as other commodities; the author implies that the British might attempt to discourage all trades through the exercise of the Declaratory Act. The mobilization of the Dublin press for the creation of the national culture for which the pamphlet is calling would not only profit writers and printers. It also could serve as the key to securing the *Monti*'s wealth by transubstantiating the nominal notion of the Irish nation into a real presence that could oppose British policies that were undercutting Ireland's economy.

A Letter of Advice makes its case for a national print culture by suggesting that literature is lacking in Ireland. The narrator complains, "I have many Years lamented the want of a *Grub-street* in this our large and polite *City*" (9:341). Grub Street, a metonymic London location where popular literature was printed, had been noted as the source of low-brow writing since John Dryden published *MacFlecknoe* in the late seventeenth century and was usually the object of ridicule by Swift and friends such as Alexander Pope and John Gay. The narrator of *A Letter*, however, is saying that such popular cultural production is needed in Dublin, which has the outlets for it: "we have here a *Court*, a *College*, a *Play-House* . . . and abundance of *Pens*, *Ink* and *Paper* (clear of Taxes) and every other circumstance to provoke WIT, and yet those whose Province it is, have not yet thought fit to appoint a place for *Evacuations* of it" (9:341). Though the books published by what Bryan Coleborne has called "the Dublin Grub Street" would be, as the scatological term "evacuations" implies, pulp fiction, it is precisely that kind of work, in the opinion of the narrator, that would help form a literary public sphere in Ireland.[12] "*A Corporation* of *Poets*," he argues, should be formed to cooperate with the "*Wardens* and *Beadles*" of the Guild of St. Luke's, and they should attend public occasions in "Gowns turn'd up with Green"—Ireland's national color—"instead of Lawrels" (9:344–345). By also recommending that the Irish government and various Irish cities have poets laureate and that Trinity College Dublin should endow a professorship in poetry to preside over that sphere, *A Letter of Advice* furthers that goal by creating living symbols of literature's power. As Ingrassia has argued, the cult of the personality of the author provided stability within print culture, giving writers the opportunity to emblematize a form of "written" proprietorship suited to the new paper economy.[13] Swift's authorial persona was the first to serve as such an emblem of value in modern Anglo-Irish literature.

As *A Letter of Advice* suggests, patronage from the landed men of the Protestant interest, who controlled many aspects of government, would launch the Irish culture industry and be its primary support: "I have heard, that a certain Gentleman has great Designs, to serve the Public in the way of their Diversions, with due Encouragement, (that is) if he can obtain some *Concordatum Money*, or *Yearly Sallery*, and handsome *Contributions*" (9:343). A public salary in the form of a political patronage job and private contributions in the form of subscriptions for publications were common means of encouraging writers and printers to wage a media campaign, but the award of Concordatum money—payments from Ireland's secret service fund—may seem an unusual means by which sponsor publications. British writers, such as Daniel Defoe, had received such fees from British secret service funds, though it remains unclear whether they were for publication or only for spying.[14] Further, there is research to suggest that secret service money was paid to printers in Swift's era and at the turn of the eighteenth to the nineteenth centuries.[15] The discussion of the Concordatum in this context suggests that members of the Irish Privy Council, who controlled the fund, may have been making the link between the support of nominally valuable paper money and the culture industry. The members of the Privy Council who were also *Monti* contributors, in short, may have envisioned a national literature as an effective substitute for coin in the post–South Sea Bubble era. A national literature could be that which produced confidence in alternative forms of currency such as paper money by constructing the idea of a sovereign economic community that could govern exchange.

Other pamphlets participated in *A Letter of Advice*'s metadiscourse on the role of the bank controversy in creating national identity. Swift's *Swearer's Bank or, Parliamentary Security for a new Bank*, for example, notes that language itself could underwrite the stock and deposits of the proposed bank. Referring to an already existing fine of one shilling levied on members of Parliament for "profane swearing," it argues that extending this fine to the whole population would yield millions of pounds in public revenue that could guarantee the bank's deposits (9:295). This proposal parodies the controversy by pointing to the sheer amount of words expended upon the issue of the bank, calling attention to how, regardless of its outcome, it has created a national public. Another pamphlet attributed to Swift, *An Account of the Short Life, sudden Death, and pompous Funeral of Michy Windybank, &c.*, refers to these words as "wind," suggesting that the bank was never anything but the sum of the papers in the controversy. It refers to the corpus of the debate as a dead "*Child*" who must be "embalm'd and lap'd in *Sheets of Paper*" for its funeral (9:309). These satires, together with more serious essays of political economy like *A Letter to the Gentlemen of the Landed Interest in Ireland, Relating To a Bank*, consider the debate itself to be a form of paper credit ultimately more valuable to Ireland than the paper currency promised by the bank projectors. These works, however, came late to a debate that began with the rise and fall of the South Sea Bubble. The controversy in the autumn of 1721 would not have taken the shape that it did if the poetry and pamphlets, together with the financial crisis itself, had not conditioned Irish readers to react to economic news politically.

Two of Swift's poems of 1720, *The Run Upon the Bankers* and *The Bubble*, exploited the financial meltdown of their year of publication while nonetheless converting their critique into the final site of economic redemption: land, the real asset backing the *Monti*. These and his other responses to the South Sea crash can be credited with inventing a heuristic that held real estate to be a sublimated site of value opposed to, yet supporting, paper credit and the moneyed interest. The poems were published a few months after the crash, in London and Dublin respectively, and they satirize paper credit as a nominal chimera not equivalent to sound coinage. Their function was to capitalize on the denigration of such notes by the public and, by doing so, to promise the immanent rematerialization of "real" value in the form of coins and land. In effect, works like these modeled desire in such a way as to maintain "the investor's imagination concerning a moment which will never exist in reality" for the *Monti*'s nation.[16] The net effect of the poems is to reify the putative "realness" of sterling and land and the corollary Tory political ideology that went with them. Yet this distinction was produced within a culture saturated by paper credit investment and in which those securities were also subject to the stock market—a culture in which Swift himself was personally investing.[17] The satire of these poems produced a division between the scapegoated world of paper credit that Swift targeted and the normative agrarianism he presented to the reader's imagination. This splitting attempted to inscribe within discourse a hierarchy that would yield an ideology in which the terms "coin" and "land" could continue to represent immanent *loci* of intrinsic value guaranteeing paper credit's merely nominal form. This strategy and its implicit scheme of commensuration mobilized Tory resentment at the bursting of the Whig bubble and modeled the party's potential recapture of political ascendancy. As satire, these works critique a problem in order to promote a different ideal, in this case a normative politics and economy oriented around agrarian capitalism—trade in land's produce.

The Anglo-Irish gentry had invested heavily in a variety of companies associated with the bubble. William Conolly, speaker of the Irish House of Commons, described some of this investment and the effects of the bursting of the bubble.[18] Archbishop William King of Dublin reported the extent to which people spent their equity in real estate and bought stock with loans secured on it.[19] The entire financial system of the Kingdom of Ireland was at stake because of these developments. Complicating matters was the Bank of Ireland project, which had arisen at the same time as the investment bubble. The project failed in part because the bursting of the bubble had undermined faith in such schemes, but also because of the Anglo-Irish establishment's anxiety that the proceeds of their investment in the *Monti* would be taken by Britain if placed in the bank and managed by it. The bank was to be one of deposit, not a *Monti*, and its opponents were concerned that by placing all of the country's resources in one institution chartered by the crown, both personal and public funds could legally be seized by politicians in London. The Declaratory Act and South Sea bills were being prepared simultaneously, and some observers feared that the managers of this legislation were creating investment confidence by backing the stock with provincial revenues that they had the potential to appropriate. Moreover, the South Sea Act was undertaken to convert outstanding public bonds into private shares in the South Sea Company, suggesting, as one gentleman remarked, that the Anglo-Irish landed class would effectively pay England's national debt.[20] In these circumstances, a variety of vested interests arrayed themselves against the bank initiative. In this crisis, all were attempting to redeem their paper securities for any real assets that remained. The bank's proposal for administering the Debt of the Nation and disseminating a national paper currency not only threatened existing monopolies in the financial sector but also presented the possibility that hard cash would migrate beyond their reach.

A Run Upon the Bankers and *The Bubble* dramatize the collapse of confidence in the financial system. The first satirizes the lack of actual commodities backing South Sea stock certificates, effectively saying that irrational and "capricious" desire, rather than what Swift would consider a secured, disinterested, and "virtuous" material personality, governed the South Sea Company.[21] This absence of real assets breaks "the bankers and the banks," who cannot possibly answer the call to redeem their banknotes for specie during the panic. The note-holding public was demanding payment immediately, and the bankers were withholding it lest they lose both their business and personal wealth: "We want our Money on the Nail; / The Banker's ruin'd if he pays" (lines 17–18). Swift unleashed his full critique of paper currency, focusing on the banknotes of Ireland's private bankers. The idea that "parchment wings" (paper) and the "plumes" of "geese" (quills) could create wealth was problematic for Swift, and the run on the banks provided him with the occasion to gloat over the fact that the popular will to convert banknotes into coin supported his Tory appreciation of hard currency (lines 23–24). He compares the fiscal-military state, which was responsible for the bubble, to a vampire bat that sucked the life out of the body politic, especially the Irish gentry.

The Bubble builds upon these observations, extending the notion of circulation within the national body politic to the migration of capital abroad.[22] Geared towards a broader British audience, it should be understood as a revision of *A Run Upon the Bankers* that focuses more strongly on the South Sea Company itself. *The Bubble* revives the "circus" rhetoric of *A Proposal for the Universal Use of Irish Manufacture* to describe paper credit schemes, likening the South Sea Bubble to a conjurer's magic trick in a carnival sideshow and describing it as having been created by imported publications that distracted the eye from what is "real." Publicity for the South Sea Company leads investors to imagine a "fantastick Scene" in which their profits lead to "a Lord's Estate" and "A Coach and Six" (lines 30, 18, 20)—unrealistic expectations for the vast majority of investors. The poem once again underscores Swift's public sentiments about the corrupt moneyed interest attempting to displace the virtuous landed interest through duplicitous promises of profits from their investment schemes.

The poem contains a cautionary note about the presumed indemnity of the company directors from the financial chaos of the South Sea investment debacle, metaphorically informing the reading public that these authors of the crisis may yet be held accountable. The satirist suggests that there will be a search for the directors who have fled and an exorcism of these parasites from the souls of investors and the British body politic. This desire for accountability enacts a search for closure—an end to the sublime excess of disappointed desire associated with the South Sea fiasco that the "real" of the satirically scapegoated bodies of the company directors can provide. Indeed, the poem's frequent and repetitious references to such words as the "deep" and "depth" (lines 42, 110, 149, 175, 207), the "drown'd" (lines 60, 147, 192, 216), and "sink" (lines

91, 136, 195, 210), all establish an unconscious undercurrent to British culture that is suddenly and traumatically being made conscious. *The Bubble* thus was instrumental in constructing a British country ideology of the real, shaped from the practical engagement with the new forms of money presented by the English financial revolution and its most notable trauma. Swift seems to have been quite aware that paper credit constituted a national sublime for Britain, and the "South Sea" was the perfect and convenient metaphor to encapsulate the connotations of that ineffable being and identity that lies deep beneath the surface of the conscious and nominal representation. As Pat Rogers notes, *The Bubble* "was one of the most frequently reprinted of all Swift's poems," and it should be understood as a central document in the shaping of the English historical imagination of that event.[23]

The analysis of Swift's reification of land and coin into normative entities in these works requires the postcolonial appropriation of the "satiric norm" or "satiric antithesis," a New Critical concept by which the negative vice or folly targeted in Juvenalian or Horatian satire, respectively, is counterbalanced by a positive meditation on a specific or implicit virtue. Classical formal verse satire followed a two-part structure in which Part A attacked "some specific vice or folly" and was followed by Part B, in which "its opposing virtue was recommended. . . . for every vice, major and minor, there must be a precisely corresponding precept of virtue."[24] The "norm" is often not in the text, but only implied.[25] In the latter case, it is context and/or reader dependent: "it is up to us to supply its 'true' meaning from knowledge tacitly shared by the satirist and ourselves. . . . the normative moral ingredient of satire follows from the fact that culpability has no meaning outside some context of rectitude or propriety."[26] This shared knowledge is usually that of a small, elite group and the satiric norm asserts a particular agenda.[27] It seeks to paint a picture of a disordered society in need of restoration: "satire presents something as grotesque: the grotesque is by definition a deviant from a norm: the norm makes the satire satiric."[28] This strategy is inevitably political: "negativity can be enlisted in the service of ideological construction. . . . satire's effects can be read as formative rather than reformative or destructive, though both reformation and destruction may advance its formative ends."[29] Scriblerian satire resurrected, or at least transubstantiated, its vision of the virtue of a social order based on agrarian capitalism: "The ideological imperatives associated with an expanding commercial nation demand not a longing backward glance but rather a re-reflection of that backward glance so that it encompasses the present, making presence itself out of satire's productive absence."[30] The Tory perspective was not simply one of nostalgia for a time before the financial revolution; their faction was an active player in the market whose cultural production in the form of satire served to assert their particular financial interests and claim their right to govern. This non-universalism of the satirist's norm is particularly manifest in Swift's work on Irish economic issues; the "normative moral ingredient" to Swift's satires on these occasions is financial and is concerned with the maintenance of the *Monti*'s property.

The satire on South Sea paper credit in the poems, accordingly, has a logic that attempts to construct the boundaries between real and imaginary value in a financial situation in which the saturation of the culture with South Sea Company paper, and its devaluation, had proven all value to be contingent. The landed ideology of real property is precisely that— an ideology, within a discursive field rather than the autonomous presence its proponents purport it to be. Consequently, the agrarian landed interest and financial moneyed interest both represented sources of capital already inscribed by writing and various forms of paper credit. The necessity for the distinction between them is that, in a heuristic sense, a difference between the imaginary and the real had to be posited—a necessary distinction if paper were to be considered redeemable for some substance like land and the nation prevented from being thought of as bankrupt. The financial work of satire "can be seen most profitably in terms of a reordering of discourses in which the real and imaginary sums present to the economy are represented within discrete and mutually exclusive discursive domains, and by the very fact of this reordering the power of representation itself increases."[31] The aestheticized promises of government bonds and South Sea stock dominated all aspects of British culture, and property "ceased to be real" and became "not merely mobile but imaginary."[32] Therefore, land became a discursive object, not a material one, and was subject to paper credit's mobilizing of property into writing. Yet the discourse surrounding paper credit had to maintain the vanished distinction between real property and paper in order to sustain the credit of the nation, the belief in the redeemability of government stock, and the monetary system itself.

Swift's skepticism in these two poems constructs such an imaginative heuristic in that it enacts one of the chief functions of satire: to arouse contempt for the scapegoated target (paper credit) while contrasting it with a norm (land or bullion). The formal operation of the genre in these two instances actuates a sublimating "reality effect" in which a boundary is constructed between the South Sea Company's debasement and Swift's presentation of an alternative of common sense, poetic justice, and fair dealing. This contrast rebuilds confidence by inferring that there is an immanent reserve of resources supporting Britain and Ireland. It is only through conveying such an impression that the myth of national solvency can be restored. This satiric strategy, in short, helped to underwrite the *Monti*.

III

Also helping the *Monti* during the post-bubble recession were practical actions like the British government's bailout of the shareholders who held now-worthless South Sea Company stock, some of whom were Anglo-Irish investors. The Bank of Ireland project was jeopardizing this bailout because if investors shifted their money to this Irish bank from the Bank of England—one of the sources for the cash and shares of financial stocks needed for the bailout—funds needed to reimburse South Sea shareholders might not be available. Though some Anglo-Irishmen were afraid that this bailout would be funded by the Irish tax revenues that rightfully belonged to the Irish Parliament and the *Monti*, the evidence indicates that many were also worried that creating the Irish bank would prevent them from being reimbursed for their stock market losses. They wanted the British government to support the stock market with a Bank of England and taxpayer-funded bailout, but they did not want Ireland's taxes to be used for it, especially if doing so meant that British political institutions would permanently establish sovereignty over what was rightly the Irish Parliament's legislative authority in money matters. In short, Anglo-Irish leaders were in no mood to risk the establishment of the Bank of Ireland, not only because the bursting of the South Sea Bubble had demolished confidence in such projects, but also because they stood to gain from the bailout and feared losing their income from Irish sources and the political power that protected it.

Robert Walpole, the future prime minister of Great Britain, formulated the bailout initially in the so-called "Bank Contract," the first part of which was a new subscription in South Sea stocks, this time floated by the Bank of England, in which investors would buy up South Sea shares with Bank of England notes. This required the second part of the contract, which was a transfer of over £3,000,000 in annuity payments in the form of Exchequer bills from the bank to the South Sea Company and a return of about £900,000 in South Sea stock to the bank at the above-market-value price of £400 per £100 Bank of England notes. As P. G. M. Dickson notes, "it was obviously hoped that the news of this would support the market price and the market in general."[33] There was a shortfall in fulfilling the full amount of the subscription, and the governor of the Bank of England said he did not want to complete the bank contract further without statutory authority. Walpole came up with another idea for a bailout of the South Sea shareholders, known as the "Ingraftment" scheme, which contained the provisions of the bank contract but also involved reimbursing shareholders by borrowing stock from the Bank of England and the East India Company upon which the British government would pay interest. In short, taxpayers would sponsor this bailout, because the government would be using public funds to buy the stock of three companies to make it happen. The final plan, the "Bank Treaty" that eventually was passed by the British parliament in February of 1721, was a taxpayer-financed bailout that involved the Bank of England's buying out part of the South Sea Company.[34]

The important part of this bailout for the purposes of the Bank of Ireland project is that South Sea investors would expect to exchange some of their South Sea Company stock for Bank of England stock, giving them a vested interest in eliminating competitors to the Bank of England, such as the Irish bank. The significance of the bailout was appreciated by Irish commentators. Archbishop William King of Dublin, for example, was worried that the South Sea Company and its allies in the British Parliament who were investors in the company would try some sort of scheme to reimburse themselves out of the public funds, such as through taxes or British national debt–creating Exchequer bills. Writing to John Stearne, the Bishop of Clogher, he said, "We are in great dread of the next session of Parlement in England in which the South Sea is to answer for all, that it is feared they will reprise themselves out of the Public. Tis feard otherwise that a great many will hang or drown themselves on the miscarriage of that fund."[35] He wrote another correspondent that he was surprised that the government would be crediting shareholders with a price-per-share four times as high as its downgraded market price.[36]

Because of these developments, in the British and Anglo-Irish public mind the Bank of England was clearly playing a regulatory function similar to that of an underwriter or deposit insurance company, at least for the period during which the Bank of Ireland project was under consideration. In a world in which some paper, namely South Sea stock certificates, had lost legitimacy and value, the Bank of England's paper maintained a putative "realness" or intrinsic value even within paper credit's nominal forms of value. The bailout scheme helped to construct a heuristic division in which the Bank of England's notes would represent a material redeemability of South Sea paper, and the fact that they were tantalizingly withheld from South Sea investors for as long as it took to settle the bank treaty could only have enhanced their reified status.

Irish South Sea stockholders would have been awaiting this hoped-for payoff and, because they would have lost so much money in the South Sea disaster, would have had some anxiety about creating a national Irish banking institution, the stock and notes of which might diminish the value of those of the Bank of England. A letter from Stearne to King suggests that the buoyancy of Bank of England stock was a concern in the establishment of a Bank of Ireland. Stearne says the managers of the Bank of England might oppose the bill in the British Privy Council if they are convinced that their Irish depositors would withdraw their money and deposit it in the Bank of Ireland instead, and that dissemination of news of the prospect of such opposition might generate earlier opposition in the Irish Parliament to the Irish bank.[37] This letter strategizes how "to convince the numerous English subscribers [to the Bank of Ireland scheme] that because of the dire economic condition of Ireland they would certainly lose their deposits if the bank went ahead."[38] Such an anxiety for the fate of Bank of England stock vis-à-vis the Bank of Ireland scheme may have been present in possessors of that stock and in South Sea stockholders who stood to gain in any scheme for stock conversions. In this scenario, the reification of the Bank of England paper that would rescue the subscribers to the *Monti* would require the sacrifice of an emergent rival colonial financial institution that threatened its solvency.

Further, by discouraging English investors in the Bank of Ireland, the Anglo-Irish leadership could guarantee that payments from the revenue would remain under domestic control. The debate that raged in Dublin's public sphere during consideration of the bill for founding the Irish bank shows that the defeat of the Irish bank project was due mostly to these dual concerns about preserving the South Sea Company bailout and protecting the constitutional rights of the Irish Parliament against British inroads, upon which the *Monti* depended.

IV

Swift's broadsides and pamphlets that were composed against the Bank of Ireland bill did not explicitly cite the defense of the *Monti* as a reason to dismiss the bill, because to do so would have made it appear that only the *Monti*'s members, not the general population, would benefit from the prevention of the bank's establishment. Most of these pieces were written during the controversy over chartering the Bank of Ireland that took shape during the Irish Parliamentary session of 1721 between the initial narrow defeat of the bank bill on a procedural vote on 14 October and its resounding defeat on 9 December. Accordingly, these writings can be taken as interventions in existing popular print culture that cultivated support for the existing credit system during this controversy. The pamphlet war over the bank that took shape during the parliamentary session apparently did much to undermine confidence in the bank and its paper credit. Swift's role in the pamphlet controversy is uncertain, as all of the pamphlets attributed to him in this affair are anonymous. Critics have been able to attribute some of the works to him by noting that he authorized two of the bank papers, *The Wonderful Wonder of Wonders* and *The Wonder of All the Wonders, That Ever the World Wondered At*, to be reprinted in compilations of his writing during his lifetime. In addition, another pamphlet, *Subscribers to the Bank Plac'd According to Their Order and Quality with Notes and Queries*, was noted as his work in the postscript of *A Letter to Henry Maxwell, Esq.* Because *Subscribers* came from the press of John Harding, critics have speculated that other Harding publications during the controversy may have been Swift's as well (9:291). Though the *Subscribers* pamphlet, which purports to be a listing of the social class of the subscribers to the bank, is probably his most important contribution to the bank controversy while the bill was before Parliament, his poem *The Bank Thrown Down, To an Excellent New Tune*, written after the bank was voted down in December, was his most lasting contribution on this issue. Whether he wrote them or not, most of the pamphlets employ metaphors that associate the project with Continental inveighling, fraud, and the punishments for debasement. Their general aim was to exploit the period's association of creditworthiness with reputation by implying that any investor or depositer who was connected with the project risked damage to his or her good character.

The Wonderful Wonder of Wonders (1720) and *The Wonder of All the Wonders, That Ever the World Wondered At* (1721) are the only two pamphlets from the controversy that we can have full confidence that Swift wrote (9:xvii–xviii). Both pamphlets satirize what Daniel Defoe called "air money," his term for paper credit. Sandra Sherman, in describing the ambivalence of Defoe's term, has suggested that "Air Money" is "never realized in a payoff or blown up in a Bubble" but hovers "in epistemological limbo, neither obvious Lie nor verified Truth"—a claim that supports her case that Augustan era paper credit is a spectacle that requires spectators or readers to reify it.[39] The *Wonders* pamphlets satirize this ambivalent status of paper credit, its "airy" qualities, and its pretensions towards literal transparency. Their scatological elements—rhetorical tactics explored in detail in the next chapter—also function to undermine the bank project's paper credit and advertisements by considering them to be printed on inferior paper worthy only of excremental use.

Subscribers to the Bank Plac'd According to Their Order and Quality with Notes and Queries was published after the Bank of Ireland commissioners published a new list of subscribers at the end of October. The text parodies the new list by attempting to show how few of the subscribers belong to the landed interest and how many are of the commercial classes and/or foreigners. The pamphlet points out that only 7 of 147 of Ireland's nobility (temporal lords and bishops) are subscribers and that only 2 of 300 members of the gentry (baronets and knights) are on the list (9:288–289). Further, it declares that only 8 of the subscribers are clergy, and that 2 of them are Frenchmen—a xenophobic epithet repeated in the list of traders among the subscribers, where a Dublin alderman is listed as "A *French*-Man," 10 of the 29 merchants as "*French*," and 8 of 59 "Masters-Dealers" as "*French*-Men" (9:290). This epithet comes to govern the pamphlet, as Swift attempted to make his larger point that very few members of Ireland's landed interest supported the bank. Those who do subscribe are commercial people with no stake in Ireland's land. Therefore, the bank's organizers and most prominent investors are said to be not of the Anglo-Irish establishment and the *Monti*. Swift implied that these people, such as William Latouche, a prominent Dublin private banker, were perhaps of French Protestant, Hugenot identity (9:290). This Frenchness was also Swift's means of stamping the bank proponents as "projectors," or adherents to John Law's Mississippi scheme in France, the bubble of which burst shortly before the South Sea Bubble. By suggesting that the "reasons for a Bank" had to do with land distribution, Swift made the case that the project was designed to redistribute property away from the landed interest. This claim, together with the text's xenophobic and classist epithets, worked to shield the *Monti* by making its members understand that the bank ultimately would undermine them.

Swift's *A Letter to the King at Arms* expands these doubts by discoursing on counterfeit subjects. It takes issue with the previous pamphlet's insinuation that the "Esquire" and other subscribers to the bank might not be real gentlemen.[40] The knight writes that he is upset with this insinuation and that he seeks from Ireland's "King at Arms" a proper coat of arms (at the cheapest price) to certify his authenticity (9:291). He complains that by a recent act of Parliament, he is not yet allowed to keep a greyhound for game hunting, but he is hoping that the new bank will help him obtain one through its influence with Parliament (9:292–293). Through this satire, the author, perhaps Swift, is able to show that lowborn subscribers fully expected the bank to corrupt Parliament, while at the same time suggesting that they were being bamboozled by the bank projectors into believing that they would make extravagant gains on very low deposits. He therefore played to many audiences and emotions—to some who laugh at the fool, to those who might identify with the letter writer's investment in the bank and learn that it is some sort of trick being played on subscribers, to those who might fear the interloper's ascendancy, and to those who might pity him and seek to put an end to his misery by killing the legislation once and for all.

Swearer's Bank or, Parliamentary Security for a New Bank has been attributed to Swift. It is not likely his work, however, because its printer was Thomas Hume, and most evidence shows that Swift was working exclusively with John Harding in this period.[41] The anti-Catholicism of this satire links it with the other anti-bank pamphlets, as the anonymous satirist is quick to connect the fictional subscriber's faith in the paper credit of the bank with the Catholic faith, tapping into Anglican anxieties that the bank would bring in a Catholic moneyed interest (9:294, 9:297). The pamphlet's satirical proposal is to extend to the whole of Ireland's population a Parliamentary injunction against swearing, the punishment for which will be a fine through which the bank, since it doesn't have anything that the satirist considers real securities, will be capitalized. This idea derived from the by-laws of printing houses, which set fines—called "solaces"—which workers paid when they were found to swear, fight, or commit other offenses.[42] *Swearer's Bank*, accordingly, more or less admits that the bank controversy is being fought in the printing houses, to the extent that the paper war itself, rather than the bank project, may serve as Ireland's main source of value. Further, this satire targets "fiat money," currency that could be established by act of Parliament; and by suggesting that swears could become capital by act of Parliament, the pamphlet pokes fun at the commodification of language implied both by the profits presses are earning through the controversy and by such a fiat. The pamphlet states, "It's very well known, that by an Act of Parliament to prevent profane Swearing, the Person so offending on Oath made before a Magistrate forfeits a Shilling which may be levied with little Difficulty" (9:291). The satirist estimates that tens of thousands of pounds may be collected from this fine (9:295–296).

A Letter from a Lady in Town to her Friend in the Country, Concerning the Bank, Or, the List of the Subscribers Farther Explain'd is likely Swift's work, because it comes from Harding's press and engages the anti-Catholicism of *Subscribers to the Bank Plac'd According to Their Order and Quality*. It tells the story, in the form of a first-person letter, of a woman who arrives in Dublin to place a subscription of £2,000 in the bank on behalf of her lady friend in the country, her meeting with an unreliable agent of the bank, and her conversion against the bank by a noble male relative of hers whom she meets by chance. Along the way, it rehearses the controversy's arguments for and against the bank, making references to particular pamphlets and their authors. Its style is undoubtedly Swiftian, and it bears a strong relationship to the *Subscrib-*

ers to the Bank pamphlet in that it exercises further ridicule of the French in its denigration of the bank's supporters.

On her way to make a deposit of £2,000 in the bank, the lady meets the noble male relative, who proceeds to praise the anti-bank argument that the project lacks sufficient security, that should it get such security it would create a moneyed interest that would overwhelm the landed interest, and that the moneyed interest would be Catholic and would put gold and silver in the hands of papists and worthless paper credit in those of Protestants (9:302). The relative also dismisses the work of Henry Maxwell, a principal propagandist for the bank, saying that his "Intentions were better than his Abilities" and "That from poring upon *Dav'enant, Petty, Child*, and other *Reasoners* from *Political Arithmetic* he hath drawn Conclusions by no Means Calculated for the Circumstances and Condition of *Ireland*" (9:303). He also says that the lord lieutenant (Grafton) had not "interested himself in Favour of the BANK" and "had behaved himself with the utmost Candor and Indifferency, which appeared throughout the whole Transaction betwixt His GRACE and the *Negotiators*" (9:303–304).

The narrator attempts to undermine the credit of the bank by suggesting that anyone associated with it will lose not only their credit but also their reputation. The heroine of the story relates that she knows of a lady who was cheated by the bank and who is trying to recover her subscription. Word of this loss, apparently, has reached her suitor and has caused him to call off their engagement (9:305). Female reputation is slandered by association with debt in a metonymy that connects the typical feminine characterization of paper credit—its personification as "Lady Credit"—with connotations of insubstantial, unreliable, and unstable value. The "redeemable" aspect of femininity in the landed interest's marriage market—the true, substantive wealth in lands that a woman might bring to a marriage—is thus troublingly absent.

After *A Letter from a Lady*, Swift's satirical contributions to the bank controversy close with *The Bank Thrown Down, To an Excellent New Tune*.[43] This poem documents the progress of the Bank of Ireland scheme and satirizes its proposals as being those of a mountebank. Its a/a/a/b/b rhyme scheme sets up a series of contrasts—such as that between "Rings," "Things," and "Springs" of wealth and the "Rank" "Bank" of poverty and decay—that highlight the distance between the satirized object—paper credit—and the normative bullion coin, land, and landed "Squire" (line 51). Swift's Tory point is that the bank will actually go against its projectors' theory that it will improve the circulation of currency in the country: the "real" money of the "springs"—coin or "fish" (lines 3, 7)—will actually be choked by the bank, stagnating the economy—an effect accomplished in the rhyming of "rank" and "bank" in the first stanza. That real money—figured as "fish" and "salmon" (lines 7–8) in the second stanza—would actually go into the pockets of the bank projectors. But in the poem the House of Commons votes down the legislation, preventing the damming of the river, making visible the absence and imaginary nature of the bank's paper money, highlighted by the rhyming of "blank" and "Bank" (lines 9–10). The poem closes with the suggestion that the landed interest has triumphed over the paper monster apparatus of the moneyed interest, securing a normative ideology through the satire of the putatively sly bank projectors. Should they become a moneyed interest or, more significantly, Irish government creditors, Swift implies, the country will fall out of the control of the Anglo-Irish *Monti*.

The seemingly naïve "bipartite" construction of a normative country ideology supportive of the *Monti* in Swift's bank satires—literary evidence which goes a long way towards supporting Michael Ryder's contention that opposition to the bank came from Irish country ideologues—may have been masking more complex financial maneuvers.[44] Given the evidence of Swift's investments in paper credit schemes, these satires should be taken as manipulations of public perceptions of value rather than as a reflection of his actual attitudes towards paper credit in general. The South Sea Company had obviously been proven to the public to be insolvent by the time of this pamphlet's publication, and the Irish private bankers along with it (according to *The Run Upon the Bankers*). Swift's satirical technique is to present the company directors, the Irish private bankers, and the "moneyed men" behind the Bank of Ireland project as sacrificial scapegoats in a performance that leads to a sublimating ritual of reading. This ritual purports to be restorative of community norms of value; however, it is clear that these norms are actually invented by the process of reading these satires for their reaction to the modernity of market fluctuation.

Swift's publications on the South Sea Bubble and the Bank of Ireland were only one part of a much larger pamphlet controversy that had begun to construct an imagined Irish national community originating in economic discourse. Though his contributions were largely literary, the fact that they both borrowed from more serious economic pamphlets and further fueled the controversy suggests that the very existence of a debate in printed works, regardless of the positions taken, was creating a political public sphere in Ireland. Like *A Proposal for the Universal Use of Manufacture*, an Irish book about the necessity of Irish books that exploited the Declaratory Act to begin to construct an Irish nation vis-à-vis the "othering" of the British one, the publications concerning the bank invented Ireland as an economic interest with distinct political needs. *Reasons Offer'd for Erecting a Bank in Ireland*; *A Letter to Henry Maxwell, Esq.*; *A Dialogue Between Mr. Freeport, a Merchant, and Tom Handy, A Trades-man*; *The Phoenix*; *Objections Against the General Bank in Ireland*, and other pamphlets addressed a variety of Irish constituencies whose opinions on the bank project could shape its fate. By doing so, they worked together with Swift's writings to hail into existence an Irish public of mutual interests, laying the foundation for later appeals to a more universal Irish patriotism. Moreover, their discourse on the sovereignty implications of the bank reveals that contemporaries were concerned about the fate of Ireland's Parliament and revenue powers— and therefore the *Monti*—in the context of the Declaratory Act. Further, works like *A Letter to the Gentlemen of the Landed Interest in Ireland* specifically link the media event of the debate itself to the formation of a national Irish culture industry.

Henry Maxwell, a member of the Irish House of Commons and a proponent of the bank, began the pamphlet debate by publishing *Reasons Offer'd for Erecting a Bank in Ireland; in a Letter to Hercules Rowley, Esq.* This pamphlet's significance lies in how it presents evidence that Ireland's sovereignty problems were central to the parliamentary debate—problems that the pamphlet refutes by reference to the successful paper currencies of the New England colonies. Maxwell responded to the question of whether the bank could help Ireland thrive as a dependent kingdom by drawing on the example of the New England colonies. In his view, because they, as successful British territories in a state of dependence, like Ireland, had central paper credit systems, constitutional objections to the bank were unfounded.[45] This comparative analysis, while it helped Maxwell make his point that other dependent British territories had had tremendous success with paper credit banks, surely would not win him friends with anyone upset about how the Declaratory Act had virtually made Ireland into a colony with fewer rights than an American colonial assembly. In short, *Reasons Offer'd* reflects an awareness that many members of Parliament were concerned that the Bank of Ireland project would undermine rights to property and, by extension, the *Monti*'s property in future Irish tax revenues. Accordingly, it continuously insists that "where ever a bank is established it will, nay it must to its Power, support the present Settlement, and Constitution of that Country. . . . For this Reason a Bank is the most steady Thing in a Government."[46] Ireland's compromised sovereignty, in Maxwell's view, would not jeopardize deposits in the bank and should not be used as an argument against it.

Bank of Ireland opponents, however, also attempted to sway popular opinion in a direction more favorable to what they perceived to be the *Monti*'s interests. Maxwell's uncle Hercules Rowley, to whom *Reasons Offer'd* was addressed, countered arguments for the bank with *An Answer to a Book, Intitl'd Reasons Offer'd for Erecting a Bank in Ireland in a Letter to Henry Maxwell* on 23 November 1721. He came out as a country ideologue in the pamphlet, making a polarizing response to what he would consider his nephew's more moneyed interest view of the issue. For Rowley, the problem of sovereignty and its relationship to risk should be a central consideration in the debate over the bank. He complained that Ireland was a "dependant Kingdom" because of the Declaratory Act. It therefore risked both the appropriation of any profit that the bank might make and bore the sole burden of any losses. He feared that the bank would "end in our Destruction, and the Razure of our little Remains of Liberty," and that England would "procure a Repeal of the Charter" for the bank or "cramp our Trade, and discourage our Manufactures" if Ireland began to grow too rich because of it. On the other hand, the Irish Parliament could be sure, he predicted, that the charter for the bank would be continued if it caused a loss of its wealth to England, so that "England *must be Sharers in the Profit, but* Ireland *alone bear the Loss.*" [47] Rowley thus saw the bank as troubling both from its constitutional questions interior to Ireland and those related to Ireland's relationship to England, viewing the former as being founded on Protestantism and the *Monti*. Indeed, his arguments seem to confirm *A Letter to Henry Maxwell*'s implication that opponents to the bank, aside from being anti-Catholic and anti-Dissenting Protestant, had other interest-bearing concerns that would be threatened by its establishment. [48]

Objections Against the General Bank in Ireland, a shorter piece, adopts this line of argumentation with some qualifications. It more stridently claims that the bank is a British imposition on Ireland that the King George I, whom the writer sees as the true guardian of the Protestant interest in Ireland, has somehow been convinced to support. It also says that the large concentration of specie in one place in the bank will be tempting to the British Parliament, who may find reasons to tap into it, to the detriment and impoverishment of the Irish. It parts ways with Rowley's pamphlet, however, in suggesting that fears of the pretender to the throne are inflated and are precisely the mechanism the British Parliament may employ to raid the bank's capital if the institution is established. The pamphlet's most important contribution to the landed interests' objections to the bank is to fully articulate why a central bank, common to other countries, is not suitable to the system of government in Ireland. It asserts that Ireland's governing institutions are too dependent upon Britain because of the Declaratory Act and previous legislation and custom and that laws for punishing financial fraud are too lenient. [49] The writer studiously avoids mentioning the Bank of England in this example, perhaps because to do so would make apparent the fact that Britain too had come to be governed somewhat like Holland, Venice, and Genoa, with a central bank largely influencing the government and life of the nation. The Bank of England's paper credit is never confused with that of the South Sea Company, referenced at the end of this passage as the "late instance" in England, in which men had robbed the public. [50] The argument that central banks are not unsuitable to monarchical systems of government thus breaks down under close analysis, but it is nonetheless entirely in keeping with the rhetoric of the writer's side of the question.

Objections is central to understanding the *Monti*'s opposition to the bank because it states more clearly than other pamphlets how Britain might appropriate the bank's deposits, or at least force a loan from the bank, in times of real or imaginary threats of war:

> May not Four or Five hundred thousand pounds in one Chest, move the Desire, and Incite the Inclinations of our Masters beyond, who in process of Time may not be so Indulgent of us, as the present Set are, who in many Instances have given us Reason to believe that they are not Unmindful of us; and may not Imaginary as well as Real fear of Danger be made use of as a Handle: may it not be given out that under some secret Designs, (God knows what) are Forming against us abroad, and under a Pretence to keep out the Pretender, or in Reality to keep in a Ministry. May not our Bank be Call'd upon to Lend this Money, if they Refuse, they will be thought Undutiful, if they give it, they will injure their Trust.[51]

The pamphlet makes a clear case that Ireland's dependent status as a kingdom under the Declaratory Act would impede its ability to guarantee the security of the capital of its own bank, especially given the survival instincts of British ministries, described as constantly looking for sources of funding for jobs and projects in order to stay in power. The writer perceptively sees the anxieties of Rowley about the pretender as the kind of chimeras a ministry could manipulate to gain concessions from parliaments and the public, an observation that sets up a discourse on the imaginary versus the real, with money at its center.

Framed this way, the questions that Rowley asks about whether the bank's subscriptions constitute "real" securities is subject to another question about reification: whether Ireland is a real nation with sovereign powers. Did it have the political and legal power to refuse to hand over the bank's deposits in time of war? *Objections* says that if the Irish Parliament is asked by the British Parliament for the bank funds, it must, "declare the Money well Apply'd, and that our Friends in England will Refund it when they are Able, perhaps at the same Time, that they will Restore our Lords to their Jurisdiction; and if this doth not make the Complainants Easy, we will stop their Mouths another way, by Voting them *Tories, High-Flyers,* and *Jacobites.*"[52] This rather cynical view of the poor political and governmental position in which Ireland had been placed, and the suggestion that Ireland was as likely to get any funds back from the English Parliament as it was of obtaining a repeal of the Declaratory Act, is the major source of the writer's opposition to the bank.

The sovereignty debate concerning legal and political control over the bank's funds—a debate taking place in the context of the Declaratory Act—governs the remainder of the pamphlets published during the controversy. For example, a sign that the fears of the landed members of the *Monti* were winning the debate over the bank was John Irwin's *The Phoenix: or, a New Scheme for Establishing Credit, Upon the Most Solid and Satisfactory Foundation, and Intirely Free from All Objections Made to the Former Intended Bank.* Irwin's pamphlet is strikingly different from others in this controversy in that it attempts to balance the competing moneyed and landed ideologies with a patriot rhetoric that invents Ireland as one community. Although this strategy is suspect inasmuch as he supports the bank as one of its founding members and therefore can be perceived as being of the moneyed interest, his appeal hijacks country ideology's constitutional conceit and ideal of disinterest while constructing an Irish public body: "By our happy Constitution this Nation is but one Community, and as that centers in the Legislature, 'tis presumed they are composed of such worthy Patriots, as will discard all private Views, when the Publick calls for their best Council and Aid."[53] His proposal very much follows this plan of repressing the private, keeping the bank as a public entity in full view, supervised by the government without the presence of private stockholders who might deceive or tax the public. Further, in a major concession and appeal to landed investors, Irwin's plan offers loans at 5 percent interest to those who provide land as security, whereas commercial men will have to borrow at a much higher rate.[54]

A Letter to the Gentlemen of the Landed Interest in Ireland, Relating To a Bank—a pamphlet in favor of the project—is the most interesting one in the controversy, because it critiques the debate as a whole and regards it as an object constitutive of a new Irish public. The author positioned himself as a critic of all of the pamphlets written in the controversy to that point and even indulged in a metacritical commentary on how those pamphlets were being received. The piece makes a comparison between the composition of Rowley's pamphlet and the incorporation of the bank, suggesting that Rowley's book, being made of paper, is like paper credit, undermining Rowley's case against the bank's proposed paper currency by saying that Rowley is already trading in it. Alluding to claims that Rowley's pamphlet had many authors, this anonymous writer suggests that *An Answer to a Book* is like the bank in having many subscribers. Rowley's book, in his view, should therefore be an example of how many hands acting together in a project, whether it is a bank or a book, can create better "credit" for it.

> My answering this last Project, brings to my Mind the Judgment of the Criticks of this Town, who pretend to say, That though the Gentleman, whose Name is in the Front, hath been content to make himself the Father of it all; yet, in reality, the Book it self is a *BANK*, into which several Subscribers have cast their Contributions. I speak not this for a Reflection. I am so much for a BANK, that I wou'd have all Books be such; and I own, that this Book is such; and the Reason why it is no better, is because my Subscribers were few, and not so careful as they should have been, in paying their Subscriptions. But this is not to the Purpose.[55]

The writer, if we can call him such given this information, tells us here that both Rowley's and his own pamphlet, and perhaps other pamphlets in the controversy, are collaborative works penned by many hands, which creates a certain crisis in authorship. It does, however, explain the anonymity of *A Letter to the Gentlemen of the Landed Interest* and some of the other works. The problem of finding the real author in these works apparently caused an epistemological crisis for some critics, who "pretend to point out the Authors of the several Pages."[56] The critics' search for the real author of certain sections of Rowley's pamphlet is part-and-parcel of the bank debate's analysis of what constitutes real money and intrinsic value, so the authorial function becomes a means of limiting the proliferation of the nominal values of the texts' arguments with an intrinsic property and responsibility. The pamphlet's attribution of this search for an author to critics is also problematic, however, as the writer is ventriloquizing them as authors of an interpretation that, for all we know, is a backhanded critique of Rowley's inconsistencies in his pamphlet. The function of anonymity, as the searches for both the pamphlets' authorships and the origins of paper money's value testify, may be to create the impression that a public of writers and readers invested in Ireland's political and economic future immanently existed.

VI

In this reading, the rhetorical strategies and technical descriptions within the various tracts in which the controversy played out may not be as important as the existence of the debate itself. The larger significance of the Bank of Ireland project may lie in the fact that it launched a decade of political economic writing obsessed with the financial ramifications of Ireland's constitutional status vis-à-vis Britain. The economic crisis generated by the South Sea Bubble caused a surge in the production of Irish writing devoted to improving Ireland's economy, and because those works focused on the political reasons for the country's poverty—British governmental policy—they helped construct "Irishness" as a distinct political and economic identity.[57] Though the constitutional argumentation in these publications of the 1720s harkens back to the arguments concerning trade made a couple of decades earlier by Molyneux and others, the discussion of the problems of finance and monetary policy inspired by the bank controversy gave birth to the imagined nation of Ireland, forming a distinctly Irish political public sphere. This newborn public discourse on Irish finance laid the groundwork for a domestic book market within which a modern Anglo-Irish literature could emerge.

CHAPTER 3

Arachne's Bowels

Scatology, Enlightenment, and Swift's Relations with the London Book Trade

Swift may have aimed to cultivate a domestic Irish book trade, but there can be no doubt that for the majority of his life, he preferred to publish his more important literary works in London.[1] *A Tale of a Tub*, *The Battle of the Books*, *Gulliver's Travels*, and several significant essays and poems were first put into print by Benjamin Tooke, Benjamin Motte, and other London publishers. This does not mean that he did not value the Dublin print culture, which he was helping to create, nor does it mean that he fully embraced the British culture industry, which his London publications were helping to deconstruct from within. His residing in Ireland may have served his publishing strategies in both cities, providing a haven from the consequences of works he published in London and a good location from which to foster an interior market serving Irish political and economic needs. Michael Treadwell has noted that Swift preferred to be back in Ireland after leaving manuscripts to be printed in London; he may have thought of his trips to England as sorties into an inhospitable political environment and print culture that he was critiquing from a position of safety.[2] The London friends who were handling his publishing matters, however, were vulnerable to arrest, and this often led them to cut controversial passages from his manuscripts.[3] Most of his major London publications were anonymous at the time of their first printing, though, and are therefore not evidence that he directly sought credit with English readers. Many of these works did not even list their publisher's name; Swift and his publishers used trade publishers and their imprints on title pages to conceal their identities and shield themselves from harassment and prosecution.[4] This is not to say that publishing in Ireland posed no risks; Dublin printers were on occasion arrested for manufacturing one of Swift's publications, and many printers were afraid to publish his writings.[5] In short, Swift's reasons for working with the publishers and printers of either city were complex.

It is evident that until the 1730s, the Dublin book trade's relationship with London's was less one of succession or competition than one of concurrence and occasional cooperation. Part of the reason for this concurrence may have been the family relationship between the Crookes and the Tookes, publishers in both Ireland and England. The Crookes held the patent of King's Printer for Ireland and technically had a "total monopoly of the book trade" there until 1732.[6] The Tookes and their employees were Swift's main London publishers. John Crooke, who obtained the patent in 1660, married Mary Tooke, sister of his apprentice Benjamin Tooke Sr. Later, Benjamin held the patent in trust for the Crooke family, from 1669–1693, passing it to his nephew Andrew Crooke II, who held it from 1693–1732. Andrew Tooke (1673–1732), Benjamin's second son, was also part of the business, participating by occasionally translating and editing, although he spent the majority of his life as a professor. Though not always resident in Ireland, the Crookes published "titles of Irish interest or origin" in both Dublin and London.[7] Benjamin Tooke Sr. "reaped some benefit from his office in the Irish business that came his way through his connection with the Crookes," and his name "appears on scores of Irish imprints" until the mid-1680s.[8] Swift may have chosen to publish with Benjamin's son Benjamin Tooke Jr. for that reason, particularly because some of those imprints were by fellow Anglo-Irishmen, like William King and William Molyneux, though Swift also worked with John Barber for more explicitly political tracts.[9] Even when Benjamin Motte, who had a long-standing connection to the Tookes, took over the operation of their shop in 1724, Andrew Tooke continued to hold a majority stake in the business and was responsible for cutting passages from *Gulliver's Travels* when it was published by Motte in 1726.[10] In short, the firm of Tooke and Motte seemed to be a London outlet for the work of Swift and other Anglo-Irish writers, in part due to the Tookes' relationship with the Crookes and their experience of profit from Irish titles. The relationship between the two families ended, at least symbolically, in 1732, the year in which both Andrew Crooke II and Andrew Tooke died and the family lost the patent. Motte, however, continued to work with Irish material until his death in 1738.

Conversely, Dublin publishers like John Hyde and George Faulkner seem to have handled Irish distribution and/or reprints of some of Swift's London publications and occasionally provided London publishers with material by Swift and others in Ireland to reprint. Hyde, a stationer and bookseller to Trinity College Dublin, distributed and reprinted some of the London publications of Swift and his friends through a variety of Dublin printers. There was correspondence between Hyde and Motte concerning the first Irish reprinting of *Gulliver's Travels* in 1726, and Hyde's widow Sarah functioned as the intermediary for Motte's letters to Swift in the 1730s.[11] Faulkner, who had been a journeyman with London printer William Bowyer at various times in the 1720s, collaborated with Bowyer throughout his life. Bowyer reprinted Faulker's publications of Swift, and Swift assigned Bowyer copyrights to several of his Faulkner-printed pieces. However, Faulkner had a legal dispute with Motte over the distribution of Faulkner's Dublin edition of Swift's works, and that dispute eventually led to a 1739 act forbidding importation of "foreign" reprints into England. As I discuss in Chapter 6, these and other events in the 1730s marked a split between Dublin and London publishers, contributing to the very autonomy of Irish publishing for which Swift had been advocating.[12]

Despite the cooperation of some British and Irish publishers, then, there were some signs that the Dublin book trade was becoming a competitor to London in English-language printing. As early as the 1720s, some of the satires that emerged in the wake of the Bank of Ireland controversy targeted the London culture industry for political, economic, and ideological reasons. These works critiqued the British Enlightenment as the governing ideology produced by that industry and in the process identified the Dublin printing press as the manufacturer of an alternative Anglo-Irish Enlightenment. As Richard Sher has contended, the development of publishing in the eighteenth century was "intimately tied to the espousal and promulgation of the Enlightenment," implying that the narrowest definition of "Enlightenment" is "the ability to disseminate texts and to produce a readership." Accordingly, when regional and national print cultures distinct from Britain's developed, they produced their own Enlightenments, which, while connected to an international intellectual movement, nonetheless served national ideological needs.[13] The Declaratory Act, the South Sea Bubble, and the Irish bank controversy, I argue, formed a nexus of media events that made possible the splitting of the Irish print trade and Irish Enlightenment away from Britain's. This act of division is most apparent in scatological satires by Swift and other Anglo-Irish authors that targeted both popular and high British art—satires that deconstructed the ideology of "politeness" that was the prerequisite for the performance of British Enlightenment values. In doing so, however, they drew upon Swift's more notable prior— London-published—critiques of British book culture in *A Tale of a Tub* and *The Battle of the Books*. This chapter, consequently, first examines these major works' attitudes towards these developments before demonstrating how Dublin scatological satire transformed this parody into an external critique of imperial print culture by a colonial press. These observations support a reading of *Gulliver's Travels* that links its parody of the genre of the English novel to its counter-Enlightenment satire.

I

A Tale of a Tub and *The Battle of Books*, published in a single volume with *The Mechanical Operation of the Spirit* in 1704, are fundamentally deconstructive satires centered on the problem of the book as a material object and the related issues of reception and interpretation. They challenge the veracity of textuality and, by doing so, call into question the book's status as a medium of truth and an object of value. They are books about books and therefore inherently engage in a metadiscourse about the business that they are part of, commenting both on the ideas contained in books and the means and motives behind their production. Their critique is made in a way that undermines the importance of the materiality of the book and calls attention to its valuation in an abstract schema of commodified cultural capital. These two books explore "the relationship of the literal to the allegorical, the equation of books to persons, and the reduction of books to the materials of which they are made" to make the point that meaning does not inhere in the text but lies outside it, in the hands of readers.[14] Thus, they question the importance of the London book trade by which they themselves are published and sold, seemingly setting out, as *A Defence of English Commodities* complained in 1720, to ruin that business. Simultaneously, they are profitable products of that business that attempt to enhance their value by criticizing other products of the business. Consequently, they partake of their own commentary on Arachne and other literary spiders, not only revisiting the textile/text homology of *A Proposal for the Universal Use of Irish Manufacture*, but engaging in satire drawn from their own bowels and containing the remains of half-consumed writers and texts they have critiqued. Swift's scatological satires on the book suggest that Arachne's bowels—a symbol for the national press—produce nothing of worth, only material for the next critic to digest in yet another forgettable book. Yet Swift also implies that the national media is a "modern" phenomenon, necessary to the age of rising vernacular nationalism and the decline of the "ancient" order of Classical languages and texts.

A Defence of English Commodities, an anonymous, London-published pamphlet produced in 1720 in response to *A Proposal for the Universal Use of Irish Manufacture*, discusses Swift's deconstruction of the London culture industry and encouragement of the Dublin one in a manner that sheds light on the reception of Swift's London works.[15] It begins by identifying the author of *A Proposal* as "a *Tory* Doctor of Divinity"—Swift—calling him "one that has done all that in him lay to ruin his own Trade" and that has "set up for an Improver of other Peoples" (9:269). On a literal reading, this passage would seem to indicate that Swift has been destroying the Anglican Church, in which he was a clergyman. Given the pamphlet's appropriation of *A Proposal*'s metadiscourse on textiles as texts, however, it appears that Swift is being accused of trying to destroy the British book trade throughout his career even as he helps develop Ireland's. "The Woollen Manufactory" (the publishing industry), the pamphleteer explains, is important to the British because it is "the Foundation of their Power, and even necessary to their Existence" (9:269). Swift's essay is undermining that foundation by sowing "the Seeds of Discord and Contention"—encouraging the Anglo-Irish to think of themselves as distinct from the British (9:269). *A Defence* further claims that *A Proposal* unfairly libeled British publicists, such as Martin Bladen and William Luckyn Grimston. Swift, it says, "butchered their Reputations with the Cruelty of an Assassin and Barbarian, without the least Grounds or Foundation; a Madman, a *Grubstreet* Translator, and the Standard of Stupidity, are the best Titles he can afford to Persons of the greatest Worth, Rank, and Distinction" (9:270). The author of *A Defence* quips that it will not be long before Swift recommends making this textual butchering literal.

The textile allegory of this pamphlet is then extended to encompass legal issues in publishing—a matter that Swift had tacitly addressed in his use of the fable of Arachne (Ireland) and Pallas Athena (Britain). Referring to the prosecution of Edward Waters for printing *A Proposal*, *A Defence* argues that the British support their cultural foundation by using the courts for censorship, "setting their Magistrates upon Wool-Packs in the supreme Tribunal" (9:269). The author hopes that the "Gentlemen of *Ireland*" will "make it their Choice to be content with their own Manufactures, tho' dearer and worse than the *English*," but he warns of "Reprisals" from Britain if the press is used to produce "Rebellion" (9:271–272). Acknowledging that "it is very natural for every Man to covet to have a Mill [printing press] of his own," he hopes that the Protestants of Ireland will use their press in a manner consistent with their constitutional dependency and its accompanying "Restrictions" (9:276). He gives dire warnings of punishments for violating these rules, referring to how Athena made Arachne "Hang her self" for the hubris of presuming to compete in spinning [printing] with her (9:272), although he observes that Athena "cut the Rope" and was merciful, giving Arachne the alternative sentence of being metamorphosed into a spider. Athena is not a jealous rival, but "the Deity" has "the Wisdom and Justice of the Creator" and a mandate to "humble the proud" who, like Adam and Eve, "meddle with the Forbidden-Tree" (9:273, 9:276). Because *A Defence* was published in London, it may be taken as the British printing industry's attempt to defend its market in Ireland and with it, its political sovereignty in that kingdom. The pamphlet is significant not only because it documents how Swift's project for Irish publishing was received by the British government but because it contributes to our understanding of the contemporary interpretation of Swift's intent in his earlier London-published works.

The Battle of the Books (1704) is clearly referenced in *A Proposal* and *A Defence* for its appropriation of Aesop's fable of the spider and the bee. This appropriation establishes these insects as figures for writers in a manner that anticipates the use of Ovid's tale of Arachne in those later writings. It is located within a satiric allegorization of a controversy between the "Moderns"—contemporary scholars disputing the origins of the *Epistles of Phalaris* and *Aesop's Fables*—and the "Ancients"—Classical writers and their modern interpreters. Richard Bentley, William Wotton, and their supporters were considered Moderns because they were revising the Classical curriculum to reflect that many often-taught works were not composed in ancient times at all but much later. Bentley, the keeper of the library of St. James, had established that the *Epistles* were a forgery and that many printed editions of the *Fables* contained material added after Aesop's time. Wotton criticized William Temple's embrace of the *Epistles* and his theories that the pre-Classical East had had advanced forms of knowledge and that cultural history followed a cyclical pattern. The Ancients, including Temple, Charles Boyle, and Francis Atterbury, produced their own edition of the *Epistles of Phalaris* and challenged Bentley and Wotton in other writings. A pamphlet controversy between the Ancients and Moderns erupted over the course of the 1690s, and Swift satirized it.[16] *The Battle of the Books*, consequently, functions as a critique of the London book trade because, though it discusses the ideas involved in the controversy, it personifies those ideas as material texts. I argue that Swift emphasized the materiality of the books in question because he was calling attention to how this controversy was ultimately about competition between the publishers of Ancient and Modern works. The way he did it, however, indicated that the brand identity and corollary marketability of the book was more important than its materiality. The publishers of the Ancients were the shareholders in the English Stock, a patent granted to the London Stationer's Company, and they had a monopoly over publishing the Classics and other books used in schools. The publishers of the Moderns, who were sometimes publishers of Ancients as well, were seemingly competing with that monopoly—in Swift's words, attempting to "raise their own side of the hill"—and both sides were profiting from the controversy.[17] *A Defence of English Commodities* may have been correct in suggesting that Swift was attempting to ruin the London book trade, because he did not take a side in the issue but rather satirized the material means and commercial motives of the purveyors of ideas.

The allegorical form of *The Battle of the Books* helps Swift accomplish this satire, moving from the abstract realm of intellectual disputes to their physical manifestation and back to another abstraction, that of the book as imaginary cultural capital with a particular brand identity within the marketplace. *The Battle* personifies both living and dead Ancients and Moderns as books; the names of writers are not to be understood as actual people but as "only certain sheets of paper, bound up in leather, containing in print the works of the said poet."[18] These objects seemingly invent their authors rather than the reverse, suggesting that names and opinions are not necessarily what are at issue, but rather how those names and opinions, through controversy, construct markets for bound printed paper.[19] From the outset of this satiric allegory, it would appear that the material book proper, not what its pages convey, is the object of the action; and the royal library of St. James, in which the action between the books takes place, becomes the location of a post–1688 Revolution canon war. Yet such a war signifies that the materiality of the book, while an important literary device by which to convey scholarly debate as physical combat between tomes, is ultimately rejected, because the books, after all, exist as mere symbols on the pages of Swift's allegorical text. As intentionally allegorical figures, their names—their signifiers—are without signification, an effect of the genre that leaves readers in the position of both supplying meaning and assigning value to it. "Virgil," for example, is a brand name signifying the quality of the content as "ancient" and therefore worthy of a particular price point in the market, but it is not the content itself. The culture wars of the 1690s that Swift was satirizing, in short, are presented not only as legitimate intellectual disagreements but also as profitable ventures in which publishers and authors are brands signifying readers' participation in those debates and their proprietorships of cultural capital. The brand identity of bound printed paper and how it translates into sales in a competitive book market, *The Battle* suggests, is at the root of the dispute between the Ancients and the Moderns, with all living parties being modern stakeholders—and sometimes literally stockholders—in those titles.

The Battle makes the most of the message that bookmaking is a business operated by workers whose contributions are as important as the author's. It comments on the various crafts (pen and ink production, papermaking, binding, etc.) that construct the book as a material object, yet it does so in a way that transforms those literal trades into metaphors for the rhetorical actions of authors. Book craftsmen, via the allegory of textual war, are metamorphosed into makers of weapons and war machines.

Ink, "the great missive weapon in all battles of the learned," for example, is made of "gall and copperas . . . compounded by the engineer who invented it." Quills are a "sort of engine" of war by which ink is "darted at the enemy." Titles are "trophies" of the learned combatants that, sometimes in the short form of title pages that advertise books, are "fixed up in all public places . . . for passengers to gaze at." They are preserved in libraries, which, like munitions storehouses, are "magazines" from which they later can be extracted in times of war.[20] The "book of fate," possessed by Jupiter and other gods (presumably Ancients), is "three large volumes in folio" and is made of the finest materials: "The clasps were of silver double gilt, the covers of celestial turkey leather, and the paper such as here on earth might pass almost for vellum."[21] The books of the Moderns are produced with cheaper materials and inferior craftsmanship. Compared to those of the Ancients, they are "sorrily armed" and "worse clad" (bound in material of lesser quality). Further, they are "out of case" (printed with poor type faces and designs).[22]

The rising action of the Moderns' dispute with the Ancients is described in similar terms, allegorizing the alliance between Wotton and Bentley in the jargon of the print trade. Bentley has wounded Aesop materially in his essay; he "tore off his title-page, sorely defaced one half of his leaves, and chained him fast among a shelf of Moderns." Bentley and Wotton, accordingly, worship "Criticism," a monstrous goddess who reclines on "half devoured" books and dresses up her daughter, "Pride," in "the scraps of paper herself had torn." The metamorphosis of this immortal into her disguise as Wotton's friend, the mortal Bentley, is figured in the sequence of the printing of the latter's book as an octavo edition:

> She therefore gathered up her person into an octavo compass:
> her body grew white and arid, and split in pieces with dryness;
> the thick turned into pasteboard, and the thin into paper, upon
> which her parents and children artfully strewed a black juice, or
> decoction of gall and soot, in form of letters; her head, and voice,
> and spleen, kept their primitive form, and that which before was a
> cover of skin did still continue so.

Papermaking, ink production, typesetting, and binding are represented as processes in the monstrous birth of Modern books in a manner that paints the art of printing, practiced in Europe only since the fifteenth century, with the tincture of illegitimacy when compared to the medieval monastic book production by which the Ancients were preserved. Criticism, as the goddess of academics and wits at Gresham College and Covent Garden, has an interest in continuing to produce scholarly and satiric printed works that parasitically feed on the Ancients.[23] Yet it is unclear how making such books is different from printing contemporary editions and translations of Ancient ones.

Swift's stake in the controversy—whether he was an Ancient or Modern or both—may be apparent by examining both the representations of a book's identity in the text and external evidence of his work with publishers. For example, Criticism may be the figure for publishers of works that fall outside the English Stock, a profitable monopoly that included the exclusive right to publish "Psalm books, almanacks, the Primer, and a number of popular classical and other works, many of them widely used in schools."[24] Benjamin Tooke Sr., father of Benjamin Tooke Jr., the publisher of the volume containing *A Tale of a Tub*, *The Battle of the Books*, and *The Mechanical Operation of the Spirit*, had been treasurer of the English Stock from 1687–1702 but had been dismissed for "irregularities." Benjamin Jr., according to Treadwell, seems to have possessed shares in English Stock copyrights, and his brother Andrew, who later edited *Gulliver's Travels* for Motte, was the Classics editor for English Stock titles.[25]

Swift could be said to be allied with the Ancients by this connection and because he worked for William Temple, who left him the publishing rights to his manuscripts in his will.[26] Swift saw Temple's works through the press initially with Ralph Simpson, but then switched to working with Benjamin Tooke Jr. for the third part of Temple's *Miscellanea* and for his own *A Discourse of the Contests and Dissensions Between the Nobles and Commons in Athens and Rome*.[27] He continued to work with Tooke for more than a decade, obtaining for him and their publishing friend John Barber another monopoly, though one that fell outside the English Stock: a jointly held patent to be Queen's Printer in England beginning in 1739. This patent, like its equivalent in Ireland, granted exclusive rights to print Bibles and Books of Common Prayer—which could qualify as Ancient works—as well as statutes, proclamations, injunctions, and other governmental material.[28] Though Tooke and Barber sold this patent before they could assume it in 1739, the patent itself, together with Tooke's shares in the English Stock, provides further evidence that Tooke had a stake in the Ancients side of the controversy. *A Tale of a Tub* and *The Battle of the Books*, for which Tooke also owned the copyrights, are, however, clearly the kind of Modern works of criticism and satire that Swift, paradoxically, was parodying within them, indicating that neither he nor Tooke was working only one side of the divide. Tooke is said to have been the publisher of "all the most valuable folio and lesser tomes of classical and general literature" in the period, encompassing both ancient and modern works.[29] Tooke clearly had a stake in Temple as well as Swift and Pope, and Swift was probably commenting on how the controversy could generate profits for publishers, sometimes a single publisher.

Swift's appropriation of Aesop's fable of the spider and the bee, who watch the battle from the library's corner, shows the Moderns to be more characteristic of the age of rising British nationalism than were the Ancients—more vernacular than Latin or Greek and therefore having a larger audience and more sales potential. The spider is shown to be a Modern because he embraces cognitive modernization—his webs are evidence of "great skill in architecture and improvement in the mathematics"—and because he is a critic and satirist. Like Arachne in Swift's later usage of the spider figure, he is independent in that he is "drawing and spinning out" from within himself, secure in a domestic property that he has created from "materials extracted altogether out of [his] own person." He is therefore a figure for a self-sufficient nation and book trade that is guarding its nest—its imagined community and home market—writing native "English" cultural resources in the national vernacular, not Latin or Greek. The bee, on the other hand, is an Ancient who is "without house or home, without stock or inheritance" and whose "livelihood is an universal plunder upon nature"; he is a "freebooter" who steals and robs from the property of others. Nonetheless, he gives man "honey and wax, thus furnishing mankind with the two noblest of things, which are sweetness and light." It is the spider, however, who is more like Swift. His cobwebs (writings), though they may survive only by "being forgotten, or neglected, or hid in a corner," are "a large vein of wrangling and satire." They are often scatological in that they are like "excrement" and "dirt," yet they may be so because their consumption of "insects"—the work of other writers—generates those elements within him. The spider is also the figure for a publisher who benefits from "acquisitions" of dirt from other writers, using the pre-text exemplified in one book as the fodder for another, which in turn becomes fodder for another. The publisher, like the spider, therefore has a permanent and self-reproducing supply of native materials for publication. Like Arachne, both writer and publisher are challenged by Athena, "Pallas, the protectress of the Ancients," again supporting the idea that *A Proposal for the Universal Use of Irish Manufacture* and *A Defence of English Commodities* were drawing on the themes and figures of *The Battle of the Books*.[30]

This satire of the London book trade is extended in *A Tale of a Tub*, which, though written after *The Battle*, comes first in the volume in which both were published. *A Tale*, another commentary on the British culture industry, associates publishing with the values of the new bourgeois public sphere, which had emerged with the fiscal-military state after the Revolution of 1688. Swift was skeptical of this sphere because it was emblematic of all other aspects of the modernization taking place under Whig auspices throughout Britain, one feature of which was the rise of a national aesthetic within a new mass media. He felt that this new print culture was an arena of proliferating textuality that disavowed the role of authority in making meaning. *A Tale of a Tub* set out to satirize the English book trade, which had brought this arena of debate into being. It not only challenged how the excessive number of texts and commentaries diffused interpretive authority, but it did so in a religious allegory and a description of the process of reading a will, showing the political and social consequences of that diffusion. As a satire of religion and a variety of exegetical traditions, however, it was not proposing a return to the political theology that print culture had replaced as a means of reconstituting authoritative interpretation.[31] Rather, it was instructing readers to be wary both of the ideology of interpretive freedom that this culture encouraged and of various claimants, especially religious ones, to that authority. *A Tale*, via its description of the fate of a will, targets the materiality of the book as "a threatening false orthodoxy" of the British public sphere and the fiscal-military state that gave rise to it.[32]

As Christian Thorne has contended, satire was the preferred method by which Swift, Alexander Pope, John Gay, and other Tory writers critiqued this development. They targeted "the very idea of a public sphere and a critical press" because they considered it a false promise to deliver a "dictatorship of the public, as a catastrophic attempt to predicate power on public opinion rather than on virtue."[33] The critical theory of satirical form put forth by Thorne is that satire is in the market but not of it, in that satire constantly undermines the very formal conventions that hold that market together. It challenges the idea of the public sphere not merely contextually but also formally at the level of the epistemological believability of print.[34] Tory satire, Thorne argues, points to values and truths that are elsewhere than in print, yet it does not necessarily define them explicitly—it merely gestures to them. Far from being a site for the revelation of truth, the public sphere, in this formulation of satire, is insincere and corrosive of more established norms and truths: it is a venue for propaganda for a corrupt public. The Scriberlians thus challenged the growing focus on the materiality of the book, what Paula McDowell has identified as the project of Daniel Defoe and other Whigs "to strengthen the credibility of print."[35] It was not the signifiers printed on the page that conveyed truths transparently but the consensus on what they signified.

A Tale of a Tub demonstrates this Scriblerian attitude, presenting the material of English books themselves as being composed of disorganized, unauthorized fragments—a "grotesque body" or disjointed literary corpus mirroring what they considered to be the disordered body politic of the new fiscal-military state.[36] *A Tale* mimics the form and materiality of other books, parodying customs like prefacing the work with dedicatory epistles and apologies, using footnotes and other hypertexts, and engaging in digressions. Throughout the work there are places where large blocks of text are missing, presumably where the printer is supposed to insert text that has not yet been written. This strategy of omission is a major way in which Swift satirizes the book as a material product of an industrial process of bookmaking and suggests that every book risks being a sequence of cut-and-pasted chunks of text reassembled by a press corrector and compositor according to their own design. In short, Swift presents the parts of a book as if it were interrupted before the process of its production was finished, making *A Tale* look like a book, but an incomplete one lacking any overarching scheme that would make it a whole.

The most appropriate stylistic description for the satire in the *Tale*, accordingly, is Menippean, a species of the genre often referred to as an "anatomy" of the targeted object—a term well-suited to the parodic critique of the English book as the corpus of imperial power.[37] Menippean satire can be employed both passively and actively, merely recording observations of a breakdown in a culture or strenuously working to shatter the norms of an oppressive society. On the one hand, it descriptively "lives in a precarious universe of broken or fragile national, cultural, religious, political, or generally intellectual values," but on the other, it prescriptively is "good at destroying and bad at building."[38] *A Tale of a Tub* does both, observing the weakening of traditional English society and its values after the rise of the fiscal-military state, yet also working to further tear apart its ideology. It shows how cultural production, particularly in the arena of religious dispute, was distracting readers from political and economic developments: "God is a perennial tub, thrown out to divert restless leviathans that might otherwise disturb the ship of state."[39] By demonstrating textual instability in its discourse on the interpretation of texts, its author bequeaths responsibility for finding this message to readers. The *Tale*'s ideology is derived from its form: the effects of Menippean satire mirror the political order from which they emerge, and *A Tale* thus operates as a critique of empire.

The *Tale*'s central allegory concerns the interpretive anarchy created by a father's death and consequent reading of his will, which is supposed to dictate how his three sons should wear and care for three identical coats that he leaves to each of them. A will, at the time of its formal reading, is an "orphaned text": as Robert Phiddian has explained, "set loose in a culture orphaned from seminal origins of legitimacy by the willfulness of its recent history, the orphaned text generates myths of origins and authenticity in a frantic attempt to claim or forge a legitimacy to which it has no natural claim."[40] A text is described in Plato's *Phaedrus* as a composition that "drifts all over the place, getting into the hands not only of those who understand it, but equally of those who have no business with it." When it is "ill-treated and unfairly abused it always needs its parent to come to its help, being unable to defend or help itself," but the father, the writer, is dead.[41] Further, the written word has the tincture of illegitimacy. Only the audience who treats writing as a mere "reminder" of the father's truthfulness—not those who regard writing as truth itself—are the legitimate heirs to interpretive authority. Plato says that "these people are the author's own legitimate children—a title to be applied primarily to such as originate within the man himself, and secondarily to such of their sons and brothers as have grown up aright in the souls of other men."[42] Jacques Derrida has said that interpretation is a matter of the sovereign's authority: "The value of writing will not be itself, writing will have no value, unless and to the extent that god-the-king approves of it."[43] Plato's fable says that what authorizes the written word as truth—what establishes that it has any meaning at all—is the decision of a human agent who is sanctified by a divine origin. The *Tale*'s device of the father's will, therefore, can be read as a discourse on interpretive authority. As Stephen Karian has argued, Swift, in other works, for example "Verses on the Death of Doctor Swift," as well as in *A Tale*, used wills to respond to the way "eighteenth-century readers sometimes recreated texts for their own purposes by selectively reproducing and inferring available textual material."[44] The eighteenth-century English book, if it was the vehicle by which culture replaced political theology, can therefore be seen as only furthering the interpretive difficulties it was meant to resolve.

The *Tale*'s allegory of the three brothers and the coats they inherit is directed at the religious dimensions of this problem. Of the three sons, Peter represents Roman Catholicism, Jack represents Dissenters or Presbyterians, and Martin stands for Anglicanism. In this religious characterization, scripture and various religions' attitudes towards its exegesis are the central object of the sons' interpretive disagreements. The brothers are a "multiplicity of *godfathers*" who attempt to "christen" the orphaned text in the name of their various interpretive schemes and communities.[45] Right from the beginning of this allegory, then, Swift staged the will as the Bible and the three brothers as children who are attempting to find the proper method by which the document can most truly be deciphered and lived, or at least worn publicly. The clerical context is signaled by how the three coats represent interpretive authority through investiture. Deborah Baker Wyrick writes, "As the word *investiture* attests, the ceremony's visible focal point is the giving and the wearing of special clothing symbolizing the power of office: . . . investiture is both a putting in and putting on; the vestments, as outward signs of inward power, are badges of distinction, of privileged authority and proper placement within a preexisting order."[46] Once again, textiles, in Swift's lexicon, are metaphors for texts and their interpretation. The coats of the brothers are the means by which God the Father has invested them with authority, yet their different interpretations of how to wear them threaten the destruction of vested authority itself.

Peter's claim that shoulder knots, gold lace, satin linings, silver fringe, and Indian embroidery on the coats are approved by the father is supported by forged codicils that Peter has added to the will. This behavior satirizes Catholicism's emphasis on oral tradition as the key to the continuity of authoritative interpretation: "'there is nothing here in this Will, *totidem verbis* (written), making mention of shoulder-knots, but I dare conjecture we may find them inclusive, or *totidem syllabus* (oral)."'[47] Martin and Jack rebel against Peter, get excommunicated, and proceed to unravel Peter's doctrine; yet they too are shown to be nonauthoritative interpreters who "deal entirely with invention, and strike things out of themselves."[48] The radically dissenting Jack not only strips his coat down to the point that he almost destroys its basic cloth, but he also mistakes the text of the will for substance. His interpretive method is described by the narrator as "zeal," which "proceeded from a notion into a word, and thence, in a hot summer, ripened into a tangible substance."[49] Jack goes mad, not only because his theology is purely negative, in that it comprehends itself only by opposition, but also because his fetish for the written word—a fetish that leads him to strip the coat of all adornment—threatens to destroy the will by saying that there was no divine intention in it at all. Jack, as Howard Weinbrot has argued, may be the figure for the narrator, who "certainly is a Modern in letters, a Dissenter in religion, and a madman allied with many other powerful madmen who abuse both religion and learning."[50]

Martin, the figure for Anglicanism, removes from his coat only some of the fringe, silver points, and gold lace. Startled by Jack's bloodthirsty desire for revenge on Peter and his willingness to destroy Christian unity altogether, Martin reminds Jack that Peter is still their brother and that their father's will "was no less penal, and strict, in prescribing agreement and friendship and affection between them."[51] In short, Martin's Anglicanism is shown to combine the best of Peter's Catholicism with the reformative impulses of Jack. He is therefore elevated by Swift to be the proper mediator not only between denominations but also between the Bible and man. The body of Christ, in Swift's view, must establish an authoritative interpreter, like the established church, to control the kind of schisms caused by differences in interpretation. For the maintenance of peace, Swift believed, there was an overriding need for all in society "to accept existing institutions, political as well as religious."[52] This logic, as Judith Mueller has argued, seems strangely Hobbesian for Swift inasmuch as it assumes the need for a central authority figure who can order both interpretation and society itself by fearful necessity, but, on the other hand, the logic is in keeping with Swift's staunch royalism.[53]

By satirizing the process of interpreting a will within a work that itself is a parody of the English book, *A Tale of a Tub* demonstrates how the Whig culture industry was creating what Swift saw to be an unsustainable form of society. The work comments on the relationship of war to literary interpretation, religious practice, and political authority, modeling how the dissemination of English books was creating a form of value that was replacing the central authority and hierarchy that had stabilized value previously. Though it is a critique of religious enthusiasm and dispute, it nonetheless satirizes the anarchy of having no arbiter of value—no God or monarch—in a manner that reifies the character Martin, representative of Swift's own position as an Anglican clergyman. Put simply, Swift believed that the endlessly proliferating and distracting textuality of the postrevolutionary period required authoritative mediation, and the public sphere was inadequate for these tasks. *A Tale of a Tub*, however, does not overtly supply a mediating figure—not even Martin—but leaves it to the reader to consider how the loss of the father set this interpretive anarchy into motion.

II

Swift's critique of the British culture industry was as epistemological as it was political; he understood that the project of the English book was inseparable from the British Enlightenment's attempt to disseminate social and behavioral ideals by which the financial revolution could achieve legitimacy. The printing house was understood by contemporaries to be "the source, the literal engine, of the textual forces that created and sustained Enlightenment values"; and by creating skepticism about books, Swift was implicitly challenging the contemporary philosophy produced by them.[54] The British Enlightenment's discourse of "politeness"—the central ethic of social performance and judgment by which enlightenment was to be actualized—was recognized by colonials such as Swift to be a repressive mode of behavioral control enabling the hegemony of the fiscal-military state.[55] Because colonials received London publications as imports, they could see, often more clearly than English readers, how Britain's politicized book trade could not have done without this emerging cult of refinement. As Adrian Johns has explained, contemporaries all over the British Isles were perceiving print culture "not as a realization of the rationalizing effects now so often ascribed to the press, but as destabilizing and threatening to civility." Information overload may have been disrupting social and behavioral norms, which may explain why Enlightenment thinkers became focused on issues of politeness and decorum.[56] As Clifford Siskin has argued, eighteenth-century philosophy was grappling with how to value the proliferation of printed texts, an impulse to categorize that also required clearinghouses for epistemological control in the form of new state administrations. Consequently, the Enlightenment might be understood as both cause and effect of the necessity for a rational mode of criticism by which to convert information into knowledge.[57] Accordingly, the fiscal-military state's move to authoritatively define reason and common sense through the book trade could be interpreted as an attempt to reestablish standards of taste in the wake of the commodification of culture by the boom in publication in the eighteenth century.[58] The reader was taught to value the market's standards of taste and to desire to rise in the market's hierarchical scheme of cultural capital. The reader's worship of the market's standards caused further reification of the value of English cultural production and fostered its dissemination. Because the arts of writing and manners occupied "a privileged place in the legitimation of the bourgeois state during the period of expansive colonialism," as David Lloyd contends, intellectuals in favor of decolonization recognized that there would have to be a "connection . . . between the erosion of the aesthetic domain and the demise of colonialism itself."[59] The scatological writing of Swift models this erosion, showing how the ideology of refined politeness could be exposed as cover for exploitive forms of political, economic, and cultural management. What has been called Swift's "excremental vision" was made possible by the "excremental reality" of politics in his home country, Ireland, under the policies and ideologies of the British empire.[60]

Ireland's importance to the critique of the fiscal-military state's hegemonic desire to control representation through the book trade, I argue, is rooted in its cultural offensive during the moment when modern Britain established itself in the late seventeenth and early eighteenth centuries. Borrowing from classical critiques of the alliance of money and art in corrupt empires, Anglo-Irish writers of the period deployed scatology to question the motives, formal strategies, and social effects of the imperial print media. Swift's satires denigrated the British book trade, in part to deflate the fiscal-military state's investment bubbles and reverse the exportation of Ireland's resources. Projects like the Bank of Ireland and the South Sea Bubble he called "Politic FARTS," so publicity for them was an excremental form of literature.[61] Those who worried about the sovereignty of the *Monti* in the face of this kind of project linked what appeared to be the disinterested and rational arguments for the bank to the imperial war machine's appetite for revenue, which suggests that contemporaries understood how the financial revolution was the economic basis of cultural production. Scatology was not only unmasking this rhetoric, however, but doing so to assert a less culture-centric set of assumptions about what human relationships and community should be. If Swift was "a distant precursor to the excremental writers of postcolonial Africa and Ireland," as some have argued, it is because what has been called his "Counter-Enlightenment" attitude is actually the assertion of the "more ethnographically sensitive Enlightenment."[62] The Irish Enlightenment, of which he was a part, was not only a critique of the philosophy and values imported in English books, but an integral component of an aggressive move by Dublin to become the second city to London in Anglophone printing.[63] The *Monti* was the economic base that necessitated this publishing offensive. In bringing about these counter-Enlightenment transformations, Ireland's emerging organic intellectuals were appropriating British publishing technology and producing a national ideology and distinct literary decorum, mimicking the cultural imperialism of their governors in a bid for sovereignty.[64]

The immediate motivation for Swift's financial satires was an indictment of the fiscal-military state's culture industry because it had failed the economies of both Great Britain and Ireland. The collapse of the South Sea Bubble created a situation in which the most expedient rhetorical method by which to rebuild confidence was to imagine that foreign creditors, imported commodities such as books, and the vices of luxury were to blame. Swift's mission was to moderate unstable and fluctuating desires that had been inflated by publicity for the South Sea Company and Bank of Ireland and which had then been deflated by the market crash. This purpose was served best by scatological technique, the effects of which were to interrupt the flights of fancy generated by the Whig media and bring the readers' imaginations back towards the body and pragmatic reality, from which they had been severed. Swift's parodies of British models of polite living, accordingly, reveal them to be advertisements for a mode of behavior and grandiose lifestyle impossible for most people to reach yet appealing enough to encourage many to risk investment. By targeting the ideology of politeness produced by London presses, Swift and other Anglo-Irish writers were critiquing a doctrine of appropriate manners, etiquette, body comportment, and language by which the British could claim to be "a polite and commercial people" who had reconciled Enlightenment refinement with voracious capitalism.[65] The failure of the period's investment schemes, in their view, was also the failure of that ideology and its form of art, and it was clear to them that the reconstitution of the market required the inculcation of more realistic expectations. Satires published immediately after the crash, such as the anonymous *The Benefit of Farting Explain'ed*, I argue, worked to both breed disgust in the books that flatulently had inflated the bubble while reconstituting a normative aesthetic by which economic recovery could be achieved. This reading of the "economimesis" of scatological satire—its argument that "politics and political economy . . . are implicated in every discourse on art and the beautiful"—contends that this genre's discourse on disgust paradoxically stabilizes the financial system it critiques.[66] By doing so, it also contends that Swift's bank tracts served to remind the Anglo-Irish public that Ireland's strength and ability to resist the empire lay in its agrarian capitalism and in funding of the *Monti*, arguing that the bubble and bank crisis actually presented an opportunity to assert an alternative to the fiscal-military state.

The more scatological poems of the Bank of Ireland crisis, such as *The Wonder of All the Wonders that Ever the World Wondered At* and *The Wonderful Wonder of Wonders*, appropriated both classical sources and internal British counter-Enlightenment critiques of the fiscal-military state's cultural production. Though the literature of decolonization initially "repeats the master narrative of imperialism, the narrative of development which is always applied with extreme rigour and priority to colonized peoples," in the Irish case, it also borrows objections to the excesses of empire that were issuing from within the metropole itself.[67] Swift, as an exponent of that internal critique while writing in England for the Tory party, could be said to be the vehicle for the migration to Ireland of this literary form, or at least of its counter-aesthetic uses during this period. Initially, his parody of the discourse of politeness, a component of the ideology of the public sphere said to be emergent in this period of British history, was directed at English Whigs, though it would later target their Anglo-Irish counterparts.[68] Because politeness emphasized the propriety of written and spoken linguistic performance as the means by which more enlightened civil society might be achieved, Swift viewed it as the central pillar of the British Whig book culture's hegemony. By attacking this conceit of superior language etiquette, Tory writers were attempting to undermine the emergent Whig culture industry's claims to being an "improving" force in British politics. By scatologically parodying Whig genres circulating in print culture, the opposition hoped to generate disgust among readers for both Whig politicians and the propaganda that justified their often self-interested aims. Swift's satires best exemplify the relevance of this internal critique to postcolonial critical ethics. Having returned in 1714 to write for the sovereignty of colonial Ireland, he could see how the primitivizations and infantilizations of Irish culture which had been constitutive of the hegemony of the British book masked the expropriation of Ireland's resources.

The Earl of Shaftesbury, who set the tone for an epistemology that "distinguishes the enlightenment as the single most important moment in the history of the concept of the aesthetic," is generally credited with developing the philosophical basis for this discourse in the first decade of the eighteenth century.[69] In his essay *Sensus Communis* he outlined how consent to the revolution could be produced through the emotions, arguing that a universal "public spirit" could be formed "only from a Feeling or *Sense of Partnership* with Human Kind" and that "where Absolute Power is, there is no PUBLICK."[70] Echoing many seventeenth-century advocates for the control of the press, he worried that people might "be so wrought on, and confounded, by different Modes of Opinion, different Systems and Schemes *impos'd by Authority*, that they may wholly lose all Notion or Comprehension of *Truth*."[71] The communication that would "at length carry us," the new state, was an invisible one that would "hide strong Truths from tender Eyes," a practice which might require "wise Men to speak in *Parables*, and with a double Meaning, that the Enemy may be amus'd, and They only *who have Ears to hear, may hear.*"[72] Factions participating in the new system could mask their antagonism in a sign of class solidarity by this self-restraint. Religious enthusiasts' "Spirit of *Bigotry*," which had jeopardized the state in the previous century, could be prevented if they remembered that "the Publick is not, on any account, to be laugh'd at, to its face" and that they should not "affect a Superiority over *the Vulgar*."[73] At the same time, he argued that print culture must not be censored, but must remain like a "Free-Port" so as to prevent the visibility of the lines of authority in the new regime.[74]

Shaftesbury was drawn "towards the sort of legitimation of the 1688 Whig regime" that could be made possible if the revolution "put forth a new vision of polite English culture under Whig auspices."[75] By cultivating polite standards of manners, speech, and other behavior, he speculated, a national aesthetic that would manufacture favorable public opinion could emerge. He theorized that this new fiscal-military state—patently paternalist but anti–absolute sovereignty—was achievable in the abstract process of reading, spreading affections "not sensibly, but in Idea: according to that general View or Notion of a *State* or *Commonwealth*."[76] In short, he envisioned an Enlightenment culture industry that would further the process of the liberalization of the economy and society, one "waiting to flourish under the patronage of a civic-minded, classically cultivated aristocracy."[77] It may be that all postrevolutionary societies attempt to manufacture consent in this way, and Shaftesbury's project may serve as a model for decolonizing intellectuals hoping to use the media to imagine sovereignty. The "lack of style" of the genres required to forge this fiction of community, and the internal political opposition to this project and its art, however, may have produced ambivalence in the provincial intellectual towards Enlightenment—an ambivalence that would be echoed by postcolonial writers three centuries later.[78]

Joseph Addison and Richard Steele's newspapers *The Tatler* and *The Spectator* attempted to bring Shaftesbury's culture industry and its standards of decorum into being. Their general project for the reformation of taste recommended reading and writing as the means by which the cultural capital and social mobility of politeness could be actualized: "It is likewise necessary for a Man who would form to himself a finished Taste of good Writing, to be well versed in the Works of the best Criticks both Ancient and Modern." Access to such refinement is improved by conversation, the means and end of education in taste: "Conversation with Men of a Polite Genius is another Method for improving our Natural Taste."[79] Steele's essay on polite conversation imitates Shaftesbury's *Sensus Communis*, arguing for forms of conversation that either distance speakers if they are "too intimate" or mask difference if they are from separate social classes. His discourse on conduct centers on the "Evil" of "indiscreet Familiarity," which leads to perceptions of inequality among both insiders and outsiders. His explanation, while it deconstructs notions of rank and hierarchy, simultaneously reinforces them:

> Equality is the Life of Conversation; and he is as much out who assumes to himself any Part above another, as he who considers himself below the rest of the Society. Familiarity in Inferiors is Sauciness; in Superiors, condescension; neither of which are to have Being among Companions, the very Word implying that they are to be equal. When therefore we have abstracted the Company from all Considerations of their Quality or Fortune, it will immediately appear, that to make it happy and polite, there must nothing be started which shall discover that our Thoughts run upon any such Distinctions. Hence it will arise, that Benevolence must become the Rule of Society, and he that is most obliging must be most diverting.[80]

On the one hand, this focus on the centrality of "the very Word" in making or breaking ideas of difference between people attempts to actualize the Enlightenment idea that all men are created equal. On the other hand, the use and misuse of language discussed in this passage makes the word appear to be a ruse by which thoughts of class hierarchies are concealed. Steele ultimately defaults to the moral concept of charity in terms of both finance and conduct as the means by which solidarity among classes is secured. In this, he follows Shaftesbury, who helped develop the Anglican Latitudinarian doctrine of benevolence into a national virtue.[81]

Politeness, if one followed the dictates of the period's conduct books, was above all the restraint of one's controversial opinions, an investment in the status quo that was revolting to some eighteenth-century provincials who recognized the paradox that such silences were complicit with political and economic inequality.[82] The eighteenth century developed early modern courtesy rhetoric into particular forms of social discipline that helped one to accumulate marketable behaviors appropriate to philosophers' "aestheticization of the social order as 'beautiful.'"[83] Politeness, however, became more visibly an instrument of cultural and class warfare; as Brian Cowan has argued, "Whig politeness was a form of policing" behaviors not in keeping with the political and economic order that had been established after the revolution.[84] This "art of pleasing in conversation" was inextricably linked to progressive ideas of liberty and equality, yet it was the very emblem of the empire's repression of cultural diversity and autonomy.[85] This problem was made even more visible to colonial subjects by the uneven development that followed on the heels of the empire's appropriation of their revenues and resources to feed its creditors and armies. They recognized that the beneficiaries of politeness amounted to nothing without its other: filth—that which is left behind in its refinement process, like the subjects who underwrite that narrative of progress. The "Citizen of Enlightenment" requires a wild Other who is always present yet repressed by the citizen as the very condition for the formation of his or her status as "the reasonable human representative of culture."[86]

Swift's Irish scatology, however, was part of a larger project of the Scriblerus Club, an informal group of English Tories consisting of himself, Alexander Pope, John Gay, and many others, who saw the doctrine of politeness as a mask for Whig political and economic interests. They sought to "tutor the reader in the insincerity of print" so that readers would learn not to be duped by partisan journalism that was encouraging them to purchase a set of cultural products and attitudes.[87] They did not believe that the polite public that Shaftesbury sought to create would bring about what Jürgen Habermas has termed a "bourgeois public sphere of disinterested, rational political criticism."[88] Daniel Defoe, for example, often regarded as a novelist who survived by sales of his work, was a partisan Whig publicist who received secret service money for his publications when the Whigs were in power.[89] Early-eighteenth-century print culture was not an arena of discourse on the general good or an appeal to the "reader's reason which was crucial in political writing," but an "appeal to his emotions and self-interest."[90] The Scriblerians continuously called attention to this fact, attempting to undermine the putative transparency of the public sphere and expose the partisan powers that lay behind it.

Swift critiqued the ideology of the Whig public sphere on its own terms, exposing it as a mask for Whig power, demonstrating that its aesthetic values were inferior, and promoting an alternative Tory decorum that destabilized the discourse of politeness central to its hegemony. His *Proposal for Correcting the English Tongue* laments "young Men at the Universities" who "think all Politeness to consist in reading the daily Trash sent down to them from hence: This they call *knowing the World*, and *reading Men and Manners*," complaining that bad poetry is corrupting conversational norms (4:12). Swift's *Hints Towards an Essay on Conversation*, a parody of politeness that was never published in his lifetime, begins in the Shaftesburyian manner but progressively undermines the potential of Shaftesbury's "maxims" by which conversation may be "regulated" (4:87). For example, Steele's contempt for "familiarity" is parodied by Swift by saying it was introduced by a Whig hero of the previous century, Oliver Cromwell. If "the Folly of Talking too much" is a vice of familiarity, the narrator can't "remember to have seen five People together where some one among them hath not been predominant in that Kind, to the great Constraint and Disgust of all the rest" (4:88). Human nature dictates that a person "will run over the History of their Lives" without understanding that one's "Affairs can have no more Weight with other Men, than theirs have with him" (4:88–89). Swift's full disdain for the taste promoted by the Whigs is leveled at Will's Coffee-house, known for its literary gatherings, where he witnesses "the worst Conversation I ever remember to have heard in my Life." (4:90). Far from generating polite conversation, Whig cultural production is the vehicle for "pedantry" (4:90). Against the view that the new public sphere was to be a "cleaning and purifying operation" on culture, a "*will to refinement*" cultivating taste and decorum, Swift presents the "Politeness, Criticism and Belles Lettres" circulating in it not as cultural capital but as "Trash."[91]

Scatology, accordingly, became the preferred satirical technique by which Tories could expose that cleansing operation as a project for obfuscating the new state's corruption of the culture, customs, and rights of the very "Britishness" for which it falsely claimed to be advocating. Tories were skeptical of the Whigs' attempt to form what Benedict Anderson has called a national "imagined community" of readers in which "each communicant is well aware that the ceremony he performs is being replicated simultaneously by thousands (or millions) of others, of whose existence he is confident, yet of whose identity he has not the slightest notion."[92] Because "the novel and the newspaper," the "two forms of imagining which first flowered in Europe in the eighteenth century," had become the Whigs' principal genres for cultural hegemony, they were targeted by the Scriberlians as the archetypes of the "bumfodder" that was disavowingly producing nationalist ideology.[93] As Catherine Ingrassia has argued, the financial revolution replaced traditional forms of wealth such as gold, silver, and land with paper money, stocks, and bonds, all of which signified "a symbolic imaginative economy or value system based on paper."[94] By exposing Whig cultural production as "bumfodder" supporting this paper wealth, the Scriblerians also can be said to have been targeting what they considered to be false money. Counterfeit currency is often portrayed as an infantile attempt to appropriate parental sovereignty and is therefore, psychoanalytically, "a function of fecal values"—an attempt to substitute the only gift an infant can offer—"excrement"—for gold.[95] As Sophie Gee has argued, "Augustan writers realized that filth was powerful not as the antithesis of valuable matter, but because the two could be made to look the same," suggesting that scatology was used as a blanket indictment of what was projected to be sound money and fine art.[96] These Tory writers were painting a picture of the infantile in their scatological satires of Whig texts, attempting to recover—or invent—"hierarchies of meaning and power" that identified the high cultural position of Tory art, politics, and persons by comparison.[97] Twentieth-century psychoanalytic readings of Swift's scatological texts contend that they are projections of his personal, infantile neurosis, but this misrepresents what is clearly a battle of wits in which scatology is used to critique a rival author's or party's writing.[98]

The Tories were attempting to represent themselves as the legitimate heads of the body politic and their Whig rivals, lower in society, as the asses of it. This metonymy was part of a neoclassical rearticulation of an ancient discourse warning of the role of wealth in the state—one appropriated to critique the financial revolution and its steadily increasing substitution of paper money for coin. Tory writers were eager to exploit classical metaphors of filth to hold up a mirror to the grotesqueness of

the modern age. The trope of feces establishes the analogy between counterfeit money and the pulp literature that spins it, and critics of the fiscal-
military state often cited Aristophanes's *The Clouds*, which suggests that
sophists inflated their talk with rhetorical *copia* as a means of deferring
payment of their debts.[99] For Tories, the term "rump" brought these political, economic, and literary significations together. The Republican
parliamentary government ruling after the death of Oliver Cromwell
and before the Restoration had been referred to as "The Rump," not only
because it was a body trying to govern without a head, but also because
it was a vocal minority within what was supposed to be a democratic legislative assembly.[100] Accordingly, "all the money and blood spent during
the civil wars has been digested by the Republican government, which
has now excreted it out of an enormous rear-end (the Rump)."[101] The
excessive number of laws that it produced and the volume of speeches
and printed propaganda associated with it, as a satirist explained in
"Upon the Parliament Fart," were understood as the uncensored emis-
sions of the posterior.[102] Samuel Butler's *Hudibras*, for example, carica-
tured Oliver Cromwell, leader of Parliament and lord protector of England, as a man with "enormous buttocks."[103] Eighteenth-century Tories
were able to appropriate these significations to smear the fiscal-military
state and imply that the balance of power had shifted too strongly in
favor of the war industry's representatives in Parliament. *A Vision of the
Golden Rump*, a play attacking the corruption of Robert Walpole, the
Whig prime minister of the 1730s, was perhaps the greatest eighteenth-
century appropriation of earlier English scatology, one that led to the Licensing Act of 1737, which censored dramatic performances.[104] The Whig
ideology of politeness was aiming for the "meticulous disciplining of the
body which converts morality to style," and Tory scatology was declaring
this project a failure, the excremental incontinence of an undisciplined
body politic.[105]

The Benefit of Farting Explained, a satire bundled with some of Swift's
miscellaneous pieces, is perhaps the most exemplary post–South Sea
Bubble scatological satire because it brings these critiques of the literature of politeness and economic projection together anatomically. It does
so by figuring its materiality—the ostensibly medically oriented conduct
book about the proper care and presentation of the self—as an excremental body. The front matter announces that the publisher has inverted

the normal assembly of the corpus constituting a book, beginning its argument not with the head but with the behind in a "Postscript by way of a Preface." This section follows the title page's claim to be "Proving *á Posteriori* most of the Dis-ordures *In-tail'd* . . . are owing to *Flatulencies* not seasonably vented." This double entendre parodies both the inflated class expectations generated by the "polite" ballooning, rather than expulsion, of gas from the body and how most explanations of the disaster were flawed because they proceeded after the fact. The author is "Don *Fartihando Puff-indorst*," an attribution that puns on the practice of employing publicists to write puff pieces, favorable advertising and publicity, for investment schemes and other projects, like books.[106] English printers are implicated for producing the bad taste that led to the investment bubble. They are mocked in the name of a flatulent, windy publishing house, "*Simon Bumbubbard*, at the Sign of the *Wind-Mill* opposite *Twattling-Street*."[107] Paradoxically, however, the text, translating a passage from Virgil scatologically, endorses puffery as the solution to the crisis caused by the repression of so much printed gas: "If you're opprest by rumbling Wind, / Strain hard, to squeeze it out behind. / From Puffs, and crackling Farts Relief you'll find."[108] Moreover, it revisits the circulatory theme of *The Run Upon the Bankers* by suggesting that the ideology of politeness has made the body ill by interrupting the normal flow of language and capital:

> A Fart, tho' wholesome, does not fail,
> If barr'd of Passage by the Tail,
> To fly back to the Head again,
> And, by its Fumes, disturb the Brain:
> Thus Gunpowder confin'd, you know, Sir,
> Grows stronger, as 'tis ram'd the closer;
> But if in open Air it Fires,
> In harmless Smoke its Force expires.[109]

As a critique of politeness, this verse argues that language, like money, must circulate freely to create value. The Whig culture of conduct, as an ideology of the English financial revolution, has repressed the free discourse necessary for a healthy conversation about political economy and by doing so has masked the accumulation of the nation's capital in the hands of the few. By claiming to be published in "County LONG-FART"

(Longford in Ireland), this London pamphlet implies that these scatological "Scent-iments" are issuing from the periphery of empire.[110]

Scatological satire was associated with Ireland in part because of the Irish tradition of countering English claims of cultural and behavioral superiority. Swift viewed the imperialist deployment of the Whig conceit of politeness as the latest in a historical series of claims about Irish barbarism and English civility—claims used, particularly during Queen Elizabeth I's conquest of Ireland, to justify the English right to govern it.[111] As Clare Carroll has explained, "the Elizabethan conquest was enacted through the new discourse of civility, carried out through enforcement of laws, colonial settlement, and warfare."[112] Edmund Spenser, secretary to the lord deputy of Ireland in the reign of Elizabeth, described Irish language and customs as "uncivill and Scythian-like"; and John Milton, secretary for foreign languages to Oliver Cromwell, felt that Ireland could "waxe more civill by a more civilizing Conquest."[113] By the eighteenth century, another English secretary in Ireland, none other than Addison himself, was responsible for spreading similar ideas about the universal superiority of English manners (*Dictionary of National Biography*). Accordingly, Swift chose to make his case for Ireland's rights by eviscerating the pretensions to decorum of Addison's immediate superior, the Earl of Wharton, lord lieutenant of Ireland, in *A Short Character of his Excellency Thomas Earl of Wharton*. Wharton governed for only two years (1708–1710), partly because of the success of this satire in showing that he was "generally the worst Companion in the World" due to his lack of decorum (3:180).

As the controversy over Wharton's lord lieutenancy and the Bank of Ireland crisis of a decade later attest, the oppositional mobilization of the press for scatological critique of the empire and British books was more likely to produce pragmatic action in the provinces and colonies than in England itself. The Bank of Ireland controversy, as a media event splitting the Irish political public sphere away from the British one, made use of scatology. For example, *The Wonderful Wonder of Wonders* presents a character who is a Dublin member of Parliament in the pay of the British, describing him as a "Person lately arrived at this City" whose character is "very inconsistent, improbable, and unnatural"—much like Swift's view of paper credit and the stock market in general (9:281). Like paper credit, he is immaterial—the writer says, "I cannot directly say, I have ever *seen* him" and that he "was never seen *before,* by any Mortal" (9:281). As "*Receiver General*" he also seems to be one of the commissioners of the revenue, constitutionally part of the executive branch of government and therefore not always representing the interests of Ireland (9:282). He is a descendant of a "Member of the *Rump* Parliament," and when he rises to speak, he is farting-out British law and propaganda to get Ireland's money: "He has the Reputation to be a *close, griping, squeezing* Fellow; and that when his Bags are *full,* he is often *needy*; yet, when the Fit takes him, as fast as he gets, he *lets it fly*" (9:283, 281–282). He is all in favor of the Declaratory Act and the eclipse of the Irish Parliament's consent to laws binding on Ireland. These positions smell fishy to those around him: "He lets nothing pass *willingly,* but what is *well digested.* His Courage is indisputable, for he will take the boldest Man alive *by the Nose*" (9:283). It may be true that "the whole piece rests on the metaphor of excrement equaling money," in that money is associated with filth when it is counterfeit, suggesting that Swift's subversiveness in this piece is his denigration of the fiscal-military state's law, texts, and currency as illegitimate.[114] In the midst of favorable publicity for the bank and the prospect of growth that investment in it offered, he "reodorizes money," reminding readers that such publicity may be masking the stink of a scheme to defraud them of their wealth.[115]

Other pamphlets published during the bank controversy continued this scatological critique. *The Wonder of All the Wonders that Ever the World Wondered At* furthers this accusation of deception by calling the project's organizer the excremental name "*John Emmanuel Schoits*" (9:285). Further, *An Account of the Short Life, Sudden Death, and Pompous Funeral of Michy Windybank, & C.* portrays the bank scheme as being from the start an investment bubble inflated with the print equivalent of farts, impossible for the Rump-ish Irish parliamentary minority in favor of it to nourish with its limited amount of "*Asses Milk*" (9:308). Swift continued to use references to filth in his Irish writing throughout the 1720s, forming an "outhouse ethos" that associated his rivals not with excrement *per se* but with its visibility as waste not properly concealed in domestic architecture—a contemporary symbol of the nation that he travestied by suggesting that all nations are latrines.[116] Scatology was his means of communicating his awareness that the putatively universalist cultural production accompanying finance "was not one of diversity but of *domination*, in that one usurping tradition repudiates dialogue in favour of the subjugation and destruction of other cultures or ways of life."[117]

Swift had crafted a form of satire that undermined the kind of realist conventions upon which the market depended. As an anti-realist form, this style modeled more sublime values within its very negativity, generating an ideological recognition of the virtue and material propriety of unnamed objects that lay outside the market, or beneath it—those real essences that underwrote the immaterial and unstable commerce in paper credit. Its strategy was to upset the formal transparency upon which paper credit relied for its reification as putatively having "real" value. Like much Tory art, it was seeking to produce, as Christian Thorne put it, "a new kind of writerly object, one that can survive commodification intact, one that can make it through the marketplace without being mugged of its excellence. . . . it is with the satirists that culture begins its long and stuttery history of secessionism, trying again and again to claim autonomy from the degraded spheres of politics and economics."[118] Yet Swift's work was political and economic, too, participating in the very print culture it critiqued, though he claimed that it was advocating for a higher standard of ethics and aesthetics. He was participating in the market both in popular literature and in certain kinds of paper credit investments, and his satire, accordingly, can be said to be doing important ideological work upon the market.

Swift's satires intimated the arrival of a reconstituted sovereignty capable of securing the inhabitants' property against British theft. They affirmed that the *Monti*'s land-banking strategy would continue to work for its members, if not for the kingdom as a whole. Their scatology correspondingly deflated the English financial revolution's more abstract aesthetic by reminding it that it had a body, resituating the location of real wealth and sovereignty in the labor and land of agrarian capitalism, a particularly Anglo-Irish *nomos* of the earth. In this sense, any account of the transformation in Ireland's relationship with Great Britain in the 1720s, focusing on the Declaratory Act of 1720, must begin with a study of Swift's financial satires on the bank and the South Sea investment bubble. These satires begin the work of sublimating an ideology of an Anglo-Irish public sphere that the *Drapier's Letters*, *A Modest Proposal*, and later tracts further develop.

Gulliver's Travels, though begun while these Anglo-Irish scatological satires were being published, was more of an internal critique of the London culture industry, along the lines of *A Tale of a Tub* and *The Battle of the Books*, than a text arguing for the formation of a domestic Irish book trade. Swift, following a pattern, returned to Ireland before *Gulliver's Travels* was published in 1726, suggesting that the book, though primarily a British opposition critique of the Walpole administration and its cultural production, also had an Anglo-Irish nationalist dimension.[119] It was not until the 1730s, however, that his publication patterns reveal less an interest in internal British political opposition than outright Irish patriotism and an embrace of Dublin publishers for his important literary works. So, though launched from the legal safety of Dublin, *Gulliver's Travels* seems to have been primarily a British text. Given that Swift also had chosen to contract with Motte, in London, for *Miscellanies in Prose and Verse*, featuring his work and that of Alexander Pope, in 1727, it is apparent that in these years he continued to work with London presses, albeit for the purpose of satirizing the English culture industry itself.[120]

Gulliver's Travels amplifies the skepticism of textuality characteristic of *A Tale* and *The Battle* and adds to it a critique of the British Enlightenment—a critique he was well-equipped to make because of his own participation in the Anglo-Irish scatological satire of polite English letters. He may have prepared the work for the English rather than Irish sphere of letters because, as a more strictly literary work, it stood to benefit from England's broader market in *belles lettres*, the domestic Irish trade being focused on pamphlets and religious books, not literature, until the 1730s. If *Gulliver's Travels* is read, as some critics have done, as a satirical appropriation of the stylistic conventions of the popular literature emerging from English presses, it may be considered "a satire of the travel narrative, and of the naïve empiricism with which it is so closely associated."[121] It simultaneously is a "parody . . . of what we now see as the novel and the assumptions that enable it," largely because the travel narrative is considered the formal basis for novelistic discourse.[122] It may be argued that Swift's satires of these genres—genres that were beginning to dominate the literary market of the British Isles—were attempts to undermine the English culture industry. Given that the Enlightenment and the book were united aspects of this media environment, Swift's challenge to the formal realism of these genres, a style that obtains the reader's suspension of disbelief through thick description and other techniques, simultaneously subverts the empirical epistemology accompanying Enlightenment thought.[123] Consequently, *Gulliver's Travels*, a skeptical assessment of a "new kind of writing" that "was beginning to codify a 'modern,' significantly new way of perceiving the world," must also be understood as a text combining its parody of the English book with a form of counter-Enlightenment critique that may have been proposing the Irish Enlightenment as an alternative.[124]

This book's compositional and publication history provides evidence that there was some cooperation on it between London and Dublin publishers from its earliest editions, in which case it may be regarded, in part, as an Irish text from the periphery of empire critiquing the cultural imperialism of the metropolis.[125] Swift began writing it in Dublin in 1721 and had largely finished it there by 1725, though it probably was not completed until he traveled to London in 1726.[126] In August of 1726, he disguised himself in a letter as "Richard Sympson" and offered its copyright for £200 to Benjamin Motte, who had taken over the operation of Benjamin Tooke Jr.'s firm in 1724. Motte agreed to publish the manuscript, which carried no author's name, in two volumes by December 1726 and did so on 28 October. It was edited, probably by Andrew Tooke, who held a stake in his family's firm, to such an extent that Swift later complained that its more controversial passages satirizing the court, nobility, Parliament, the legal profession, and the Atterbury treason trial had been "mangled and murdered."[127] Swift's first attempt to correct these alterations was made with John Hyde, who in December 1726 produced a Dublin edition, mostly working from Motte's first edition and a list of twenty-three revisions supplied by Swift from marginal notes he had made in that edition (now known as the "Armagh copy"). It appears that Swift attempted to take advantage of his proximity and close relationship with Irish publishers to quickly provide a more accurate printed copy. He did not find satisfaction on this matter, however, until he worked extensively with George Faulkner in the 1730s. Faulkner may have constructed his Dublin text of 1735 from Motte's first edition, transcripts of corrections that Swift had sent to his friend Charles Ford, and maybe an original copy of Swift's manuscript that had been in the possession of Matthew Pilkington.[128] It is clear, though, that Motte tried to make improvements on the first edition (known as 1726A) in three succeeding editions (known as 1726AA, 1726B, and 1727 [an octavo edition]). Motte worked with a variety of printers, who printed different parts of the text before he, as publisher, collated them into a whole. Treadwell suggests that Motte used this method for the sake of speed in publication, to prevent piracy by rival printers, and for fear of the current government's interference in the bookmaking process before the book was published. Because William Bowyer was responsible for printing Part Four of the 1726B edition and the whole of volume one of the 1727(8°) edition, and because Faulkner was a journeyman in Bowyer's printing house for much of 1726, it is likely that Faulkner had been exposed to the printing of *Gulliver's Travels* far earlier than the 1730s, when he produced his own Dublin version.[129] Though Motte sued Faulkner over the London sales of that version, there is evidence, namely the correspondence between Hyde and Motte concerning the December 1726 Dublin version and Faulkner's work with Bowyer, that *Gulliver's Travels* was the product of collaboration between Irish and English publishers.[130]

The book, consequently, may be regarded as an opposition text with Tory leanings, a general critique of the London culture industry in which, paradoxically, it was a part, and an Anglo-Irish colonial response to cultural imperialism in the form of the British Enlightenment. The modernization of British society that was part and parcel of the Enlightenment, accordingly, is a central target of the book's satire. Swift had reservations about how Britain had developed through processes of cognitive and social transformation that were mose manifest in the existence of the printing press as well as in its products. The cognitive changes were connected to the scientific revolution and encompassed "the growth of scientific consciousness, the development of a secular outlook, the doctrine of progress, the primacy of instrumental rationality, the fact-value split, individualistic understandings of the self, contractualist understandings of society, and so on." These were combined with social and political change, "the emergence and institutionalization of market-driven industrial economics, bureaucratically administered states, modes of popular government, rule of law, mass media, and increased mobility, literacy, and urbanization."[131] The social transformations, associated with the rise of the fiscal-military state and bourgeois forms of government, can be understood as the economic base for the cognitive transformations, which formed the intellectual and ideological superstructure of British society.

This "societal/cultural modernity," in Swift's view, brought about a form of enlightenment that was specifically nationalistic, giving rise to a culture industry that supported Britain but not necessarily its provinces and colonies.[132] His counter-Enlightenment attitude, consequently, was related to his status as a provincial intellectual objecting to cultural products imported from London. Though he wanted Ireland to have its own book trade, which would have necessitated an accompanying domestic Enlightenment, he did not always approve of modernization or wish Ireland to imitate the pattern of British development. He was ambivalent about enlightenment, presenting readers "with what he understood to be the contradictions—dangerous, and potentially antihuman—inherent to Modernity."[133] For example, his central character and narrator, a representative of the modern medical profession and, by association, the scientific revolution, is a caricature of cognitive modernity whose increasingly unreliable observations work to undermine the hegemony of empiricism and scientific method.[134] Swift may more properly be said to have been cultivating a cultural/aesthetic modernity that would redeem humanism in the face of the financial, scientific, and related revolutions in society and thought.[135] Ireland, largely because of the agrarian capitalism of the *Monti*, served as the site for the cultivation of this proto-Romantic alternative vision and of a print culture capable of sustaining it.

Like *A Tale of a Tub*, the *Travels* was a Menippean satire, modeling the fragmentation of the fiscal-military state's authority over Ireland by showing how Gulliver, a symbol of the imperialism of English cognitive modernization, found his methods and expectations travestied by exposure to other societies. This satire's observation that a "modern Colony" was the product of piracy and violence critiques the political effects of the English financial revolution. It suggests that this revolution had eliminated acceptable forms of imperialism, making more coercive means necessary in the effort to feed the fiscal-military state's appetite for revenue.[136] The book narrates this critique by demonstrating how the colonial contact zone portrayed in Gulliver's voyages reifies cultural difference in a manner that calls into question the validity, applicability, and universality of his British Enlightenment knowledge. Clement Hawes calls this satirical strategy "dismantling the colonizer": the reduction of Gulliver's status as a standard of the "Englishness" of civility, advancement, and modernity via "assaults on the coherence of his identity."[137] The plot of the work consists of continuing reversals of this standard, creating a situation in which "Gulliver, the English narrator, is himself colonized" by those he encounters on his voyages.[138] The central motif actualizing these reversals is scale, which calls attention to the positionality of Gulliver's English empirical observations and points out that each society has its own logocentric means of establishing the benchmarks by which value is measured. *Gulliver's Travels'* discourse on incommensurability, accordingly, is also one on the epistemological effects of sovereignty—effects most visible when the printing press and the scale of monetary valuation are considered components of national identity.

Swift's commentary on the English print trade and its relationship to the epistemological ethos of the Enlightenment is located in the third book, "A Voyage to Laputa," a satire of Britain's Royal Society and the scientific revolution with which it was associated. In the speculative learning wing of the Academy of Lagado, the first professor whom Gulliver meets is working on "a Frame, which took up the greatest part of both the Length and Breadth of the Room."[139] This machine, a figure for the Royal Society's printing press, has been invented to help people "write Books in Philosophy, Poetry, Politicks, Law, Mathematicks and Theology without the least Assistance from Genius or Study."[140] The professor's assistants crank machine handles attached to wooden cubes, the sides of which have letters and words engraved upon them. The book is created by combinations of these words: "where they found three or four Words together that might make part of a Sentence, they dictated to the four remaining Boys who were Scribes."[141] The product of this labor has been "several Volumes in large Folio already collected, of broken Sentences, which [the professor] intended to piece together, and out of those rich Materials to give the World a compleat Body of all Arts and Sciences."[142] The scientific approach to textual production, Swift cautions, leads to the kinds of flawed, trashy books that the fiscal-military state was producing. He contends in this *argumentum ad absurdam* that, by adhering too closely to methods of cognitive modernization, England has formed a print culture that defies the kind of common sense and reason that the scientific revolution ostensibly stood for.

By solely relying on a machine in book production, the professor's modernization of printing has neglected the human element in writing. Part of Swift's message here is a call for the redemption of humanism in the face of the new culture industry. This call, however, comes from the colonial periphery of empire, and Gulliver may be taken as the symbol of an imperial book trade and form of sovereignty satirically deconstructed by provincial intellectuals seeking to control public opinion and politics through their presses. Gulliver initially comes across as a brainwashed, pliable spokesman for the unhealthy fiscal-military state—"a parrot-like mouthpiece . . . of his militaristic culture" who is "defenseless against an external critique of its failings" by characters representing provincial intellectuals that he encounters in the colonial contact zone.[143] The body politic prior to 1688 had been represented positively in the image of a healthy royal incorporation of the branches of the state, and satirists like Swift appropriated that model to render the newly emergent public, portrayed in the dissection of Gulliver's character, as a grotesque, malformed body of nonintegrated parts. As Hawes has argued, this dissection represents not only an appropriation of the imperialist's position but also a travestying of the expectations of the English book inasmuch as it defies the expectations of character development in the genre of the novel: "Gulliver simply cannot be understood without some minimal concept of an evolving 'character.' But he exists in a surrealistic historical dimension that cannot be adequately represented within the conventions of formal realism."[144] Rather than compelling the natives he encounters in his travels to adapt to his norms, as Defoe's Robinson Crusoe would, Gulliver assimilates to theirs, demonstrating a malleability eventually threatening to his sanity. Accordingly, his is a failed assimilation that works against the standard narrative of the novel, in which characters achieve a healthy balance between autonomy and belonging.[145] Ending up living in a stable with horses instead of with people, Gulliver becomes so simultaneously adaptive and resistant that there is no human community in which he can belong.

The satire's motif of scale works with Gulliver's malleability to decenter English imperial standards and place them within the culturally relativistic context of a diverse array of sovereignties competing to establish hegemony, at least within their own national boundaries. It does so by delegitimating the travel story and the novel in their capacity as narratives of imperialism, revising these genres to make the narrating character the subject of, rather than the subjugator of, the sovereign societies that he encounters. *Gulliver's Travels*, unlike *A Tale of a Tub*, is almost wholly secular, engaging the problem of sovereignty in modern terms as one concerning economies of scale in relation to one another. It nonetheless is a critique of modernity and secularism, at least in the imperialist form that the standard travel narrative and novel promoted. Though Swift had begun to operate within the new modern order and his satire was becoming less that of a traditional, clerical intellectual and more that of an organic intellectual unifying an oppositional constituency, what gave him perspective on modernity was his knowledge of what had come before. The sovereign of political theology, though problematic from a democratic point of view, had provided a clear standard of signification and meaning in the person and body of the monarch. The flaw in British Enlightenment thinking, as he saw it, was the depersonalizing of these standards and the one-size-fits-all approach to the problems of value that cognitive and social modernization had brought about. This approach did not account for cultural relativism, and these standards were unworkable in Swift's Ireland, given its unequal status under the fiscal-military state.

This problem of scale and value is expressed best in the *Travels'* critique of the materialism of modern epistemology, which is extended to encompass the materiality of the book and the status of language within the new science. Words were a problem for the Royal Society, the academy of cognitive modernization, because they have no ontological being aside from their existence as letters on the page. For example, there is a conceptual connection in John Locke's work between the social contract, epistemology, and language that is derived from the distinction between "nominal" and "real" essence in the vocabulary of *An Essay Concerning Human Understanding*. This difference is perhaps most significant in his construction of empirical objectivity, inasmuch as "nominal essence" refers to "that *abstract* Idea *to which the Name is annexed*," and "real essence" refers to "that particular constitution, which every Thing has within it self, without any relation to anything without it."[146] In this view, there is a gap between names, or the abstract ideas that are the signified objects of those names, and what Locke calls "insensible" ontological things. His description of this distinction, however, relies on the example of the difference between "words" and "gold": "the *nominal Essence of Gold*, is that complex *Idea* the word *Gold* stands for, let it be, for instance, a Body yellow, of a certain weight, malleable, fusible, and fixed. But the *real Essence* is the constitution of the insensible parts of that Body, on which those Qualities, and all the other Properties of *Gold* depend."[147] "Real" gold, in this passage, is said to be the material "other" of immaterial language and ideas: gold is an *a priori* and autonomous "real" thing that does not need us to name it, for which reason the "nominal essence" of gold, its name, is constructed as an inferior, dependent on this "real essence." Words are not to be mistaken for objects: "it often happens that Men, even when they would apply themselves to an attentive Consideration, do set their Thoughts more on Words than Things."[148] It is the ontological, real "thing" which is to be valued, not its mediation in linguistic representation. Books, according to Locke's theory, are problematic because they are ontological "things" containing nominal essences—words.

Swift parodied Locke's view of how "things" should tell books' stories in the third voyage, the account of the academy of Lagado. Gulliver observes a linguistic experiment designed to abolish "all Words whatsoever."[149] This scheme to eliminate signification for the sake of the thing-in-itself was written by Swift as a satire of the Royal Society's attempts to find a transparent language, one free of the duplicity that often dogs the relationship between sign and thing-in-itself. The particular target of this attack was Thomas Sprat, who "envisioned a 'return back to the primitive purity and shortness, when men deliver'd so many things almost in an equal number of words.'"[150] In this scheme, the object speaks for itself and requires no mediator to establish its identity. Swift was also recognizing the evidentiary function of the thing in empiricist method and realist narrative by showing how the desire for the thing—its presentation in lieu of sign—redeems the absent formalism of representation with a present ontological reality. Yet he portrayed such a fantasy of redemption, particularly when its realization is attempted in representation itself, as merely an erroneous literalist conceit. Swift's satire suggests that in Sprat and Locke's view the book's materiality itself certifies the word and idea of the book, not the other way around. As *A Tale of a Tub*, *The Battle of the Books*, and *Gulliver's Travels*—all allegorical works—

testify, Swift, contrary to cognitive modernists, privileged the idea of the book over its materiality.

Accordingly, the *Travels* itself, though regarded as a literal object like other travel narratives, is shown to be, like the narrator himself, an unreliable mediator of material events and places. As Richard Rodino has noted, Swift not only demonstrated the error of Gulliver's purist empiricism through the parody of thick description but, through Gulliver's tendency to respond to challenges to his narrative by other characters, he mocks the Lockean impulse to use things, not words, to tell a story.[151] In the last chapter of "A Voyage to Lilliput," Gulliver legitimates the claims that his tale makes by showing the captain of the ship that rescues him many Lilliputian objects. Gulliver convinces the captain of his "Veracity" by presenting presences—tiny cattle, sheep, and gold coins—to redeem and render true his absent, merely re-presentative words.[152] In the Lockean epistemology that he follows, such forms of material evidence redeem the narrative; yet in the *Travels*, they are not attached to the text as supplementary objects but only represented in the medium of words.

Swift's post-Brobdingnagian version of the drama of fact-production is different from the post-Lilliputian one in that the things presented to certify the authenticity of the tale are more completely finished products of labour. Gulliver demonstrates the veracity of his tale to the captain who rescues him from Brobdingnag by showing him the outsized goods he has made and collected in that country such as a comb, stumps of the king's beard, needles, pins, and so forth.[153] Once again, these "foreign" things serve as presences that authenticate Gulliver's narrative, supporting his putatively merely mediatory words with material "proof." These Brobdingnagian objects, as finished products of the labour of another society, also serve as commodity fetishes, which in British society constituted representatives of the other that helped the British imagination appropriate that otherness.

Gulliver's Travels may be read as a text challenging the stylistic conventions of popular literature such as Defoe's *Robinson Crusoe*, which Swift considered to be an extension of such Lockean and Whig epistemology. Swift links those conventions to the objectivity claims of the empirical historicism rehearsed in the realist novel. The "Sinon problem" in *Gulliver's Travels*—the question of whether Gulliver is a reliable narrator—

is one mechanism by which this connection between epistemology and language is examined.[154] The story's textual details document the adventure by following scientific method: "*Gulliver's Travels* is adorned with all the claims to historicity and all the authenticating devices of 'modern history' in general, and of travel narrative in particular. . . . The narrative is interspersed with documents—letters, maps—that attest to its own documentary objecthood."[155] Swift was parodying not only "travel narratives per se but also . . . a larger developing class of first-person fictional narratives that make extraordinary claims for the importance of the contemporary, the knowableness through personal experience of large cosmic patterns, the significance of the individual, and the imperialistic possibilities of the human mind."[156] The project in which Swift was engaged through this undermining of modern historicist conventions, paradoxically, was to create a modern literature based in an alternative sphere in which the "real" existed: "By subverting empirical epistemology, Swift contributes, as fully as Defoe does by sponsoring it, to the growth of modern ideas of realism. . . . Swift's parabolic pedagogy can tacitly justify its return to an anachronistic attitude toward how to tell the truth in narrative in part because it has, as it were, earned the right to it through a self-conscious evisceration of the more modern alternative."[157] By satirizing how a story is authenticated, Swift underwrote the notion that there is, or should be, an authentic truth and reality.

The chief and most obvious device that Swift deployed to satirize the problems of the pure empiricism of realist form was scale: the difference in size that Gulliver confronts both as a giant in Lilliput and a dwarf in Brobdingnag. Gulliver's observations in both locations are coolly detailed in descriptive prose seemingly communicating accurate facts free of value judgments. This kind of descriptive technique is particularly evident in matters of money. In Lilliput, Gulliver adapts himself to the standard weights and measures of the little people, ignoring the fact that his body's own size renders such extensions meaningless. He writes that his maintenance by the kingdom "cost his Majesty above a Million and a half of Sprugs, (their greatest Gold Coin, about the bigness of a Spangle)" and that later, "His Majesty presented me with fifty Purses of two hundred Sprugs a-piece."[158] He makes a similar mistake in Brobdingnag, when the European coins that he values are misperceived as of little value by the first giant he meets when he presents them as a form of communication in lieu of language. Supposedly a universal medium of exchange, the value of which lay in its "intrinsic" properties, his comparatively tiny gold and silver coins are rendered unrecognizable in the eyes of the giant.[159] He begins to understand the idea that conceptions of value are not empirical in the sense of being universal objects of nature, but rather are particular to different societies, as he reports when his owner sells him to the Brobdingnagian queen. He says that his master "demanded a thousand pieces of Gold, which were ordered him on the spot, each piece being about the bigness of eight hundred Moydores; but, allowing for the proportion of all Things between that Country and *Europe*, and the high price of Gold among them, was hardly so great a sum as a thousand Guineas would be in *England*."[160] Yet, even here, Gulliver is making a scientific judgment of difference between cultures, revealing that he still believes it is possible to make an empirical case for societal difference through an objective understanding of cultural relativism. He cannot see that it is sovereignty that establishes standards in epistemology, language, and currency.

If Gulliver is a subject produced by England's new fragmentary social order, he is one who cannot see that fact and value are both socially determined. He is "thoroughly empirical, he can follow modes, but cannot grasp principles."[161] This depiction suggests that those educated in the new style of learning fail to realize that standards are local and depend upon a clear conception of sovereign authority. Gulliver suffers in his transition from one country's standards to another. When first in Brobdingnag, he records, "I could never endure to look in a Glass after my Eyes had been accustomed to such prodigious Objects, because the Comparison gave me so despicable a Conceit of myself."[162] Eventually, however, he becomes so converted to this Brobdingnagian scale that he is initially unable to readapt to English standards. He writes that he looked upon the sailors who rescued him as "the most little contemptible Creatures I had ever beheld" and that his very vision, even at home with his family, has been altered by his stay in Brobdingnag.[163] He attributes this problem of his distorted perception to "the great Power of Habit and Prejudice," thinking that these more culturally specific biases can be rooted out by better empirical practice.[164] Yet he does not confront the roots of that prejudice, the politics of how each state that he visits establishes weights and measures.

The *Travels* informs us that this epistemological arrogance is not Gulliver's alone; even the Lilliputians blind themselves to the problem of scale in measurement, particularly when they take an inventory of his pockets. When confronted with Gulliver's human-scale money, they attribute immense value to the quantities of silver and gold they encounter, misrecognizing the physical properties of the objects for their worth in human terms. The Lilliputians make the same mistakes as Gulliver; in their naïve empiricism, they acknowledge the difference in scale but they are overwhelmed by it, turning back to their native scale in panic.[165] If they were to change their perspective to accommodate the differences in value between Gulliver's human scale and their own, they would cede a crucial part of their sovereignty: "To accept Gulliver's scale would force the Lilliputians to cede their place as dominant species, and so they don't accept it. . . . The Lilliputian world would tumble if Gulliver became the measure of it, and so the mites refuse to take his measure."[166] By calling attention to the relationship of a culture's symbolic order of commensurability to its political power and administrative apparatus, Swift undermined the revolution's claims that its "natural" methods were universally valid. His decision to arrange his narrative as a pastiche of different cultural standards therefore attempts to make modern society recognize itself as a fragmented, "grotesque body" and endeavors to explain the necessity of a general equivalent by reference to other societies.

The cultural relativism explored in the motif of scale may have been the product of a colonial consciousness recognizing that the scale of value in the metropolis was not suited to the periphery. Swift may have been saying that Ireland, which valued coins at a different rate than England did, exemplified the different standards possessed by such fictional lands as Lilliput and Brobdingnag. What connects *Gulliver's Travels* to the exploration of the coinage problem in his Irish publications is the theme of sovereignty and its relevance to problems of measurement and value. *Gulliver's Travels* and the Irish tracts, such as the *Drapier's Letters*, should be seen as two faces of the same sovereignty dispute, not only because they were written at approximately the same time, but also because where one makes positive claims on behalf of Irish independence the other paints an unflattering portrait of English imperial power. While works like *A Proposal for the Universal Use of Irish Manufacture* supported domestic efforts to control Ireland's economy, *Gulliver's Trav-*

els critiqued the modern forms by which the British fiscal-military state legitimated its authority, the very reasons the Anglo-Irish had to assert themselves in the first place.

IV

Gulliver's Travels is an Irish text critiquing the British culture industry from the inside. As such, it may be taken as part of the general effort to protect the *Monti* by promoting the Irish book trade at the expense of its British counterpart. The Irish book trade was essential for the mobilization of Irish national public opinion against the fiscal-military state's political inroads into Irish property in the form of revenues. The travel narrative—a dominant cultural form in the British book trade and a means by which the fiscal-military state's economic interests were masked and displaced—was the object of *Gulliver's Travels'* parody. Swift may have been using this satire to articulate resistance to both cultural and financial imperialism. The satire links the political problem of sovereignty to the epistemological concerns that the formal realism of the English novel attempted to resolve. Its refusal to permit this resolution from taking place within its own pages—its active undermining of the genre's referentiality of word and thing—eviscerates the novel as a vehicle for truth telling and, by doing so, undermines the validity of the public sphere of which the novel is supposed to be emblematic. Enlightenment epistemology and the English book are rejected simultaneously, suggesting that if the Irish print industry were to compete, its products would have to challenge the hegemony of British ideas. Only by doing so, Swift implied, could Ireland obtain political, economic, and cultural sovereignty.

"*Money*, the Great *Divider* of the World, has, by a strange Revolution, been the great *Uniter* of a Most *divided* People"

From Minting to Printing in The Drapier's Letters

Swift's skepticism of British publications reflected his belief that the book trade was deeply intertwined with Enlightenment discourse, and his call in 1724–1725 for a boycott of a different medium of communication and exchange—currency—linked print to money in an epistemology that integrated political, fiscal, and linguistic components of sovereignty. The needs of the *Monti* after the collapse of the investment bubble provoked his awareness of the interrelationship of these seemingly distinct categories of knowledge, a synthesis that could be regarded as the spark of an interdisciplinary Irish Enlightenment. The *Drapier's Letters*, published in 1724 and 1725, was a series of pamphlets written in reaction to the crown's move to introduce copper halfpence into Ireland via a minting patent granted to William Wood.[1] The pamphlets concerning Wood's halfpence, however, were not so much about the coin as a material object as about what the constitutionally suspect way it was introduced said about Ireland's legal standing within the three kingdoms. Swift understood that in the post–South Sea Bubble era, the definition of what constituted "real" money had become more slippery. Consequently, his overt concern about the type, weight, or fineness of the metal in the copper halfpence may have been a pretext for a more subtle message: that the legitimacy or illegitimacy of a currency could shape public opinion into a national form. He exploits a coinage crisis "to generate anticolonial intellectual coin," cultivating a more universal Irish public sphere that would be useful not only for the political defense of the Irish Parliament's revenue authority but also for the nationalization of the Irish book trade, the cause and effect of that sovereignty.[2] Thus, his discourse on political economy migrates from minting to printing as the source of value, indicating that coins and words were homologous signifiers of sovereignty to the extent that "it would be otiose to quibble about the nice issue of which is the 'base' and which the 'superstructure,'" writing or coin.[3] The term "ware," which could include both currency and written materials in this period, functions in the *Drapier's Letters* to signal this homology and to mark this migration in a manner that would have been apparent to Dublin book craftsmen.

Swift, in the persona of a Dublin drapier (textile merchant), used the *Letters* to help expand Anglo-Irish identity, initially constructed in *A Proposal for the Universal Use of Irish Manufacture* and the bank satires, into a broader, more universally Irish subjectivity. The *Letters'* consequent hybridity—their attempt to mix Ireland's diverse identities into a whole—however, should be taken as an attempt to help the *Monti's* interest appear to be the same as that of the Dublin merchant community and other domestic constituencies. As many critics have contended, there is evidence that Swift was recruited by prominent members of the Protestant Interest to write these letters, which suggests, in this context, that what was at stake were the revenues feeding the creditors to the Debt of the Nation.[4] The reason that the *Letters* should be read skeptically is that, while the founding of the *Monti* and its creation of a private public of government creditors had formed the economic basis for an autonomous provincial identity, the migrations of its members and their cash undermined their patriotic claims to be acting in the interest of Ireland's population as a whole. There were many complaints from Swift and members of the Irish Parliament about absentee landlords among them, who lived in London and elsewhere, taking with them currency and capital that would otherwise have been reinvested in the domestic economy. Yet, the unanimous concern of the Anglo-Irish landed class and churchmen about the payments of their rents, as the Earl of Abercorn documented in his petition for the Bank of Ireland charter, suggests that these complaints were little more than apologetics. Their loyalty to British sterling, rather, was an expression of their regard for their English sovereign; and despite advocacy for an Irish mint by some of their writers, their appetites demanded that sterling be yielded from their tenants in ever-increasing amounts. The Wood's halfpence, intended to resolve Ireland's chronic shortage of smaller denomination coins by introducing debased copper tokens in their place, threatened the *Monti*'s supply of this ultimate sign of Englishness to the extent that the members paradoxically had to invent a more universal "Irishness" to obtain this token of Englishness. The *Drapier's Letters* were the vehicle for this task, manufacturing a broader patriotic public convinced that the halfpence initiative would be bad for them. As such, this corpus of work is one of the better examples of how a small circle can engineer public opinion in such a way as to enlist a vast majority to a cause not necessarily in their interests. The manifest gap between the economic base and the ideology of this new imagined community suggests that colonial contexts present extraordinary opportunities to examine the use of print culture to manufacture consent. Further, the *Letters*, if taken as texts commissioned by the *Monti*, demonstrate how a literary market can emerge as a parasite on the national public formed by political intervention in available media.

The *Drapier's Letters*, like the bank satires before them, exploited the homologies of money, power, and print to both constitute value in the absence of intrinsically valuable currency and ensure that what remained of the latter gravitated toward the *Monti*. Their protest against the copper pennies was therefore also a nearly treasonous assertion of Ireland's sovereignty vis-à-vis Britain. Its subtext of sterling functioned to render the legal tender as much cultural as it was political and economic, making it not only the general equivalent but also the final ground for the epistemology that governed identity in the Anglophone Atlantic. Because sterling presented both mobile private property and the fruits of immobile landed property in the Anglo-Irish mind, it was an expression of the certainty which the traditional concept of the state had provided.

The Wood's halfpence affair thus became a referendum on the relationship among currency, sovereignty, and identity; and it therefore marks, more strongly than the Bank of Ireland affair of 1721, the moment when the seeds of colonial nationalism were forged out of a resistance to the centralizing societal modernization that empire was consolidating over the course of the eighteenth century. This "forging" of identity matched the essential "forgery" that was the *Drapier's Letters*—the Let-

ters were a fiction about a copper currency that the Anglo-Irish regarded as counterfeit and "fictional"—yet the *Letters* nonetheless attained legitimacy for this national identity through their success in mobilizing the population. Examining this controversy and its impact on Irish political economy may help explain how the Anglo-Irish category of the literary emerged as the product of a discourse on currency.

I

Wood's halfpence were threatening to the *Monti* in two ways. The first was the base coin's challenge to members' private incomes from the rent of land, for if landlords began to receive rent payments in the halfpence, the value of their leased land would decrease dramatically. For example, the speaker of the Irish Parliament would need "Two Hundred and Fifty Horses" to transport the halfpence that would be used to pay just a half-year's worth of his "Sixteen Thousand Pounds" in annual rents (10:7). Swift tells his readers that absentee Anglo-Irish landlords living in London would be most affected and offended by the inferior coinage: "do you think those who live in *England* upon *Irish* Estates, will be content to take an Eighth or a Tenth Part, by being paid in *Wood's* Dross?" (10:22). Second, the base coin would cut into landed gentlemen's income from public sources because it would undermine the value of Ireland's revenue and decimate the all-important interest payments on the Debt of the Nation. Because of this problem, "the Officers of the King's Revenue . . . had already given Orders to all the inferior Officers not to receive any of his [Wood's] Coin" (10:44), not least because they were "obliged by Act of Parliament, to take nothing but *Gold* and *Silver* in Payment" of taxes (10:46). These tax officials were paid out of the revenues that they collected, and they knew that they would "be Losers of Two Thirds in their *Salaries* or *Pay*" if they accepted Wood's money in payments—a strong disincentive that ramified into all aspects of tax-supported civil service and military employment (10:47). Because money was "neither *Whig* nor *Tory*, neither of *Town* nor *Country Party*" (10:59), even "the People sent over hither from *England*, to *fill up . . . Vacancies, Ecclesiastical, Civil and Military*" were all opposed to the new halfpence (10:61). The *Drapier's Letters*, consequently, can be regarded as a media campaign engineered by the landed class and the government to protect their profits. A close reading of the Wood's halfpence controversy, however, reveals that this overt concern for the income consequences of accepting the halfpence is only part of the drapier's message; its more covert argument concerns the capability and profitability of sustaining future media campaigns—the health of the book trade—due to the halfpence's effects on the economy. This argument is conducted subtly by the drapier "in the Terms of his own Trade," the language of textile production, a code for the jargon of those employed in the printing industry (10:83). In these letters, the narrative persona of the drapier, a dealer in cloth, can be regarded as a figure for a bookseller.

The term "ware," already meaning both coin and cloth in the *Drapier's Letters'* literal text, underwrites this metaphorical figuration in its capacity to also signify manuscripts, printed pages, and other raw materials for bookmaking. "Ware" is mentioned no fewer than twelve times in the seven letters to identify Wood's profession and the commodities in which he deals. He is said to be a *"Hard-ware Dealer"* (10:4), a *"Hard-Ware-Man"* (10:16, 10:18, 10:23, 10:29, 10:105, 10:119), and one whose base copper pennies are "merchantable Ware" (10:135) that is "so bad" (10:136) that the Anglo-Irish should have "nothing to do" (10:57) with the *"Cart-Loads"* of it (10:46). In the eighteenth century, it would not be unusual to refer to any commodities as "wares," and, according to the *Oxford English Dictionary*, a drapier, as a textile merchant, would certainly use the term to describe the cloth in which he dealt (*OED* "ware, n.3." Def. 3b). *"Hardware,"* internal evidence suggests, clearly signifies Wood's halfpence as well.

The word has a further, metaphorical meaning in the *Letters*, however, because it was also used in contemporary documents to connote texts. For example, the narrator of *A Letter of Advice to a Young Poet* speaks of Grub Street as "a Market for *Small-Ware* in WIT," using italics to lend emphasis to the fact that he is describing writing (9:341). Further, Lisa Maruca has documented several cases in which literature was referred to as ware. She cites the *Monthly Review* of 1766, which says that "retailers of every kind of ware aspire to be the original manufacturer and particularly in literature," and reveals that a printer's dictionary of 1753 referred to "printed sheets" as "this ware" before they become bound in books.[5] Using this definition, she describes manuscripts as "ware like any other," discusses satires as potentially "libelous wares," and writes of "hawkers" of pamphlets "who strolled the city crying their printed wares."[6] In short, this etymology, particularly in this context, suggests that though Swift was certainly describing Wood's halfpence with this word, *"Hard-ware"* was also referring to British books that were being imported into Ireland. The *Drapier's Letters*, accordingly, may be taken as a call to boycott both Wood's halfpence and London presses, an act that would simultaneously create a market for Dublin-printed wares like the *Letters* and a distinctly Irish imagined community. These works, via the persona of the drapier, revisit the text/textile homology with which Swift had been working since at least 1720, yet they extend it to encompass currency.

The first of the *Drapier's Letters, A Letter to the Shop-Keepers, Tradesmen, Farmers, and Common-People of Ireland*, employs the weaving/writing metaphor, from the outset referencing *A Proposal for the Universal Use of Irish Manufacture*, describing it as "a little Book" about the plight of "WEAVERS" that was published "ABOUT four Years ago" (10:3). Given his use of capital letters in his discussion of a "POOR PRINTER" who was found "GUILTY" by a "JURY" consisting partly of "WEAVERS," Swift can be said to be announcing on the first page his intention to exploit that metaphor (10:3). He refers to the copper halfpence—*"base metal"*—as "TRASH," a word that, given its uses in his critique of politeness to signify bad literature, serves as a transitive term mediating the homologous relationship between imported books and debased coin that he is constructing (10:4). The halfpence, Swift implies, are the visible sign of a much larger, invisible crisis of general equivalence and commensurability that Ireland is experiencing due to its lack of sovereignty's legal, textual, and monetary components. "Trash"—a few pages later revised to *"Filthy Trash"* (10:11)—therefore imputes to false coin not only a disturbance in monetary exchange but also a much larger crisis in the political and cultural processes, including those associated with the print industry, which produced the "trash." Accordingly, when the narrator, the drapier, says that he has "a pretty good Shop of *Irish Stuffs* and *Silks*," Swift is borrowing from *A Proposal for the Universal Use of Irish Manufacture* to refer to a bookstore specializing in domestically produced Irish publications. He is implying that the most important "Shopkeepers" that he is addressing in this letter are booksellers and others in the publishing trade, whom he again asks to support the fledgling Irish print industry (10:7). The fact that he alternates between referring to the halfpence as

"*Brass*" (metal associated with counterfeit coin) and "*Lumber*" (pulp associated both with the minter's name—Wood—and with inferior paper products, including books, imported from Britain) further highlights the minting/printing homology that this letter is presenting (10:7).

The drapier's second, third, and fourth letters, *A Letter to Mr. Harding the Printer*, *Some Observations Upon a Paper*, and *A Letter to the Whole People of Ireland*, play upon this homology via a metadiscourse on the sovereign right to produce coin. *A Letter to Mr. Harding* begins and ends by calling attention to that homology, not metaphorically, but with a literal description of a minter as a writer. By reference to a paragraph by William Wood published in Harding's newspaper, the drapier observes, "Wood is generally his own News-Writer" and that his printed words, like the minted halfpence, are "an Imposition upon the Publick" (10:15). This direct, rather than implied, connection between minting and printing is exploited further, in a comparison of the quality of Wood's writing to the quality of his coin: "this Publick Enemy of ours, not satisfied to Ruin us with his Trash, takes every Occasion to treat this Kingdom with the utmost Contempt" (10:15). Wood's writing lacks civility just as the metal of his coin lacks refinement. Ending the letter by saying that Harding is "much to blame" for giving Wood a public forum in his newspaper, the drapier requests that Harding publish more copies of the *Letters* instead, and Swift invents a domestic demand for them: "Several Hundred Persons have enquired at your House, for my *Letter to the Shop-keepers*, & c. and you had none to sell them. Pray keep your self provided with that Letter, and with this; you have got very well by the former; but I did not then write for your Sake, any more than I do now" (10:24). This statement points out that patriotic writings, which should be for the public and not any private interest, are nonetheless profitable to printers; and it sends a signal to other Irish publishers not only to protect their interests as shopkeepers, who would suffer from the circulation of Wood's halfpence, but also to profit further from publication of domestic texts like Swift's, though he asks them "to sell them as cheap as you can" (10:24). Irish printing, in these passages, ceases to be a perfect homology for minting and instead replaces minting as a source of national Irish value, though it may benefit from the products of proper mints in payment for its texts. Because this letter is addressed to Swift's own printer, it should be regarded as the central one in this reading of the series, because of these direct links between Dublin's print industry and the problem of currency.

The third letter, *Some Observations*, continues in this vein via a discourse on the origins of a document entitled *A Report of the Committee of the Lords of His Majesty's Most Honourable Privy Council in England, relating to Mr. Wood's Half-pence and Farthings*. It seems to have been reprinted in Dublin from an edition published in "the *London Journal*, or some other Print of no Authority or Consequence" (10:27). The drapier refers to the document as "a Contrivance to *Fright* us; or a *Project* of some *Printer*, who hath a Mind to make a Penny by publishing something upon a Subject, which now employs all our Thoughts in this *Kingdom*" (10:27). Swift once again calls attention to the homology between writing and coining by suggesting that any paper published on the Wood's halfpence controversy is as good as money to printing houses and booksellers on either side of the Irish Sea. He implies that Wood also, in addition to the news item in Harding's paper, authored *A Report of the Committee of Lords*, and insinuates that "the *Committee* had a greater Concern for his Credit and private Emolument" than for Ireland's institutions of government. Indeed, writes the drapier, the report has "the Turn and Air" of a pamphlet pitting Wood against those institutions (10:27). Swift suggests that the report is tantamount to an illegal printing because it was published without the permission of the committee in question and before the government and privy council of Ireland had received it (10:28).

A Letter to the Whole People of Ireland even goes so far as to claim that "*Wood* prescribes to the News-Mongers in *London*, what they are to write," further linking minting and printing by saying that Wood works in both professions in England, where he has authority that he does not yet have in Ireland, due to the successful boycotting of his coins. The drapier here discusses a Dublin reprint of one of Wood's London articles as something produced by "some obscure Printer, (and certainly with a bad Design)" (10:53). The phrase "bad Design," in this passage, denigrates not only the intentions of the publication, which threatens to divide the population because of its anti-Catholicism, but also the style of both the publication and Wood's coining, smearing Wood and those printers who collaborate with him. But, he writes, "If the Pamphlets published at London by Wood and his Journeymen, in Defence of his Cause, were Re-printed here, they would convince you of his wicked Design, more than all I shall ever be able to say" (10:63). He highlights the distinction between himself as working in the public interest and writers for Wood as working in the private interest, referring to the latter as "*Hirelings*" (10:63, 10:66). Further, he says that Wood so censors the English public sphere "that no *London* Printer dare publish any Paper written in Favour of *Ireland*" lest they offend him by circulating opinions unfavorable to his project (10:64). The drapier smears Wood's writing style and personal manners by reference to his mint work, claiming that both savour "too much of the *Kettle* and the *Furnace*; and came entirely out of *Wood's Forge*" (10:67). The term "forge" functions to link the production of metal with the production of counterfeits, suggesting that Wood's coin is a forgery and that his words are fiction.

Because this covert discourse on the metaphorical coining of words by printing presses relies on the literal coining of money in mints, the *Letters'* overt discussion of the legal relationship of minting to issues of sovereignty is central to the effectiveness of this strategy of homogenizing coining and printing. When the drapier calls attention in the second letter to Ireland's former "Liberty of Coining for our selves" (10:16), he simultaneously invokes *A Proposal for the Universal Use of Manufacture's* plea for "the liberty of spinning and weaving" wool and publications, extending it to encompass currency. In questioning whether the king's outsourcing of minting to private sources is legal, he asserts the right of Ireland's inhabitants to refuse Wood's halfpence. Doing so provides him with the opportunity to discuss not only the history of coining in Ireland but also traditional, medieval, notions of the sovereign's responsibilities in the fiscal arena. John Harding was prosecuted for printing the fourth letter, an indication that Swift, by calling attention to this relationship too subversively, crossed the line, actually infringed on the territory of the monarch by advocating for Irish independence in this arena too explicitly. Because the pattern of the *Drapier's Letters* is to migrate from a discourse on minting towards one on printing, his discussion of the right to coin brings the discourse back full circle, suggesting that publishing can be Ireland's medium of coining.

When Swift spoke of Ireland's former liberty to mint for its own territory, he was referring to a right that it had had throughout the Middle Ages but which had been eliminated in 1506. Ireland had continual problems maintaining an adequate supply of coin in the early modern period because it was deprived of this central prerogative of government, one that would have enabled the kingdom to regulate its economy for its own purposes. Because the English monarch regularly drew coinage out of Ireland in the form of rent to the tune of £20,000, he or she traditionally provided a subvention to the Irish Exchequer to keep the economy it managed prosperous.[7] During Charles I's financial difficulties in the 1630s, the king reversed this subvention; the lord lieutenant of Ireland insisted that, in the exceptional circumstances of the king's fiscal emergency, Ireland should contribute to the English Exchequer.[8] Further, Charles I proclaimed that sterling would be Ireland's official currency in order to make this reversal of currency flows meaningful for the English economy.[9] In the eighteenth century, Ireland lacked circulating coin primarily because it had no means of encouraging its traders to bring gold and silver back to Ireland in exchange for their exports instead of imported commodities. If there had been an Irish mint, they could have taken any foreign bullion and coins they received for their exports and converted them into sterling that could be used in domestic commerce.[10] In these circumstances, foreign commodities like English books served as a form of commodity money that merchants received in exchange for the Irish goods they exported. In light of this history, the wool trade explored in *A Proposal for the Universal Use of Irish Manufacture* looks even more like a metaphor for the book trade, for if wool was Ireland's main export, the problematic imported products can be seen as "counterfeit" English publications received in lieu of coin.

Swift's strategy in arguing against the halfpence, given the history of minting for Ireland, is threefold. First, he claimed that the halfpence were compromised because they were being coined by a private minter, not by the king's mint. Second, he complained that the halfpence being coined were base, mixed with more inferior metals than copper, which recalls earlier impositions by arbitrary monarchs incapable of circulating coin without the use of force. Third, he contended, by reference to precedents, that the coins were minted outside of Ireland, which was related to the fact that they had been produced without the consent of the Irish Parliament. All three of these strategies, though they revisited a more medieval understanding of minting's role in sovereignty, attempted to assert the more modern and democratic idea that the Irish Parliament should have had some say in whether Wood's halfpence were to be disseminated in Ireland.

In the first argument, the question of the *extent* of the king's power to mint money for Ireland and England dominates the second, third, and fourth letters. The drapier stipulates that the monarch so clearly has the sole "Prerogative of coining Copper for Ireland and for England" that it is "not the present Question" being debated (10:34). As Jotham Parsons has argued, this prerogative was so ingrained in Western thinking that it went without saying throughout the early modern period and well into the eighteenth century, partly because it was regarded also as the sovereign's obligation.[11] The problem that Swift was confronting was not the prerogative itself but the twofold question of whether the monarch could privatize that right and compel subjects to take privately minted coins in payment. For example, a passage in *Some Observations* says that the drapier does not think that "the King can by Law Declare *any thing* to be current Money," though "the King hath a Prerogative" to outsource coining (10:37). Countering the latter claim, the drapier objects to the notion "that a King of *England* may, at any Time, coin Copper Money for *Ireland*; and oblige his Subjects here to take a piece of Copper under the Value of half a Farthing, for half a Crown, as was practiced by the late King *James*; and even without that arbitrary Prince's Excuse, from the Necessity and Exigences of his Affairs" (10:39). James II had indeed coined base money for Ireland, to pay for troops during the Jacobite War of 1689–1691 when he was defending his right to the throne of the three kingdoms against William III of Orange. By invoking this historical precedent, Swift exclaimed that the imposition of coin by an English monarch without consulting the people of Ireland was "*derogatory*" and "*evasive*" of the "*Liberties, or Privileges of the Subjects* of Ireland" (10:39). The first letter had cited ancient law that ordained "*that no* King *of this Realm should* Change, *or* Impair the Money, *or make any other* Money *than of* Gold *or* Silver *without the Assent of all the Counties, that is*, as my Lord *Coke* says, *without the Assent of* Parliament" (10:9). Further, Swift claimed in the fourth letter that "compelling the Subject to take any Coin, which is not Sterling, is no Part of the King's *Prerogative*" (10:55), further reminding his Irish readers that they are permitted under the law to refuse Wood's coins.

In the second argument against the halfpence, Swift conveyed that the quality of Wood's coinage, not just the fact that it was not sterling, was even more derogatory to the Irish people. The terms "Brass" and "Brass Coin"—references to the base metals intermixed with the copper of Wood's halfpence that recalled the coinages of James II—are used repeatedly throughout the *Drapier's Letters* to signify that the coins are not even copper. This epithet compares Wood's halfpence with that earlier, debased coinage of a monarch considered arbitrary and failed, who could not get his coin to circulate and thus lost the right to be king (10:19). Wood "certainly produced the worst Patterns [of coins] he could find; such as were coined in small Numbers by *Permissions to private men, as Butchers Half-pence, Black-Dogs*, and the like; or, perhaps, the small St. *Patrick's* Coin which passeth now for a Farthing" (10:33). Even those coins, the drapier argues, were heavier and of a "better Metal" than what Wood has produced (10:33). Further, he claims that the coin is unworthy of being stamped with the king's face (10:21, 10:137).

This observation concerning debasement leads to his third argument—that even if outsourcing minting has been proven to be legal, past royal patents granting that right had stipulated that the coin at least be subject to Irish legal authority by being produced at private mints in Ireland. The seventeenth-century coinage of John Knox, for example, had required the minter to "be obliged to receive his Half-pence back, and pay Gold or Silver in Exchange for them" (10:30), language that Wood's patent did not contain. In 1694 and again in 1698, an Irish minter named Roger Moor was forced to stop production because too many people had come to him to redeem his copper halfpence for gold and silver (10:30). Swift argued that, even if these earlier private minting contracts provided a precedent for Wood's patent, their coinage was better and of more certain legal authority than his. Further, the fourth letter disputes the legal basis for Wood's contract via a discussion of the processes by which the Knox and Moor patents were approved. These previous patents had been "passed under the great Seal of *Ireland*, by References to *Ireland*; the Copper to be coined in *Ireland*," whereas "*Wood's* Patent was made under the great Seal of *England*, the Brass coined in *England*, not the least Reference made to *Ireland*" (10:56). In short, the drapier says, the coinage has not obtained the consent of the Irish people or their representatives and "all *Government* without the Consent of the *Governed*, is the *very Definition of Slavery*" (10:63).

All three of these argumentative strategies attempt to attribute hubris to Wood; he is setting himself up as a king by claiming powers of minting that were not only not specified in his contract but would be considered illegal even if they were. Swift called Wood a "little impudent *Hard-ware-Man*" and a "diminutive, insignificant Mechanick," but naming him a "little Arbitrary *Mock-Monarch*" most thoroughly encompassed his infringements upon the rights of Irish subjects and perhaps the king himself (10:18–19). For this reason, the Irish should be "ashamed" to have to tell foreigners that the "*Image and Superscription*" on the halfpence is that of George I, when their caesar, in this case, is really William Wood (10:21). From the perspective of the drapier, a David defending the true sovereign, Wood is the "*uncircumcised Philistine*" Goliath, who, in a chainmail coat and helmet made of "*five Thousand Shekles of* BRASS," has attempted a breach of Ireland's sovereignty (10:49).

The drapier's fifth, six, and seventh letters—*A Letter to the Right Honourable the Lord Viscount Molesworth, A Letter to the Lord Chancellor Middleton*, and *An Humble Address to Both Houses of Parliament*—react to the prosecution of the printer of the fourth letter and attempt to "keep up that spirit raised against this destructive Coin of Mr. *Wood*" (10:106). John Harding had been arrested for printing two passages of *A Letter to the Whole People of Ireland*: its discussion of the King's answer to the Irish House of Lords' letter concerning Wood's patent and its discourse on whether Ireland was an unequal kingdom dependent on England's institutions of government. The latter item was taken as inciting rebellion (10:69–70, 10:84, 10:xviii). In the course of legal proceedings, a Dublin grand jury refused to indict Harding, which led to a contentious debate over whether a judge could legally dismiss a grand jury in such circumstances (10:73). Further, no witnesses came forward naming the author of the *Drapier's Letters*, a fact regarded as a gesture of the drapier's success in generating patriotic Irish public opinion (10:81, 10:xix–xxiii). The controversy surrounding the fourth letter was, in essence, an authentication crisis in which initially the drapier was considered by legal authorities to be an illegitimate, counterfeit public voice, but his victory in the case constructed a new form of Anglo-Irish political legitimacy out of that opinion. Consequentially, the three letters that followed *A Letter to the Whole People of Ireland* were "written by one who knows that his cause is almost won" (10:xxiv).

A Letter to the Right Honourable the Lord Viscount Molesworth reads as further incitement of the Dublin book trade to keep publishing tracts condemning Wood's halfpence and can be taken as a key to the *Letters* that reveals the meaning of the metaphors governing the weaving/writing trope. It first apologizes to printers, self-effacingly saying that "*as you deal in the most worthless Kind of trash, the Penny Productions of penniless Scriblers; so you often venture your Liberty, and sometimes your Lives, for the Purchase of half a Crown*" (10:79). The drapier complains that because the Dublin press is under "*so strict an Inspection*" due to the fourth letter, printers ignorant of the legal content of such writings often are "*punished for other Men's Actions*" (10:79). As a consequence, he feels compelled to reveal his identity via an autobiographical passage in which he claims authorship of *A Proposal for the Universal Use of Irish Manufacture*. He explains to Molesworth that in 1720, he was the one who took him into his shop and showed him "a Piece of *black and white Stuff*, just sent from the *Dyer*; which you were pleased to approve of," signaling not only that the textile "stuff" was the textual earlier pamphlet, but that it had received the sanction of the Anglo-Irish nobility (10:82). He recounts how he wrote the pamphlet against those who argued that "the People of *England* would be offended, if our Manufactures were brought to equal theirs," further indicating that his discussion of the wool trade was also a metaphor for the creation of a domestic Irish print industry (10:82). He describes the *Letter to the Shopkeepers*—the first letter— as a continuation of the 1720 pamphlet geared towards "*the lower and poorer Sort of People*" who wanted "*a plain, strong, coarse Stuff, to defend them*" against British publications, which are referred to as "*cold* Easterly Winds*" (10:82). The "*second* and a *third* Kind of *Stuffs*"—*A Letter to Mr. Harding* and *Some Observations*—were "for the *Gentry*" (10:83). But the "*fourth* Piece"—*A Letter to the Whole People of Ireland*—was fit for "the best Lord or Judge of the Land" (10:83). However, those nobility who wore it (read it) felt a *Shuddering in the Limbs* and had thrown it off in a Rage; cursing to Hell the poor *Drapier*, who invented it" (10:83). As a consequence, said the drapier, he had resolved "never to *work for Persons of Quality* again," except for Molesworth and "a *very few more*" (10:83). Because, however, he gave "the whole Profit" of these tracts to "the *Dyers and Pressers*"—the skilled print trademen, commoners of the kind that made up a city's juries—he is protected from both the nobility's wrath and that of the British (10:83). The drapier refers to his current letter as a *"Piece of Stuff"* that is "made only from the *Shreds and Remnants of the Wool employed in the Former*" but that will only be good enough to distribute to Molesworth's tenants (10:83). Finally, he calls upon "the Makers of *Songs* and *Ballads*" to continue the boycott, expanding the print campaign into another medium (10:93).

A Letter to the Lord Chancellor Middleton is the only one of the letters to be signed by Swift as himself, yet it nonetheless ranks as one of the *Drapier's Letters* because it helped maintain the boycott of Wood's halfpence. In it Swift says that he was "offering new Arguments, or enforcing old ones, to refresh the Memory of my Fellow Subjects, and keep up that good Spirit raised among them" by the drapier (10:100). It encourages the further dissemination of patriotic opinion by saying that "it is every Man's Duty, not only to refuse this Coin himself, but as far as in him lyes, to persuade others to do the like" (10:100). Further capitalizing on his victory in the aborted prosecution of the printer and writer of the fourth letter, it links "foreign" opinion and bad coinage to England and, by doing so, builds a conception of faithful Irish public opinion as equaling sound coinage. The letter says that to advocate against the halfpence is not seditious because the letters claimed to be defending George I and his ministers, but it intimates that the letters may have exploited an already existing rivalry between the Irish and the English (10:103). Defending press freedom in Ireland, it claims that the controversy over Wood's halfpence would be regarded as normal in London, where Parliament is "very reserved in limiting the Press" and where it is customary for legislative disputes to be handled in pamphlets (10:107). He says that if Wood's halfpence were imposed upon the English, "many Drapiers would have risen to pester the World with Pamphlets" in London (10:112), suggesting that the print controversy in Ireland is only exceptional because it is taking place in what increasingly appears to be a colony, not a sister kingdom. The letter expresses concern that poorer people might still be tempted to adopt the halfpence because they "are easily frighted, and greedy to swallow Misinformations," so Swift claims that he may have to carry the torch of the drapier, "to revive and preserve that Spirit raised in the Nation" (10:111). He tips his hat to the drapier for successfully mobilizing a national Irish public sphere: "For several Months past, there have more Papers been written in this Town . . . than, perhaps, hath been known in any other Nation, and in so short a Time" (10:113).

By the time Swift wrote the final letter as the drapier, *An Humble Address to Both Houses of Parliament*, he was able to claim that he was writing in "great Security" because the Irish public had risen to his call for a boycott and defended him from prosecution (10:123). He was performing his "Duty in serving [his] Country," a phrase that capitalized upon and expanded the patriotic enclosing of a national public sphere that his earlier letters accomplished (10:123). The letter revisits the spinning trope, complaining that Ireland's wool (writing) is "returned upon us, in *English* Manufactures, to our infinite Shame and Damage" and of the "Affectation among us, of liking all Kinds of Goods made in *England*" (10:129). To encourage the domestic literate classes to consume Irish publications, he recommends that the "*Clergy* would set us an Example, by contenting themselves with wearing Gowns, and other Habiliments of Irish Drapery," which would be "some Incitement to the *Laity*" (10:135). He again condemns Wood's publicists—his "*Favourers, Abbettors, Supporters*" and "*Softners, Sweetners, Compounders*, and *Expedient-mongers*" (10:138). He does so in a manner that links false representations of the public's interest to counterfeit currency, arguing that these writers "thought they were better *Representers* of his Majesty, than that very *Coin*, for which they are *secret* or *open* Advocates" (10:138). In this phrase, public opinion and coinage are linked under the sign of the sovereign, pitting the drapier's faithful coin/opinion against Wood's attempts to undermine legitimacy and legality in Ireland. Swift, accordingly, requests that Ireland be granted a limited "public Mint" to match his public prints (10:138).

Given how the *Drapier's Letters* expand *A Proposal for the Universal Use of Irish Manufacture*'s wool-based trope with the minting/printing homology, they should be taken as evidence of the existence of a sustained media campaign on behalf of the *Monti*. The Anglo-Irish elite had established the economic base of their fledgling state with the founding of the Debt of the Nation in 1716, and that base required a superstructure of ideology to sustain it. *A Proposal* may have mobilized the Dublin print industry for the production of domestic cultural capital, but the Wood's halfpence controversy provided Swift with the opportunity to assert the importance of that capital by comparing sovereignty over the printing press with sovereignty over minting. The *Drapier's Letters* thereby linked the components of early modern nationalism—power of the word, authority over minting, and prerogative over the law—in a way that made the case for Irish independence. They did so, however, in manner that did not argue for new rights but asserted a traditional semi-independence that claimed loyalty to the English monarch but freedom from the intrusion of England's other branches of government.

II

By the time Swift began writing the *Drapier's Letters*, he was a latecomer to a fight that had largely been fought by the Irish Parliament, the Commissioners of the Revenue, and the rest of the Anglo-Irish elite in government positions. As Christopher Fauske has noted, "It is too easy to forget that the work Swift [had] undertaken in the guise of M.B. Drapier was begun only when the matter it addressed was all but resolved."[12] The significance of his letters, however, lay not in any official role they played in the culture but rather in how they mobilized public opinion. It is important to note that the first of Swift's *Drapier's Letters* was published by Harding a month after the Irish Parliament was prorogued in February 1723/24—a Parliament that in several addresses asked the king and the lord lieutenant to cancel Wood's halfpence for its revenue consequences and other reasons. As Swift noted in the fall of 1724 in the drapier's seventh letter, *An Humble Address to Both Houses of Parliament*, he saw the Parliament as the representative voice of the Irish nation: "I look upon your *unanimous Voice* to be the *Voice* of the Nation; and this I have been taught, and do believe to be, in some Manner, the *Voice of God*" (10:127). Swift, however, became this "voice of the nation" when Parliament adjourned. The public sphere, or more specifically the Irish print culture, had assumed the representing function in the absence of parliamentary meetings, and Swift became the icon of this nationalist world of print. It would take Lord Lieutenant Carteret's offer of a reward for the name of the author of the fourth letter and Chief Justice Whitshed's unsuccessful attempts to prosecute the printer of it to fully lionize Swift in the public eye. M. B. Drapier was everybody and nobody, the perfect vehicle for a rebellious Irish Anglican nation, and as such stood as the perfect forged identity for a population suffering from a lack of voice in its affairs, especially after the Declaratory Act.

The history of Wood's halfpence affair began in 1719 when William Wood obtained a royal patent for coining copper halfpence and farthings for the Kingdom of Ireland from the Duchess of Kendal, the mistress of King George I. The Irish Commissioners of the Revenue became aware of the patent's existence in 1722, as the patent permitted coining to take place from 25 March of that year, the beginning of the fiscal calendar. Besides the political concern in Anglo-Irish circles that the patent was granted without consulting the Irish Parliament, the sheer amount of copper to be coined was daunting because of its potential Gresham's Law effect—the fear that a huge influx of copper halfpence would drive silver and gold coinage out of the country. Irvin Ehrenpreis wrote, "In fact, whatever polemicists might say, the kingdom could well have used ten or twenty thousand pounds in copper coins. What terrified the Irish was that Wood was entitled to ship them more than a hundred thousand pounds worth, with no effective regulation of the quality or even of their number."[13] The patent provided that over a fourteen-year period, Wood could coin "Three Hundred and Sixty Tonns of Copper," a figure that translated into at least £100,800 worth of copper coinage. Given that contemporaries estimated the total coin circulating in the Kingdom of Ireland to be £400,000 in various denominations, this worry was justified.[14] One of the reasons given for the patent was that Ireland had a shortage of small coin. The small coin was mostly in sterling silver, and it was already being lost to Britain because bankers and others were profiting from exchanging this silver for gold, which was more valuable in Ireland than in surrounding countries. For this reason, gold and silver British sterling coins were valued at a premium much higher than other European coin circulating in Ireland, and they were the standard currency for payment of Irish rents and taxes.[15]

The amount of actual circulating currency in Ireland in the mid-1720s was open to conjecture. The quantity of paper banknotes of private Irish bankers in circulation during this period is not known, as they were not receivable by the revenue collectors, but some have ventured to guess that these notes made up the majority of the currency, over and above these specie amounts.[16] Of the coin in circulation, little seems to have been in the form of actual British sterling gold and silver, only "a few

Moydrs and pistols" in Portuguese and French currency, respectively.[17] These high denomination foreign gold coins came to Ireland because gold was more valuable by the standards of Ireland's money of account than elsewhere and thus had more purchasing power in currency exchange and when foreign traders bought Irish commodities.[18]

These monetary facts of Ireland under Britain's mercantilist economic policy render problematic some passages in the *Drapier's Letters* that refer to an insistence on sterling payment of rents. Sterling comes to play a much larger, more ideological role in the letters: it is not merely a medium of exchange but comes to stand as a symbol for the community of readers Swift is constructing. The *Letters* are a mix of monetary and constitutional argumentation and indicate that Swift was primarily concerned for the fate of his own Anglican class, or at least those subscribing to the *Monti*. *A Letter to the Whole People of Ireland*, the fourth letter, makes it clear that Swift was addressing not "everybody in Ireland" when he addressed the "Whole People," but rather only the Anglican Irish. He spoke of an Anglican triumphalism when he wrote, "One great Merit I am sure we have, which those of English Birth can have no Pretence to, That our Ancestors reduced this Kingdom to the Obedience of ENGLAND" (10:55). The "we," here, is exclusively those Anglicans who conquered and colonized Gaelic and Catholic Ireland. "Our *Neighbours* [the English] *whose Understandings are just upon a Level with Ours* (which perhaps are none of the Brightest) have a strong Contempt for most Nations, but especially for *Ireland*: They look upon Us as a Sort of *Savage Irish*, whom our Ancestors conquered several hundred years ago" (10:64). Here, the "Englishness" of Swift's Anglican class is constructed by a disavowal of the "Irishness" attributed to it by British natives, a disavowal constitutive of the hybrid Anglo-Irish identity of the Irish Anglicans. To fend off the allegations of Irishness that Englishmen attributed to Irish Anglicans and to preserve Englishness in the refusal of nominal hybridity, Swift rejects the claim by William Wood that it is the Irish who are opposing his halfpence (10:67). Admittedly, this rejection of an Irishness for the Anglican community is made to refute Wood's inference that the resistance to the halfpence is a Jacobite effort; yet this does not diminish the significance of Swift's construction of a distinctly Anglo-Irish readership in these comments. Swift's efforts to assert the proper identity of the opposition to Wood's halfpence demonstrate that the opposition was primarily Anglican in character and could demand, or "take it for granted," that the disenfranchised Irish Catholic majority of rent-payers would follow its opinions on monetary policy. The public opinion that counts in Swift's pamphlet war, this passage seems to indicate, is that of the Anglican Irish nation.

The *Letters*, however, while concerned with Anglican identity and public opinion, needed to broaden their appeal. For Swift, there was a problem in identifying what or who the Anglo-Irish public was—an issue faced by eighteenth-century European writers and politicians in general. J. C. Beckett has tackled this problem directly, disagreeing with popular interpretations of *A Letter to the Whole People of Ireland* that say it is addressed to a demographically inclusive Irish audience.[19] S. J. Connolly concurred, writing that "the text insisted that those who rejected Wood's coin were in fact 'the true English people of Ireland,' whose ancestors had reduced the kingdom to obedience."[20] Though there were many anonymous pamphlets written in the same controversy claiming that women, Quakers, Catholics, beggars, and other outsiders were supporting Swift's effort, there is some doubt as to whether these writings were organically representative of those communities. Sabine Baltes has suggested that such tracts may have been propagandistic efforts by Swift or another member of the established church and its laity to create an echo-chamber of opinion, persuading a broader demographic of their views through the use of such personas. Indeed, she argues that high officials in the Church of Ireland and Irish Parliament may have recruited Swift to write such appeals to low culture.[21] It is not for nothing, then, that James Kelly has called Swift an "opinion maker," one who was modeling the views that all residents of Ireland were supposed to have.[22]

The earlier controversy, over the Bank of Ireland project, had been more explicit in defining the Irish public to be the wealthier elite of the established church, advantaged by the land settlements of the post-1688 era, who controlled Parliament. Hercules Rowley, an anti-bank pamphleteer, reminded readers of all the hard work that had gone into passing penal laws against allowing Catholics to serve in Parliament, work at the university, or purchase land. He predicted that if the bank went forward, Catholics would "be no longer at any Loss in disposing of their Money, for they may lay it out in purchasing *Bank* Stock; . . . in that Case they will have the sole Management of the *Bank*. Whether this will not as much weaken the *Protestant* Interest, as *the Act against the Growth of Popery* strengthen'd it, I leave you to judge."[23] Rowley not only feared that a national Bank of Ireland and its paper money would create an Irish moneyed interest that would soon become more powerful than the Anglican landed interest, but that this moneyed interest would be composed of the Catholics, who constituted a disenfranchised 80 percent majority of Ireland's population. As Edith Johnston-Liik notes, Catholics, as well as Dissenters such as Presbyterians, were not allowed to participate even when the Bank of Ireland was finally established in 1782, mainly because of the oaths that the bank's directors were required to take concerning their adherence to the Church of Ireland's articles of faith.[24] The *Drapier's Letters*, accordingly, can be taken initially as appealing to a limited, Protestant readership.

Yet, could that community of Anglo-Irish Protestants be considered the Irish public? There was a clear difference of meaning in the eighteenth century between "the public" and "the people." Roger Chartier has written that at least in France, "Between the people and the public there was a clear break. From Malesherbes to Kant, the line of demarcation ran between those who could read and produce written matter and those who could not."[25] This notion is echoed in British Studies by J. A. W. Gunn, who sees that eighteenth-century publics were small: "Undoubtedly, Britain was then the home of public opinion, though of a small public."[26] Despite the fact that so many printed works from the controversy were directed at "the people," such as Swift's *Letter to the Whole People of Ireland*, *A Word or Two to the People of Ireland*, *A Short Defence of the People of Ireland*, and many others, there is no doubt that "the people" were being roused in support of the establishment. Because more established Anglo-Irishmen received payments for rent and goods in small denomination coinage—the only coinage a common person might be in possession of—the elite had to mobilize commoners by advising them to refuse these coppers in exchange.[27] Such persuasion and behavior modification would help guarantee that the wealthy would continue to collect the more valuable silver pence as usual. This manipulation had become so patently obvious to the more literate that satire targeting the intended audiences themselves began to appear. *A Creed for an Irish Commoner* and *Wood's Confession to the Mobb of the City of Dublin*—works perhaps by Swift—push the limit of textual impersonation to the point where they are obviously ridiculing the "people" or "mob" before their very faces. Indeed, Anne Cline Kelly has described how the author and such imitators constructed such a public via the various "Swifts" in circulation.[28] Swift, over the course of his career, was engaged in the manufacture of consent in this way; but in the specific case of the *Drapier's Letters*, his work strove to secure broad consensus on the decision to refuse Wood's patent and coins, a decision that the Anglo-Irish elite had already made.

Swift's trick in this propaganda effort was the typical strategy of the eighteenth-century professional writer and politician. Keith Michael Baker, writing of the use of the term "public opinion" in contemporary France, says that it was deployed to invent constituencies that the writer could claim supported him: "one can understand the conflicts of the Pre-Revolution as a series of struggles to fix the sociological referent of the concept in favor of one or another competing group."[29] Thomas Crow concurs, "A public appears, with a shape and a will, via the various claims made to represent it."[30] Noting that the Enlightenment ideal of universality was related rather cynically to the effort to expand a writer's, government's, or movement's appeal, Harold Mah argues that "the public sphere is a fiction, which, because it can appear real, exerts real political force. The enabling condition of a successfully staged public sphere is the ability of certain groups to make their social or group particularity invisible so that they can then appear as abstract individuals and hence universal."[31] Accordingly, governments and other established groups strive to co-opt other claimants to the public's opinion through intervention in print controversies—propaganda and disinformation—in order to seem more universal and representative.[32] The "Drapier" is the perfect narrator for this strategy because his invisibility—an anonymity that still seems familiar enough to Dubliners—makes his plea seem that of Everyman. Publicity's secret, as Jodi Dean has argued, is to create such universality through the use of tactics of invisibility, anonymity, and omission.[33]

Swift's rhetoric of liberty and property was part of a general trend in Anglophone Atlantic thought occasioned by a theory of subjectivity and citizenship that was attempting to restore virtue to public action by suggesting that land ownership integrated the personality. J. G. A. Pocock has discovered this landed-class political ideal within an "ideology of real property" in which "land, whose stability—as opposed to the mobility of goods and money—set men free to be the rational political creatures which they were by nature."[34] This putatively organic means of substantiating individual authority—a means that granted "intrinsic value" to the subject and "innateness" to his soul through his land—was part of a contemporary fashion in thinking in which a naturalized autobiographical sense of an autonomous, unified subjectivity was equated with the historiographical process of transmitting land titles to the next generation. Land ownership was regarded as "necessary if the individual was to practice virtue in a republic," because it could "confer independence on the individual" and involve him in as few as possible contingent relations with other individuals.[35] The problem of binding the contingencies threatening the individual's political agency, in this model, is resolved in the pre-lapserian image of a self-perpetuating farm. The contingency of contracting one's liberty with contemporary peers is restricted by a covenant with the dead in which the land itself perpetuates, as if through the form of a single human body, a multigenerational personality whose origins are located in a redeeming but inaccessible past. Soil is taken as the substantive medium of continuous referral to that past and the natural rights and liberties it confers. It thereby serves as the proof of present "disinterested" virtue, the genealogical source of an authorizing rhetoric of identity, and the underwriting depository of the landed class's moral capital. Where societal modernity had brought about a subject derived negatively from his "extrinsic" contractual connection with the community and the state, this ideology attempted to substitute a positively derived subject constituted by the "intrinsic" properties and proprietorship of the soil.[36] The Anglo-Irish *Monti* was the most exemplary effort at institutionalizing this ideology.

Yet, the liberty promised to the Anglican nation by its monopolistic proprietorship of the land, within this theory, was mediated by property in money: rent payments. It is perhaps for this reason that Swift was able to write in the seventh *Drapier's Letter*, "When the Value of Money is arbitrary, or unsettled; no Man can well be said to have any Property at all" (10:128). Property, for Swift, was no longer prior to money; the maintenance of the "real" that land ownership represented was now codependent with the "imaginary" realm of discourse and commodity exchange. Only sovereignty could provide the proper working of these functions; legal security of the *Monti*'s land and the medium in which the income from it was communicated demanded it.

Swift's fear of Wood's copper halfpence, I argue, was partly driven by the pressure to return British sterling silver and gold to these landlords. In the first of the *Drapier's Letters*, *A Letter to the Tradesmen, Shop-Keepers, Farmers, and Common-People of Ireland*, he says that the predominantly Catholic tenant farmers are legally bound by their leases to pay their rents in sterling:

> For suppose you go to an ALE-HOUSE with that base Money
> [Wood's halfpence], and the Landlord gives you a Quart for
> Four of these HALF-PENCE, what must the Victualer do? His
> BREWER will not be paid in that Coin, or if the BREWER should
> be such a Fool, the Farmers will not take it [Wood's halfpence]
> from them for their *Bere* [barley], because they are bound by
> their Leases to pay their Rents in Good and Lawful Money of
> *England*, which this is not, nor of *Ireland* neither, and the *Squire
> their Landlord* will never be so bewitched to take such *Trash*
> for his Land, so that it must certainly stop some where or other,
> and wherever it stops it is the same thing, and we are all undone.
> (10:6)

The country squire or landlord is envisioned as the normal endpoint of the nation's exchanges of money, and one whose appetite for sterling will impede the circulation of Wood's halfpence and the commerce of Ireland. This appetite, and opposition to the halfpence, was partly driven by the fear that if landlords received other media of exchange, the currency would have to be converted into sterling at a high rate of exchange.[37] Landlords did not want to lose income through currency exchange when they attempted to get money also negotiable in Britain during periods in which they lived there, as absentee landlords. The insistence on sterling in *A Letter To the Tradesmen, Shop-Keepers, Farmers, and Common-People of Ireland* comes across as more of a stern warning to the largely Protestant commercial classes of their dependence on the landed class for the circulation of any currency, let alone a copper coinage unacceptable for rent payments. Swift wants them to know that because of sterling rent payments and landlords' appetite for them, he anticipates a catastrophe for the Irish economy if it is flooded with a huge supply of Wood's copper halfpence, which he thinks, by Gresham's Law, will drive all gold and silver, sterling or not, out of circulation in Ireland (10:7–8).

The Irish economic system was not, however, dominated exclusively by the Anglo-Irish lay landlords and their demands for sterling rent. Church of Ireland clergy were expecting tithe-payments and rents of their church lands to be paid in sterling. Most importantly, the Irish Commissioners of the Revenue were not permitted to collect taxes in any form but sterling. These additional sterling-interested forces were also arrayed against the circulation of Wood's halfpence. Sterling rent payments were the basis of the Church of Ireland's business, and clergymen opposed Wood's halfpence for that reason.[38] Swift, in the fourth letter, explained the revenue consequences of Wood's halfpence upon the church by suggesting that the Church of Ireland primate, Boulter, would have his rental income reduced by seven-eighths.[39]

The central issue concerning the sterling standard, however, was the question of the form in which government revenue would be collected. This issue affected the maintenance of the Anglo-Irish state and its obligations to the empire more directly than the private problem of rent. When the news first arrived in Ireland that Wood's patent had been granted, the Irish Commissioners of the Revenue reported that the circulation of Wood's pence would injure the Irish revenue and therefore Ireland's parliamentary patronage system: "The Mischiefs & Inconveniency which must necessarily attend it, more especially as to the Deficiency in the Revenue may be very prejudicial to his Majesty's Affairs in Parliament."[40] If revenues begin to be returned in copper halfpence, the *Monti*'s members would grow hostile to other initiatives from the crown, Walpole's ministry, and the British Parliament. This hostility might make the Irish Parliament refuse to grant the government its usual two-year revenue supply. A parliamentary committee considering the issue concurred with this report.[41] Their fear was not only the possibility that Gresham's Law would take effect and drain the kingdom of gold and silver if the halfpence were circulated, but also that government, which secures property through law, would be seriously compromised if civil servants were compelled to take pay in copper halfpence instead of sterling.

William King, a member of the Irish House of Lords as well as an archbishop, was quick to notice the implications for the Treasury, which were that great amounts of the copper halfpence would be collected in revenue. He knew that most taxes came from the ordinary consumption of common people and that the consequent surge in small change transactions in copper would affect the kingdom's financial system as a whole.[42] This concern took on large dimensions, so much so that the revenue commissioners gave orders to the tax collectors not to accept any of Wood's halfpence. In this they were guided by the Parliament, which in the fall of 1723 had composed addresses to King George I asking that the revenue commissioners not be required to receive the halfpence in taxes.[43] Wood had apparently already tried to get around this problem of the revenue commissioners' orders by attempting to negotiate with a commissioner about accepting the coins.[44] The British government had ordered the commissioners to accept them in tax collection, and the English Privy Council overrode the Irish revenue commissioners' decision against the halfpence.[45] The order attempted to take away the Irish government's central argument against Wood's halfpence—the claim that it would have negative revenue consequences—in the hope of promoting the halfpence's circulation in the kingdom. In effect, it ended official Irish government resistance to the halfpence, leaving the cause to the pamphleteers, who could only attempt to influence public opinion against the halfpence so no one would accept them.

This revenue argument displays another logic when considered with the question of payments to civil servants. Another British concern was army pay. One Irish commentator wrote, "The best and most useful part of his Majesties Army is maintained and supported by us."[46] The vast bulk of the British army's regiments were supported by the taxation of Ireland. Regiments that Ireland paid for were based not only in that country but also in Gibralter, North America, and across the empire. The use of Ireland as a barracks for the British army served the dual purpose of justifying Irish support through revenues and keeping rebellious elements such as Catholic Jacobites under control. A petition from the people of the city of Cork discussed how discontented the army would be if it had to take payment in Wood's halfpence.[47] "The Humble Petition of the Grand Jury of the County of Dublin" agreed with this sentiment, worrying that potential "great Confusion between your Majesty's Army and your other Subjects" caused by receiving army pay in Wood's halfpence would be "disabling both for a chearfull Concurrence in the Defence of your Government in case of any foreigne Invasion in Favour of an attainted Popish Pretender."[48] In this way, Anglican anxiety about the

Catholic population and the threat of Jacobitism became tied to the sterling revenue issue. Additionally, the pay of the army was an important source of currency circulation, as soldiers purchased goods from tradesmen. A recent return to Ireland of some regiments had brought £40,000 in circulating sterling back to Ireland, so military pay was viewed as a reinvestment in Ireland's economy, as long as the regiments remained within Ireland to spend it.[49]

Swift, when writing later about an initiative to lower the value of Ireland's coin or "money of account" to help resolve the gold-from-silver Gresham effect, also took notice of the appointees who would have to be paid in the consequently less valuable money. His *Reasons Why We Should Not Lower the Coins Now Current in this Kingdom* names just some of those appointees who had to be paid in sterling:

> For, first, until the Kingdom be *intirely Ruined* the Lord Lieutenant and Lords-Justices must have their *Salaries*. My Lords the Bishops, whose Lands are set a fourth part value, will be sure of their *Rents* and their *Fines*. My Lords the Judges, and Those of other *Employments* in the Courts, must likewise have their *Salaries*. The Gentlemen of the Revenue will pay Themselves; and as to the Officers of the Army, *the Consequences of not paying Them, is obvious enough:* Nay, so far will those *Persons* I have already mentioned be from suffering, that, on the contrary, their *Revenues* being no way lessen'd by the fall of Money, and the *prices* of all *Commodities* considerably sunk thereby, they must be great *Gainers*. (13:119–120)

Although he is writing on another problem entirely, and in a later period, these observations about some of the recipients who will pay themselves first is important in understanding the total stakes of the sterling revenue question in the 1720s. All of these posts went to members of the Anglican establishment (either British or Irish), and their spending, at those times that they actually resided in Ireland, supported the rest of the economy. Yet this fact does not explain the obsession with sterling in particular as the premier form of money in a country that only had a "money of account" benchmarked against it.

In one of the great paradoxes of the Wood's halfpence episode, £300 sterling was promised to whoever reported the name of the author of the fourth of the *Drapier's Letters*—a reward the irony of which lay in that it was to be tendered by Lord Lieutenant Carteret and an Irish Privy Council who were ostensibly seeking to persuade people to take the halfpence.[50] More or less admitting defeat through this offer, Carteret and the Irish Privy Council italicized "sterling"—as if it represented the highest point of desire in the kingdom. The sterling medium seems to affect government decisions in the 1720s, especially as they relate to pensions and civil employments.

The concern over the halfpence, strong enough to produce a boycott of them in Ireland, was overblown, and it would have been unnecessary if Ireland had adopted a paper currency that contained very small denomination bills. When Wood obtained a patent to coin and introduce "Rosa Americana" copper pence into the colony of Massachusetts in 1722, the colonial legislative assembly there responded by printing paper pence. There were "£500 in small change bills issued to prevent William Wood from introducing Rosa Americana base copper coinage into circulation in New England."[51] Swift was well aware of this previous successful boycott of a Wood patent, writing in his third letter, "To the Nobility and Gentry of the Kingdom of Ireland," that "He [Wood] hath already tried his Faculty in *New-England*, and I hope he will meet at least with an EQUAL RECEPTION here; what *That* was I leave to the Publick Intelligence" (10:44). Ehrenpreis noted that all the colonies suffered from this currency problem because of British mercantilist policy, writing, "The situation in the American colonies was comparable. So the Irish crisis was only a local instance of a general grievance. In the whole course of the controversy over Wood's patent I don't believe the Irish ever recognized this truth, which would of course have weakened their case."[52] To reason why no one in Ireland recommended the solution to the small change crisis of printing paper currency would be to ask how money and its institutions had developed differently in the two colonies. Massachusetts had been printing a public paper money since 1690, while Ireland had refused a public paper money in 1721. The Massachusetts notes tended to be negotiable only in the other New England and North American colonies, which limited their use internationally or elsewhere in the empire. If Ireland had adopted a similar paper money, it would likely have been passable only within Ireland. Sterling in Ireland played some sort of interkingdom role, providing a mobility to those Anglican elites who possessed it and wished to have a negotiable currency when they lived as absentees in Britain. The fetish for sterling was bound up with notions of the "Englishness" of the Anglo-Irish, simultaneously bolstering the English portion of their tenuous hybrid identity.

III

The corpus of early-eighteenth-century Irish political economic writing of which the *Drapier's Letters* are a part presents epistemological questions that very much bear on Swift's constitution of Anglo-Irish hybrid identity and literature. This corpus largely relies on the sterling fetish to perform its evaluation of economic action, which may have served to create the "facts" of Irish political economy, ones legitimated by the obsession with sterling and the "Englishness" for which it stood. The sterling fetish bridges the gap between the intrinsic and nominal value of coinage within the abstraction of Ireland's money of account. The status of evidence and fact, the Anglo-Irish economic discourse of the period suggests, was largely dependent on sterling as the sign of the presence of a "real" general equivalent organizing all commensurability in the British Isles.

This question of determining what counts as evidence of eighteenth-century Irish economic production is difficult because contemporaries faced a significant problem: how to organize a representation of a region lacking the independent political, financial, and cultural institutions—or its own standard medium of exchange—that could supply the process for making such a representation convincing. The polemical component of eighteenth-century Irish economic writing amounts to a complaint that there were no interior state governing bodies that could adequately justify any representation of the existence of an economic system. All assessment was therefore predicated on the necessity of giving written form, in the absence of a fully authorized legislative assembly, to the community that was making value judgments and producing standards. Under these conditions, print culture would have to assume some of the representing and legitimating function of institutions like the degraded Irish parliament. Print, if it were to be an effective medium of communication during this "crisis in representation," would have to contain markers that pointed to the existence of a legitimate body of readers for whom its writers spoke.[53] This necessity of promulgating a public body may help account for Irish economic writing's audience-hailing discourses on the legal constitution of Irish readers and writers who generated a body of political and economic writing supporting its internal hegemony over other demographic groups and its external fiduciary relationship with British institutions. Because of the disparity in security between Irish and English Anglicans, Ireland's ascendant minority lacked the consensus and autonomy necessary to achieve the developments their British counterparts were attaining across the water. The dependence upon the prescriptive moral character of the Anglican community of descriptive attempts to represent the Irish economy makes apparent the sectarian basis of the economic knowledge being formulated at the time.

Irish demographic conditions of the period suggest that "political economy *was* partisan, prescriptive, tendentious. Claiming to be non-sectarian and non-political, it performed a vitally important ideological function for the political and religious establishment in defending existing socio-economic relations."[54] Far from being objective, political economy was evident as a discipline that supported the ascendancy of the Anglican minority. In Ireland, it lacked the distance from its ideological support and from its object of study that would be necessary to cultivate a more purely theoretical approach to economic evaluation. Consequently, the economic writing of Irish Anglicans tended to be more practical and less theoretical.

Salim Rashid has recognized the Anglican nature of eighteenth-century Irish economic writing.[55] He also has pointed to the nontheoretical note of Irish economists, observing that they "wrote in a pre-analytical age" and that they "made an effort to relate their conclusions *only* to some immediate practical problem and not to some axiomatic foundation."[56] He suggests that the unavailability of that theoretical capacity placed writers in a position to address only single pragmatic issues not necessarily theorized within picturesque descriptions of the economic landscape as a whole.

This detachment of the Irish school's practical economic observations from theory, the product of this political situation of its writers, could, on the other hand, affirm the factuality of its observations if the period's conceptions of epistemology are considered. The category of the "fact" in seventeenth-century political economy was premised on just such a disjunction of observed particulars from a theoretical plan. Mary Poovey cites Francis Bacon's elevation of "deviating instances" to the level of "fact" in order to describe how facts were considered "nuggets of experience detached from theory."[57] Bacon's valorization of particular instances was related to the emerging idea that proper knowledge was disinterested and therefore independent of theory, which was viewed as the interested, preconceived, and formulaic structure of knowledge. To be taken as supporting evidence, facts had to have an autonomous materiality that, ironically, would nonetheless make general theoretical knowledge available.[58] Irish economic writing's focus on isolated economic problems, and its presence as a deviating corpus of writing expressing aberrant economic events, lends it factuality if we follow Baconian criteria. Facts were to be free of the theoretical structure of general knowledge by a process of independent verification in the medium of another division of labor. Ironically, only mediation could provide the immediacy Bacon valued as the practical key to the truth and factuality of the objective world.

Bacon's fantasy that this mediation would not itself be interested and productive of the representation of fact provokes this question: How, and in the medium of what body, was evidence of eighteenth-century Irish economic events established as fact? We know that economic events were indeed "deviating instances," inasmuch as they were only noted during difficult economic times: "The gloomy picture of Ireland painted in the years of suffering and scarcity has been accepted as being applicable to the period as a whole, because for the better years writings are few and a written corrective of the darker years is thus lacking."[59] These deviating conditions, and the Irish school's nontheoretical "effort to relate their conclusions *only* to some immediate practical problem and not to some axiomatic foundation," might be enough to establish the factuality of the economic information contained in these pamphlets.[60]

L. M. Cullen has promoted an opposite model for the factuality of economic evidence, stressing that the "facts" of the Anglo-Irish school of political economy were the product of a sedimentary discourse in which repetition of supporting evidence throughout these pamphlets established the very commonplace nature of "facts" that Bacon's emphasis on singularity and deviation was trying to overcome. Cullen makes this point by discussing the readerly context in which the generally scarce and contingent facts of the eighteenth-century Irish economy were legislated.[61] Facts, within Cullen's view of how they were deployed in Irish economic polemic, were established in an interaction between writer and audience that took place over the course of controversialist pamphleteering. Used enough times in the exemplum segments of these economic disputations, and assented to and repeated by other readers and writers, evidence would grow into fact. Within the context of the Anglo-Irish school's writings and contrary to Bacon's view, they were the product of the interested representations of theoretical, knowing minds that were being conditioned by the experience of writing and reading.

Given the dominance within these writings of a more deliberative paradigm for the establishment of fact, Bacon's model of the worthiness of deviating instances may only be of value in the Irish context for describing negative economic episodes. The event of a rise in publication may tell us that something economic happened, but the evidence marshaled within those documents was dependent for its factual status on the deliberations of a readership who would reproduce it in more writing. The manner in which that readership was constituted, then, becomes the primary problem to address in asking how economic information was made into fact.

The lack of interior governmental agency, the uncertain boundaries of "national" production, and the nonstandardized nature of economics forced all economic analysis into a confrontation with the problem of postulating itself as a subject and positing Ireland as a polity to be studied. Irish economic writing of the period was caught between political economy's immaturity as a discipline and Ireland's liminal status as a nation. These factors, combined with the instability of Ireland's Anglican regime, conspired to make a more theoretical viewpoint inaccessible to economic writers.

The problem in both English and Anglo-Irish political economy was finding a standard of evidence for economic action, a means through which economic data could be measured. The role of sterling in the effort to delimit and define communities subject to the British government, in both "national" schools of economic thought, was largely to provide this standardization. This function, aside from being the primary responsibility of the sovereign, had been established by English and Irish parliamentary acts that made sterling the only receivable currency for taxes. Through this process, sterling acquired an epistemological value in addition to its monetary value. Confidence in sterling was also belief in the British empire, a faith that also signified Englishness. Certitude in economic knowledge proceeded from a standard medium of exchange that, as the Wood's halfpence affair makes clear, was no longer merely intrinsically valuable but, more importantly, nominally valuable in that its English name and authorizing stamp had acquired greater value than the silver or gold content of a pistole, moidore, or other foreign unit of currency.[62] Because Ireland was already using an imaginary money of account in this period, this observation should be taken as particularly important in the analysis of colonial economies. The materiality of sterling was of significance in Ireland only after its nominal evaluation—in short, the coin itself was the certification of transactions that had already been made in the discourse of accounting.

Accordingly, value had to be modeled as a sign within the discursive apparatus of political economy, via the printing press. Political economy itself was the disciplinary process through which this modeling was accomplished. The negotiation of the value of money was not the only effect of this process; a model of the exchanging subject was also achieved: "This subject changes across the long eighteenth century, from one defined by social relations and their obligations (status) to a free and equal subject defined by exchange (contract), a depersonalized, abstract subject defined by the free and equal exchange of commodities."[63] Where sterling is the unit of measure and exchange, this subject becomes nominally or abstractly English as political economy in the British Isles performs this modeling. To the extent that a polity in Britain's inner empire measures economic effects based upon data such as sterling revenue receipts, the polity and its subjects are invented as English in character. This is particularly true of the Anglo-Irish in Ireland, the English portion of whose hybrid identity was constituted and maintained by its attachment to the mother country's currency.

Another way of understanding how the sterling fetish in Irish political economy constructed the Anglophile subject is through Bruno Latour's concept of the "factish." This term blends the processes of fetish-making and the kind of fact-making that Anglo-Irish political economy attempted. Srinivas Aravamudan has explained Latour's term by saying that it "refuses the primitive-modern distinction" inasmuch as it suggests the constructivist notion that facts, supposedly rationally evaluated empirical objects, are fetishistically constructed by belief.[64] The empirical claims of Irish political economy, when considered as the process of making "factishes," continuously defaulted to belief-claims about the Englishness of the Anglo-Irish polity. Sterling, within the discourse of Ireland's money of account, served as the site for material redemption and innate proof of nominal Englishness, a product of the factishes made by Irish political economy. In this way, the object of knowledge—sterling—shaped the general epistemological framework for an empire and nation.

The sterling "factish" linked the regions of the British Empire by providing mobility to an English consciousness craving a material proof of an identity that was more mobile than one based on land, and thus could be current throughout the empire. As an English commodity that by law could not be exported from the isle of Britain, sterling had rarity, and therefore an enhanced reified status and corollary ability to reify abstract, Enlightenment, English subjects. Ireland's decision to have all rents and taxes paid in sterling reveals not only a practical concern for acquiring currency negotiable at a high standard throughout the empire but also an allegiance to that which could connect the Irish Anglican political nation to the mother country. The rents of absentee landlords were taken as proof of this fact. Though Swift often chastised his caste for absenteeism, he mainly wished to help it sustain its wealth longer. His writings of the late 1720s, including *A Modest Proposal*, did not so much object to their rents, collection of interest on investment in the *Monti*, or transport of their wealth to England when they lived as absentees. Rather, he taught them to conceal the consequences of it more effectively and to create a print media capable of constructing a nationalism that would support their domination of Ireland.

CHAPTER 5

Devouring Posterity

A Modest Proposal, *Empire, and Ireland's "Debt of the Nation"*

Jonathan Swift's *A Modest Proposal* traditionally has been regarded as an indictment of colonial landlordism in Ireland, one asserted subtly via the play between the narrator's overt, rational tone and the author's covert critique of it.[1] This design, it has been argued, forces the reader to play the roles of three audiences, the hailing of which he or she anticipates in the process of exegeses. These are an "ideal narrative audience" who finds "the narrator's argument cogent and compelling," another who takes it as a "serious proposal" that reflects the "skewed" values of the first audience, and a third who feels privileged to recognize the author's creativity in crafting the irony.[2] Swift's correspondence and references to the satire in contemporary works document multiple receptions, but few studies have positioned the "reader among the eaters" by locating the actual audience Swift addressed when he chose to publish the work in Dublin in October 1729.[3] Newly discovered external evidence, I argue, intimates that the Irish Parliament, convening that month, may have been the pamphlet's intended target. Some of Parliament's members, who were also participants in the *Monti*, received interest on their investment in Ireland's first "Debt of the Nation" from the taxes that they had the political power to levy on the native poor, but the famine of the late 1720s had decimated the usual revenues, forcing Parliament to consider additional ones. Like the North American colonists in the decades following the Seven Years War, they were threatened by the British crown and Parliament's efforts to appropriate these potential new funds for the empire's operations elsewhere. Ireland already was financing British and American expansion into French, Spanish, and Native American territory to the extent that its sovereignty over its own resources, as James Joyce wryly put it centuries later, was attenuated in the pull "Between the Saxon smile and yankee yawp. The devil and the deep sea."[4] *A Modest Proposal*, accordingly, can be seen as an intervention in the budgetary debates of the 1729 legislative session that promoted a new means of fiscal control. I argue that, in its calculated calendar for baby slaughter, it allegorically recommended a schedule for temporal restraint in consumption—a diet in the stream of revenue—that would make the empire respect the Irish Parliament's feeding hand. By declaring such a fast, the Anglo-Irish could guarantee that they, and not the British, would devour native posterity. This chapter does not foreclose on the satire's many other interpretive possibilities—analysis of its discourses on imperialism or poverty, for example—but contends that approaching its actuarial logic in relation to the Debt of the Nation opens a new context in which those readings can be further explored.[5]

A Modest Proposal, as a parody of the serious economic essay, is also a commentary on the kinds of texts that were shaping Ireland's public sphere, a national print culture that Swift himself initially had called for in *A Proposal for the Universal Use of Irish Manufacture* and the *Drapier's Letters*. Most of the tracts circulating on economic improvement, Swift's ironic stance seems to imply, were oriented towards making Ireland a more profitable place for its owners. Because the members of the *Monti* can be regarded as the agrarian proprietors of the past, present, and future capital of the country, Swift may, in this particular satire, be turning against them and the kinds of books they sponsored and patronized. In the famine conditions of the late 1720s, during which this work was published, economic tracts inventing ways of gouging the poor even more seemed inappropriate, mostly because they were missing the point that, without long-term economic thinking about Ireland's revenue, the *Monti* itself could not survive. Accordingly, *A Modest Proposal*'s discourse on consumption is not only about how profiting from Ireland's national debt is equivalent to a particularly colonialist form of the cannibalization of children, but also about the Anglo-Irish population's taste in and consumption of books. Swift feared that the public sphere forming around these texts was an imitation of the English one, and that the Anglo-Irish were modeling their social, ethical, and aesthetic performance—their identity and manners—around British Whig trends. Though the goal of forming a domestic Irish book market was being realized via economic discourse, it was increasingly aping the culture industry of the British fiscal-military state. Swift wanted to encourage Irish readers to reject British books and adopt Irish ones, but he was ambivalent about the quality of Whig cultural production and its relationship to the sociocultural modernization of Britain and its government.

The "children" to be consumed in *A Modest Proposal*, I argue, stood not only literally for the native Irish young whose future labor would be alienated to feed the *Monti* and metaphorically for monetary profits on investment in the Debt of the Nation, but also figuratively for texts in search of publishers. Members of the *Monti* and the Irish Parliament had to be persuaded to pass a budget that would put on a diet the supply of revenue to the British fiscal-military state, and nationalist texts such as *A Modest Proposal* had the potential to sway public opinion in favor of such a measure. Those tempted to enact perpetual taxes to pay themselves back for their contributions to the *Monti*, in Swift's view, were risking the alienation of those taxes to Britain because they were under the influence of British texts and ideas, and their opinions needed to be corrected if they were to avoid destroying themselves. Only the highly reified national differences generated by Swiftian satire could call attention to the political and economic stakes of such a budgetary blunder. *A Modest Proposal* hails the struggle between the English book and the Irish book as a significant aspect of the political debate between Britain and Ireland, aligning the emergence of an agrarian capitalism–based imagined community of print with the Irish national economic interest. By doing so, it attempts to reestablish the pre–financial revolution homologies among printing, public finance, and law enforcement for which Swift was nostalgic.

I

Swift's literal and metaphorical uses of motherhood in *A Modest Proposal* form the dominant rhetorical nexus around which the satire's links among children, texts, and money are forged. When his narrator opens by calling attention to "*Beggars* of the Female Sex, followed by three, four, or six children," he seems to be describing the very real famine conditions of the late 1720s (12:109). As he starts to discuss "a Child, *just dropt from its* dam" and the prevention of "*voluntary Abortions*," however, he shifts to a figural register familiar to book trade professionals, especially those who had read Bernard Mandeville's *A Modest Defence of Public Stews* of 1724. Though no connection has been established between Swift and Mandeville, the latter's metadiscourse on the book trade deploys metaphors connecting childbirth to textual production that were explored throughout the eighteenth century. For example, such works as *The New Foundling Hospital for Wit* (1768–1773), a serial miscellany, claimed to care for literal orphans while figurally referring to satirical texts' being born from the printing press. *A Modest Defence* was the most prominent text of this kind in the 1720s. It satirized ideas for converting vice into new revenues by proposing a prostitution tax, arguing that £10,000 could be raised by a single public brothel.[6] The "*lewdness*" of this project of sexual exchange, however, is explained not as a female sin but as one indulged by prostitute male writers who "*want a* Dinner" and hope for the "*Adoption*" of their writings by "*bright* Noblemen."[7] The narrator nakedly refers to the manuscript before the reader as a "Foundling" who was "*dropt*" at the reader's door because a legitimate press—"*the* Midwife *of a Printer*"— "*was unwilling to help bring it into the World, but upon that Condition . . . of my openly* Fathering *it.*"[8] This series of double entendres intimates that the printing press is the mother of the book and the writer its father, invoking the Platonic concepts of the "death of the author" and the "orphaned text" that Swift himself had explored in *A Tale of a Tub.*[9] *A Modest Proposal* seems to closely mimic *A Modest Defence*'s style, perhaps to the extent that it could be interpreted as a response to Mandeville's request that the "Hibernian Stallion" should "*Speak.*"[10] It appears to appropriate his notion that even in an era when the South Sea Company had "*been demolish'd*," coffeehouses supplied a "*sufficient* Stock" of writing to sustain the economy and government.[11] *A Modest Defence*'s reproductive theme dissolves the "distinction between sexual pleasure and business," suggesting that both biological mothers and maternal printing presses provide the income-generating progeny necessary to maintain material and political investment in the fiscal-military state.[12] The Dublin print industry seems to have found this idea appealing in its efforts to forge Anglo-Irish sovereignty.

Accordingly, Swift's dialogue with the British book trade is of central importance when reading *A Modest Proposal*'s discourse on public finance. As discussed in previous chapters, Swift was a member of the Scriblerus Club, an informal group of Tory opposition writers whose satire targeted the Whig ruling regime. The Scriblerians despised Robert Walpole, the Whig prime minister, because they thought his machinations in public finance—his establishment of a sinking fund to pay off the national debt, his involvement with the South Sea Company Bubble, and his taxpayer bailout of major shareholders in the company—were signs of corruption incompatible with virtuous government.[13] By the late 1720s, Swift's *Gulliver's Travels*, John Gay's *Beggar's Opera*, and Alexander Pope's *Dunciad* had combined to expose Walpole's perversion of the constitution. A letter from Swift to Gay in March 1728 discusses the success of their coordinated attack: "The Beggers Opera hath knockt down Gulliver, I hope to see Popes Dullness knock down the Beggers Opera, but not till it hath fully done its Jobb . . . writing two or three Such trifles every year to expose vice and make people laugh with innocency does more publick Service than all the Ministers of State from Adam to Walpol."[14] These satires served as both partisan political critiques and literary commodities in the highly profitable culture wars of those years. It has been argued that, as a collective partisan effort, this circle's writings were not so much damning modern public finance in general as claiming that their faction possessed writers more capable of manufacturing a virtuous national image than those employed by the Whigs.[15] The Scriblerians knew that the press was not an autonomous third estate but an organ of government. (Despite Jürgen Habermas's claims that an independent public sphere of "rational-critical arguments" arose in eighteenth-century Britain, "no theory of liberty of the press was articulated" in this period.[16]) Consequently, their mission was to prove that Tories were better at statecraft, in their case the production of the "fictions of state" necessary to breed political and financial confidence. It is likely that *A Modest Proposal* was another text in this series, rivaling the productions of the author's friends yet publicizing their style and agenda. It partook of this coterie's endeavor, forging Anglo-Irish Protestant nationalism as an ideological support for Ireland's own fiscal system.

The text exhibits Scriblerian themes of finance in the character of a cannibal, the period's conventional symbol for financiers. At least since *The Merchant of Venice*'s scene of Shylock demanding a "pound of flesh," private loan transactions had been represented as the eating of the debtor's body. Francis Bacon deployed this metonym to shame Jacobean royal creditors, condemning them as man-eating *"Cyclops,* or Ministers of Terror."[17] Giovanni Marana's *Turkish Spy* later displayed the promiscuous relations between moneylenders and the defense industry in the same figure, saying that both were "employ'd by *Jupiter* in making Thunderbolts" and other weapons.[18] This understanding of the consumption of a nation by its financial obligations was encapsulated by Swift early in his career in *The Examiner,* a Tory periodical. He described how at least half of England's taxes already had been mortgaged into perpetuity to pay the interest on the debt alone, impoverishing posterity: "the Country Gentleman is in the Condition of a young Heir, out of whose Estate a Scrivener receives half the Rents for Interest, and hath a Mortgage on the Whole" (3:5). *A Modest Proposal's* allegory of children devoured by parental debts, accordingly, drawn from Swift's own canon, influenced gothic adaptations in succeeding years. In 1733, Charles Forman translated the term "vampire" into English to suggest that collectors of interest on the national debt were the undead. Comparing the virtues of governments, he wrote, "When a *Dutchman* is paying his *Taxes* . . . it is of some Satisfaction to him to know that he is not giving from his Family what he has earned . . . to gratify the Rapine of a fat-gutted *Vampire.*"[19] A year later, Swift's ally Henry Bolingbroke seized on this image of a bloodsucking monster in an allegory describing Walpole as the leader of the nation's creditors.[20]

The cannibal was not the only figure for finance that Swift borrowed from the Scriblerian lexicon, however; he also took "prostitute," "beggar," and "thief" from works like John Gay's *The Beggar's Opera.* These terms signified the moneyed interest, the Whig government, and their publicists under a single pejorative *zeugma.* Swift, Pope, and Gay denigrated Whig publicists as inferior mercenary pens fighting a culture war by disseminating smutty pulp fiction, work legitimating the desires and ethics of the new credit culture.[21] They revived John Dryden's Grub Street metonym to compare the relationship of this popular literary market to prostitution. Accordingly, they gendered literature, elevating their own work as "high art" by dismissing these rivals as writers of an emasculated literature associating with the feminized world of finance.[22] Deploying the publishing industry's cant, Pope's *Dunciad* portrayed such "dunces" as the progeny of "Dulness," a "Mighty Mother" symbolizing both Edmund Curll's "chaste press" and his leading author, Eliza Haywood.[23] This goddess of printing continuously gave birth to bastard progeny: "Dulness's procreative abilities symbolically give her the power of physical and cultural reproduction and illustrate the ease with which texts are conceived and materially reproduced in the Grub Street environment. . . . she spawns dunces, genres, and texts that she can mold in her image."[24] This press was anything but chaste, however; the soft pornography produced by it, in Pope's view, encouraged licentiousness and caused men to "neglect their real duties to govern."[25] The poem's argument is most evident in the line, "The Goddess bade Britannia sleep," implying that Whig cultural production was distracting the citizenry from its obligation to oversee public policy.[26]

A Modest Proposal incorporates Irish patriotic themes within this Scriblerian financial satire. It employs the *Dunciad's* metaphors for textual production to critique Dublin's print culture, implying that the Anglo-Irish economic pamphlet, a genre that dominated Ireland's publishing industry and public debate, was a form of political pornography entertaining to everybody but the starving poor for whom it claimed to be advocating. *A Letter to the Archbishop of Dublin, Concerning the Weavers*—an unpublished essay of Swift's, said to have been written in April of 1729—expressed his exasperation with the discipline of political economy. He wrote that he was "weary [of] so many abortive Projects for the advancement of Trade, of so many crude Proposals in letters sent me from unknown hands, of so many contradictory Speculations about raising or sinking the value of gold and silver" (12:66). These "dreams" diverted attention away from the domestic and foreign politics of the national debt and how it related to Ireland's currency problems (12:67). Though Swift parodied the formal strategies of such pamphlets in a manner that might have been meant to unmask their conventions and reduce their persuasiveness, he actually succeeds in making *A Modest Proposal* the masterpiece of the genre. It seems tailored for a leisured Anglo-Irish political caste desiring scenes of suffering and their consequent anaesthetizing economic resolutions. While the author certainly follows convention in the way he framed such plots, his inferences make readers cognizant of the fact that their pleasure is derived from their participation in the camps of both perpetrator and reformer. Because the text outlines the authoritative presence of a faceless speaker (the proposer), readers are initially hailed as members of a universal public for whom he is the spokesman. But this anonymous *vox populi* soon is revealed as a figure of loathing, and readers realize too late that they have been snared by their straight reading and implicated in the speaker's vice. The work's effect, as a parody of earnest appeals for the end of actual suffering, was to dismiss the reality of the material economic problems discussed by pamphleteers, making the genre appear to be an exercise in apologetics that bore little relation to conditions on the ground.

Accordingly, the cannibal voice of the proposer signals that the schemes for development circulating in Dublin at the time were thinly veiled attempts to fleece the population. By opening his speech with an enduring symbol of Ireland's poverty, "*Beggars* of the Female Sex," he confronted Anglo-Irish readers with the "melancholy" symptom of economic disaster that was most visible to them in the streets (12:109).[27] Dublin, due to depression and famine, was indeed rife with panhandlers, a fact Swift had documented in a sermon of 1726 and a pamphlet of 1737.[28] When regarded as a device and not an empirical reality, however, the symbol of the beggar registers the *pathos* that, in this genre, conventionally precedes the remedying proposition.[29] By mimicking the *argumentum ad misericordiam* of Ireland's economic projectors, this paragraph progressively stretches the limits of credulity and rapidly descends into *bathos*. The author italicizes the hackneyed tropes of liberal Whig political economy, announcing the text's performative stance and inferring that these terms are freighted with supplemental signification. "*Beggars*" and "*thieves*," given this *aporia*, can be taken to stand not merely for the poor in the streets but also for writers of pamphlets pursuing patronage and the creditors backing them. Via these metaphors for the printing industry, the impoverished Irish mother of *A Modest Proposal* is transmuted from a baby machine into Dublin's "Dulness," the endlessly procreative Irish press that spawned tract after tract on economic improvement. In this allegory, her "three, four, or six Children, *all in Rags*" personify texts, given that "Rags" stands both for clothes recycled in papermaking and for pulp fiction (12:109). Similarly, the *Proposal's* lamentations about "*voluntary Abortions*" and "*Women murdering their Bastard Children* ... more to avoid the Expence than the Shame" can be read not merely as a discourse on the ethics of infanticide but also as a metadiscursive plea to his printer, Sarah Harding, the "mother" of his "children" (12:109).

At least two of Swift's publishers, Edward Waters and Sarah's husband John, had been prosecuted or "shamed" for publishing some of his pamphlets.[30] The abortion reference, within the figure of a "Dublin Dulness" producing veils for the self-interest of the *Monti*, could be an argument for the political importance of continuing to do so. It also, however, may be asking Sarah not to cancel this particular dangerous print run, given that the *Proposal* clearly would be equally controversial. When John died shortly after being jailed for publishing the fourth of the *Drapier's Letters*, in 1725, a collection was taken up for Sarah via a poem, lines of which read, "He left with his Widow, two Children behind, / And little, God help her, to keep them from / Starving. . . . she suffer'd by it much shame, and Disgrace."[31] Though these verses overtly document the dangers of printing, they also can be read as metaphors for print production. Combined with derogatory comments about how Sarah's printing was sloppy, "straggling in mean Condition," they suggest that *A Modest Proposal's* pathetic discourse on the "shame" of the street-walking Irish widow and orphan also refers to these comments about the Harding family business itself.[32]

If the offspring of the poor are figures for texts, their status as orphans is triply inscribed, connoting progeny with absent biological fathers, defenseless future taxpayers, and books with no clear author. The device of the invisible, anonymous narrator invents the Anglo-Irish public as godfather of the infant in all three of its manifestations and, by doing so, grants readers the custody of its body, its wealth, and authority over its proper interpretation. The babies' economic personas, however, take primacy as the cannibal calculus reaches its more detailed scheduling. They "will not bear Exportation" to Britain because they stand for the proceeds of Swift's nationalist scheme for their retention, short-term duties renewable by Parliament every two years (12:117). This approach, by restricting the supply of Ireland's revenues, would guarantee that Anglo-Irish creditors, not the British crown, would be receiving them on a sustainable basis. The "young healthy Child . . . at a Year old" is the figure for this alternative plan because it represents such incremental, rather than perpetual, appropriation of the income of future generations (12:111). The text pushes the limits of this figuration by saying that the payment schedule in the narrator's scheme would be every March 25th, the end of Ireland's fiscal year: "INFANTS Flesh . . . will be more plentiful in March and a little before and after," or during accounting's "fore and hind Quarter" (12:112). This is so because "there are more Children born in *Roman Catholick Countries* about Nine Months after *Lent*, than at any other Season" (12:112). The *"prolifick Dyet"* of fish to which he refers signifies the ritual of Lenten fasting, which thematizes the very kind of restraint in the collection of taxes necessary to protect Anglo-Irish interests (12:112). Swift's use of the anachronistic spelling *"dyet,"* which under another of its denotations means "an allowance or provision of food . . . a constant table or dyet in the Court," suggests a reference to how courtiers in London might be fed the revenues derived from these babies if the Irish Parliament is not prudent (*Oxford English Dictionary*, "Diet, sb.1." def. 5a).

If *A Modest Proposal* registered any humanitarian indictment of Anglo-Irish legislator-creditors, it was in its damning comparison between them and the Roman Catholic landed gentry of Old Regime France. Swift, in his capacity as an Anglican clergyman, was intimating that Ireland's Catholic infants could be compared to the Christ-child, born at Christmas to be a sacrifice at Easter in payment of man's debt, and he was accusing his Anglo-Irish co-religionists of doctrinal hypocrisy for their attitude towards the bodies on the altar. These Anglo-Irishmen claimed that the "Glorious" Revolution of 1688 had overcome what they considered to be a Catholic feudalism in the name of a liberating Protestant republicanism, yet they were behaving worse towards their Catholic dependents than the most rapacious French aristocrats did. As Ian Higgins has written, John Trenchard's *Cato's Letters* of a few years before had complained of how Continental regimes ground their subjects "under endless imposts" to support "a wanton and luxurious court," and Swift may have been borrowing Trenchard's tropes of melancholy and cannibalism to make this comparison.[33] He was implying that the Anglo-Irish colonials, like French communicants, were eating these infantile hosts of their parasitic invasion, much to the embarrassment of their church's theological objection to transubstantiation. Because the parody is mocking the *pathos* of its target genre, however, any sincere concern for the children is dissolved into *bathos* and the genre of the economic pamphlet is dismissed as cathartic theatre.

The Scriblerians preferred this bathetic mode when critiquing Whig hypocrisy because its realist effect countered the sublime associated with imperial transcendentalism. *Peri Bathos, or, The Art of Sinking in Poetry*, a jointly written work published under the name "Martin Scriblerus" at nearly the same time as *The Dunciad*, linked the poetics of the "Moderns" to contemporary government finance. Its subtitle appropriated the signification of the term "sinking fund," which referred to a Treasury measure enacted by Walpole. The purpose of the fund was to pay down Britain's national debt by progressively "sinking" the amount of its interest and principal with taxes perpetually earmarked for this purpose. The authors used this word to imply that the Moderns embraced the "*altitudo*" associated with Longinus's doctrine of the sublime because it helped maintain the investment bubble supporting the ruling party.[34] The Whig ideology of the sublime, as Peter de Bolla has argued, was one that linked the age's proliferation of printed information and its incalculable debt. The ideology arose as a means of explaining how the "feeling of boundlessness" generated by these excesses produced a crisis in apprehension, reducing comprehension to the limits of the self and the boundaries of the state of which it was a part.[35] The sublime both explained and invented British national identity as the product of anxieties about debt and knowledge, cultivating a transcendental aesthetic of "transport" as a means of escape from responsibility for these problems. The Tory critique of this aesthetic was based in its potential paralysis of the political agency required to reform the empire.

What stabilizes the subject in this episteme is "inflationary rhetoric": an equally excessive literature of *pathos*, exactly the device Swift satirizes in *A Modest Proposal*'s first paragraphs.[36] Paper money, an invention of the financial revolution, had consistently been a target of the Scriblerians because it was a medium by which Britain's national debt was reified into wealth. Both popular literature and currency inflation were linked within the ideology of the sublime in the Tory imagination, and *Peri Bathos* explains that Whig writers, by valuing it, were increasing the gap between rich and poor on "Parnassus," Swift's metonym for the British state and republic of letters. *A Modest Proposal* remarks that it is "surprizing," given the "populous of our lowlands," that "all dignities and honours should be bestowed upon the exceeding few meager inhabitants on the top of the mountain."[37] *Peri Bathos* may consist of "bathetic images of the futile attempt to hold onto wealth" in the modern economy, but it also denigrates payments to public creditors by showing how the support of the few at the top of the mountain requires ever-increasing levies on those at its foot.[38] Yet the narrator of *Peri Bathos* also suggests that, given the connection between popular literature and inflation, *bathos* might be a mode of realism that could finally sink the debt, providing a bottom to the market: "I have undertaken . . . to lead them as it were by the hand, and step by step, the gentle down-hill way to the bathos; the bottom, the end, the central point, the *non plus ultra*, of true modern poesy."[39] His repeated use of the term "profund" for "bathos" connects the signification of "depth" associated with "profound" with the "pro-fund" process of "pouring forth" wealth towards Britain's sinking fund.[40] The narrator is suggesting that the ironic effect constitutive of the bathetic can be reconstructive: an attempt to rebuild a deep foundation to support "an appalling destabilisation of the national economy and its moral basis."[41] The market, the Scriblerians argued, might be underwritten more effectively by laughter than by sensibility.

In this context, *A Modest Proposal* may have evinced consciousness about overpopulation, but it unconsciously reveals a concern with national debt and that debt's relationship to financial and rhetorical bubbles. It had become clear to Swift that population growth and inflation were linked by a practical requirement of the fiscal-military state: the revenue that would be produced by an ever-increasing number of taxpayers. The proliferation of children, whether they were regarded literally as bodies whose alienated labor would pay debts or metaphorically as inflationary pulp fictions keeping the public preoccupied, was necessary for the continuation of Whig hegemony. Given Swift's use of these pregnancy metaphors, postcolonial assessments of his critique of empire can be informed by a historicization of the period's organic unification of publishing, capitalism, and legal agency under the aegis of sexual reproduction. Laura Brown's contention that Swift was a misogynist who blamed Ireland's trade deficit on women's consumption of foreign textiles can now be amplified; his metonymy does incorporate women's bodies and clothing, but also English books that Dublin publishers were reprinting instead of publishing Anglo-Irish ones.[42] In addition, Clement Hawes's view that the dietary motif censures "England's devastating exploitation the Irish poor" can be supplemented by an understanding of how it also stands for the Irish Parliament's simultaneous appropriation of economic, textual, and political space.[43] Similarly, Srinivas Aravamudan's interpretation of these homologies might be further substantiated by examining the immediate circumstances in Dublin under which particular texts were composed.[44] These compelling readings, in short, may be supplemented by a new economic methodology that brings colonial discourse analysis together with a historical assessment of the importance of writers to the state's legal and financial missions.

II

The crisis in Ireland's economy in 1729 formed Swift's most immediate exigency for the composition of *A Modest Proposal*. Generations of Swift scholars have recognized that it was written in the wake of the bursting of the South Sea and Mississippi investment bubbles in 1720, in which the Anglo-Irish political class had invested heavily.[45] They also have documented that the subsequent depression was rendered worse by the famine of the late 1720s.[46] Few commentators, however, have considered the significance of the parliamentary controversy over Ireland's revenue to the pamphlet's publication. Oliver Ferguson's long-standing contention that the satire was circulated "in the midst of superfluous reports and useless debates" in Parliament can accordingly be revised to emphasize the centrality of this context.[47] The cannibal motif had been put into circulation in the *Intelligencer* newspaper in the late 1720s, as James Woolley has documented, and it is likely that it was because of concerns about the Debt of the Nation.[48] This motif's "ironic reversal" of blame for Ireland's barbarism from the natives to the Anglo-Irish, documented by Claude Rawson, is now apparent as a condemnation of the latter's predatory loans and schemes for taxpayer financing, not their exorbitant rents.[49] If landlords had "devoured most of the Parents" and had "best Title to the Children," as the *Proposal* asserted (12:112), it was probably because they had exhausted the resources of their tenant farmers and were tempted to perpetually tax Irish progeny, to whom they had more of a right than had the crown. They were experiencing difficulty in collecting rents, so those landlords with loan payments due from the Treasury and the power to obtain them through taxation were tempted to do so.[50] They had become dependent on the Debt of the Nation for life, liberty, and property; there would be no dominant Protestant state in Ireland without this autonomous mechanism for alienating native labor. Given that Swift had invested £1,200 with the deputy vice-treasurer, he had every motivation to support that system by propagating ideas of Anglo-Irish constitutional autonomy.[51]

The Irish Parliament had been appropriating revenue for the debt on a two-year basis, instead of a permanent one, since the Glorious Revolution, copying the means of fiscal control asserted by the English Parliament. The Debt of the Nation and the Declaratory Act of 1720, however, had heightened the risk that the crown would bypass legislative approval and directly debit the Treasury accounts holding their money. *Reflections on the National Debt,* a pamphlet published in Dublin in 1731, commented on how this problem of fiscal control could potentially compromise the Irish Parliament's political agency: "Pray what is all this, but laying the Nation under the severest Bonds, to do whatever the Prime Minister directs?"[52] Because England was also experiencing the economic consequences of the failure of the South Sea Bubble, Anglo-Irish proprietorship of any fund to pay the debt would be in doubt unless a new budgetary system was instituted.

Parliament and the court agreed in 1729 that a more permanent solution was needed for servicing the debt, partly because all figures associated with the leadership of Ireland were experiencing significantly straitened circumstances. There was a significant gap between the taxes being collected and the government's expenditures, due to famine, emigration, currency markets, and payments to British army regiments abroad. Ireland could go no further without some major adjustments to its financial structure.[53] The obvious solution of raising taxes was controversial in a time of famine, but confidence in commercial transactions, the law, and the state—and the implications of that faith for the whole economy—would be necessary to receive their interest in a timely fashion. But commentators, particularly clergymen, were concerned that taxes were already disproportionally exercised on the poor rather than the rich, negatively affecting the Irish peasantry at a difficult time. Archbishop William King of Dublin had been a long-standing critic of this policy. In an earlier controversy over Ireland's finances, he had written, "His Majesties revenue here rises in small sums from hearth money, excise on ale house & c.," reflecting the almost universal, durable truth that the bulk of any government's budget is derived from the poorest members of society.[54] Archbishop King had also for decades been circulating among his friends an unpublished manuscript complaining that the Irish were so overtaxed that he could not see "how any more can be got from them, except we . . . flay them and sell their skins."[55] This use of the cannibal metaphor for overtaxation, often cited as Swift's inspiration for scenes of Gulliver skinning Yahoos, was clearly being disseminated in Anglo-Irish circles in the 1720s. It was in exactly this sense of cannibalism, and for the same purposes, that Swift deployed this metaphor in *A Modest Proposal*.[56] His intervention in the debates of 1729 required a motif so well understood by his target readership that the tax signification of it would go without saying.

Though Swift's essay was "more directed against Irish self-destruction than against English exploitation," he, "like other *colóns*, whether in eighteenth-century Ireland or twentieth-century Kenya or Algeria, disliked the metropolitan masters not for their treatment of the native subjects but for an alleged betrayal of the *colóns* themselves."[57] He was worried about British interference in the financial affairs of the Anglo-Irish. The *Proposal* needed to address this threat at a time when the Irish Treasury, under the control of the British crown, was demanding that the legislature find ways and means of servicing the debt.

Given that the Irish Parliamentarians maintained a measure of autonomy vis-à-vis the crown by controlling revenue legislation, their proprietorship of any fund to pay the debt would be in doubt, considering that the Declaratory Act of 1720 claimed British legal supremacy over all Irish political affairs. Indeed, many felt that there was a pro-Walpole "English interest" among the Irish Whigs and that it was working to undermine the Irish Parliament's fiscal autonomy. Swift had been aware of this problem for quite some time, and the articles in his *Intelligencer* periodical of 1728 indicate that he knew that this conflict was coming to a head. His dialogical poem *Mad Mullinix and Timothy*, published in the eighth number of that periodical (18 June 1728), revived the Scriblerian critique of credit financing in defense of a Tory Earl who was accused of sedition for merely asking for transparency in public accounting:

> *M.* The *Tories* are gone ev'ry Man over
> To our Illustrious House of *Hanover.*
> From all their Conduct this is plain,
> And then—*T. G.*—Damn the Lyars again.

Did not an Earl but lately Vote
To bring in (I could Cut his Throat)
Our whole Accounts of publick Debts.
   M. Lord how this Froth Coxcomb frets! (aside)
   T. Did not an able Statesman
This dang'rous horrid motion Dish up?
As *Popish* Craft? Did he not rail on't?
Shew Fire and Faggot in the Tail on't?
Proving the *Earl* a grand Offender,
And in a Plot for the *Pretender*?[58]

In a gesture similar to that of the English Whigs who rose to power in 1714 by exploiting the Tory critique of the British national debt, calling it treason, some parliamentarians accused a peer of the Irish House of Lords of harboring Jacobite sympathies merely because he asked for a statement of public accounts. Marmaduke Coghill, a judge, lamented Swift's partisan tone, as he was forwarding a copy of this poem, for it strengthened the hand of the English interest, the executive branch of government, who possessed the accounting information.

> Swift has published a paper to day which I am sorry for, it being to keep up that faction I mentioned to you in my last, and makeing that division amongst us that must do us mischeif, those he writes against are too close united allready, and this will make them more so, whereas the happinesse of this country must subsist by the good agreement and harmony amongst us all whether English or Irish protestants, the paper if I can gett itt, I will enclose it.[59]

Coghill attributes partisan intentions to *Mad Mullinix and Timothy*, claiming that Swift was calling for Anglo-Irish parliamentarians to stand firm against British desires for the passage of permanent taxes to fund the debt, an action that would only unify opposition to temporary impositions of new levies. It is possible that these verses were stirring the opinion of the Irish interest against the Walpole government, given that the "Timothy" of the poem, Richard Tighe, served the English interest in the executive as a privy counselor.[60] Though Tighe may not have been involved directly in financial impropriety, his ties with the prime minister made him a convenient figure around whom to mobilize opposition to the Whigs' efforts to appropriate Ireland's revenues without consent. Considering that Swift proceeded to spend the summer of 1728 at Market Hill, the country home of Sir Arthur and Lady Acheson, the son-in-law and daughter of a former Tory chancellor of the Irish exchequer, it is likely that he was reasonably well informed about the financial crisis. Sir Arthur himself had been considered for the exchequer post earlier in his career but had been refused it because he was not a Whig. This move on his part suggests that he was skilled in political matters and that he might have espoused alternative approaches to public finance that Swift would have found appealing.[61] Swift's narrator claims that Irish infants would "not bear exportation . . . although perhaps I could name a country, which would be glad to eat up our whole nation without it." This statement hints that the Anglo-Irish were at risk of losing control of the future profits of colonialism to Britain (12:117).

Swift's concern about the growing economic problem was ethical, though self-interested. Ireland's national debt had brought into existence a system of finance similar to that which he complained about in England, and though he partook of it himself, he felt that it could be managed more artfully. As a high-church Anglican clergyman, he did not object to the defense of Anglican property and profit from investment in it, but he felt that "the security of Protestant Ireland hardly demanded the utter impoverishment of the Catholic natives, and was indeed ultimately endangered by it."[62] Revenue was the goal of the very methodology he was parodying in his cannibal calculus, and if that income serviced the national debt, then his message was that any further attempts to tax the natives would backfire. The mechanism for funding Anglo-Irish creditors from the public purse would grind to a halt. Indeed, fears of Jacobite recruitment were rife during the famine years of the late 1720s, and the appearance of French recruiting officers in Dublin in 1730 made that risk visible to the public in a way that no writing could (12:xxx).

Swift seemed to be aware that some financial measures involving taxation would be proposed for the approaching legislative session of 1729. He visited the Achesons again the summer before it convened, a long stay described in his frivolous poem of 1730 called *Lady A-S-N Weary of the Dean*.[63] His letter from there to Alexander Pope of 11 August 1729 subtly ironizes Ireland's financial situation, suggesting that it was a topic of conversation at Market Hill in those months: "One reason why I would have you in Ireland when you shall be at your own disposal, is that you may be master of two or three years revenues, *provisae frugis in annos copia*, so as not to be pinched in the least when years increase, and perhaps your health impairs: And when this kingdom is utterly at an end, you may support me for the few years I shall happen to live."[64] Apparently aware of the leading structural cause of the country's poverty, he jokes that the Debt of the Nation makes it possible for one to own future funds indefinitely, as long as the people are still able to yield them. In his reference to times "when years increase," he may have been advising Pope that his income would go further in Ireland as they both aged. In the context of the debt crisis, however, it is difficult not to see that this passage also could be read as a statement about how the native young would finance their colonial elders, an implication tantamount to the cannibal motif of the pamphlet that followed.

A Modest Proposal, therefore, was probably composed with these concerns in mind. Herbert Davis speculated that it was begun when he was with the Achesons "in those last weeks in the country" and was printed at the end of October, given that it was advertised in an 8 November edition of the *Dublin Intelligence* (12:xix). Publishing it at that time could have been nothing other than a political act, as the new session of Parliament had convened in September and was reaching its peak of activity. The lord lieutenant of Ireland, John Carteret, the representative of the crown and executive authority in the colony, opened the session with a speech complaining that revenue was falling short of expectations and he hoped that the Parliament would "grant such supplies as will be necessary to answer the exigencies of the Government."[65] He made it clear that he desired "that the imposition of the appropriated duties should be open-ended, to cease only when the debt was cleared."[66] I modestly submit that Swift published the *Proposal* at this time to raise opposition to this request.

III

Little is known of how the *Proposal* was received during these weeks of controversy, though there is enough evidence to indicate that contemporaries understood that its covert message concerned the new taxation that most members of Parliament knew was inevitable.[67] Swift feared that these new taxes would be permanent, not only putting the poor in greater jeopardy, but also threatening the means by which Ireland retained a measure of political agency vis-à-vis the empire. Members of Parliament shared this concern.[68] At the time of the text's publication, no decisions had been made regarding these matters, though Swift warned of "a perpetual scene of misfortunes" for the native Irish and "the most inevitable prospect of intailing the like, or greater miseries, upon their breed forever" if Parliament enacted the permanent taxes that the viceroy wanted (12:117–118). I argue that patriotic advocacy of this kind helped shape the resolution that emerged from the Parliament in December: the introduction of a second biennial supply act to temporarily finance a sinking fund. With this strategy, the legislative branch preserved its check on the executive branch, giving the latter only two years worth of debt servicing at a time rather than a permanent appropriation.[69]

Swift's correspondence indicates that the *Proposal* was read by some as an allegory for the general problem of European national debts. Lord Bathurst, an old Tory friend of Swift's who helped manage publishing and financial matters for him in London, wrote to him that winter expanding on the cannibal motif for taxation. He deployed an elaborate metaphor of siblings and twins to describe not only the national debts of England and Ireland but also the predatory behavior of the former towards the latter. Referring to the *Proposal*'s lines that the Anglo-Irish had "the best Title to the Children," he wrote that funds for the debt had made possible the notion that the "youngest shou'd raise fortunes for the Eldest" in his or her taxes.[70] This phrase doubles as Scriblerian terminology for printing; it is possible that Bathurst was also implying that this young text would sell more copies of *Gulliver's Travels*, which was the "eldest" or first publication in the coordinated attack of Swift, Pope, and Gay. His references to Ireland as a "twin," a child of a "second woman," and "the fattest of the two" signal that he thought that the *Proposal* was arguing that England was preying on Ireland.

Newly discovered evidence of the satire's reception, however, points to the debt crisis as its subtext and the probable primary exigency for its composition, suggesting that its target was the Anglo-Irish parliamentarians, not the English. A few days after the *Proposal*'s publication, a letter from Marmaduke Coghill to Secretary of State Edward Southwell discussed the satire in relation to these fiscal concerns. Given that this memorandum ends with the note "the enclosed is a book of Swift's," and that David Hayton has speculated that this note was referring to a copy of *A Modest Proposal*, it is likely that Coghill was linking the pamphlet to Parliament's budgetary debates.[71] Coghill was made first commissioner of the revenue of Ireland a week later, so the *Proposal* was significant to him at the moment he wrote the letter because he would soon be responsible under any new plan for servicing the debt.[72]

Additional evidence that Swift was thinking about the national debt during this period is the unpublished pamphlet *A Proposal that all the Ladies Should Appear Constantly in Irish Manufactures* written in December 1729, a revision of *A Proposal for the Universal Use of Irish Manufacture* of nine years before. Hoping to intervene in the parliamentary debates over raising taxes to support payments to the country's creditors, he announced his awareness of the public debates: "I am informed that our national debt (and God knows how we wretches came by that fashionable thing a national debt) is about 250,000*l*; which is, at least, one third of the whole kingdom's rents, after our absentees and other foreign drains are paid, and about 50,000*l*. more than all the cash" (12:123). He recommends alternative luxury taxes on silks and on rent payments remitted to absentee landlords overseas—measures that would target the wealthy exclusively. Because the Irish Parliament had voted "larger Supplies than ever granted in any previous Session," however, "it was too late for him to protest," and he decided not to print this piece (12:xxii). The fact that the pamphlet explicitly mentioned the debt may have worked against his strategy, making its existence too apparent to the public. If his objective was to prove that Scriblerian writing produced superior fictions of state, publishing this manuscript would have undermined his previous pamphlet's more subtle approach.

Perhaps it was in part in response to *A Modest Proposal*'s advocacy that the Irish Parliament created a sinking fund financed by more progressive taxation and that preserved its sovereignty by levying only enough money for two years' payments. Supplementing its usual bill continuing additional duties on beer, ale, strong waters, wine, tobacco and other goods, which it had renewed since 1715 (3 Geo. II, c.1), it passed 3 Geo. II, c.2, a bill to fund the national debt, which imposed "a further Additional

Duty on Wine Strong Waters Brandy and Spirits and also a Tax of Four Shillings in the Pound on all Salaries Profits of Employments Fees and Pensions."[73] These acts affected the wealthy more than the poor, as the former both monopolized civil service salaries and consumed wine and spirits to a greater extent than did the native Irish.[74] These new duties on luxury items can be interpreted as a tribute to the success of Swift's pamphlet.[75] His work may have begun to alter the context for policymaking decisions.[76] Though the irony of *A Modest Proposal* has been taken to reflect Swift's final personal despair about the possibilities of reform, it is nonetheless evident that he persuaded the landed men of the Parliament to behave more responsibly.[77] In the next session of the Irish Parliament, 1731, their secondary budget bill to fund repayments on their loans to the government again targeted their own community more than any other. The act 5 Geo. II, c.2 granted "a further additional Duty on Wine Silk Hops China Earthen Japanned or Lacquered Ware and Vinegar" in addition to continuing the tax on civil servants.[78] Considering that the *Proposal* had recommended normative solutions to Irish economic problems, such as discouraging the consumption of imported luxury goods, this revenue bill was a step in the right direction.

IV

By the late 1720s, the Scriblerians no longer believed that they could actually reverse the financial revolution. The Scriblerian critique of Walpole and the Whigs, rather, was directed at the visibility of that party's corruption, inadequately covered by their writers. They were claiming that their art, and the policies of Tory politicians, would put a better face on the state and help secure the class positions of the elite of both parties: "[W]hat most Whigs and Tories were arguing about was in fact how they might best protect and preserve their own—shared—privileged position in society."[79] Swift's work was no exception, but the particularly rarified politics of immediate postrevolutionary Ireland raised the stakes of his rhetoric; he had to speak to multiple classes and to both colonizer and the colonized. By covertly addressing the revenue problem in the cannibal metaphor, he may not really have been masking it—everyone in Dublin knew the economy was in trouble and that Parliament was meeting to discuss it—but may have been proving how talented he was at disseminating a compelling fiction of Anglo-Irish independence in the face of it.

This contextualization of *A Modest Proposal*'s discourse on cannibalism has the potential to transform the critical ideology of its "stable" irony, because, though it reads as a parody of the dry economic pamphlet, it was not entirely dismissing the potential of that genre.[80] Its end was the reform of budgetary planning, but its main effects might not have been taken as the double irony that "*Swift* means what the *Proposer* says," but rather as allegory; by the parliamentary audience, it seems to have been taken as an economic proposal, and a serious one at that.[81] Its strategy of migrating the narrator's persona from master of the accounting desk to host at the dinner table brings the questions of the genres and media of Anglophilic social performance to the fore in unexpected ways. The *Proposal*'s culinary metaphors for the dieting of revenue, for example, seem also to mock the kinds of table manners and tastes that the Anglo-Irish were mimicking from the English and to slice through the bourgeois propriety fashioned in imported novels. These social imitations, by pulling the Anglo-Irish towards British cultural capital, undermined their claims of sovereignty in Ireland. What was needed was a distinctly Irish aesthetic and culture industry to support these claims.

CHAPTER 6

"A Mart of Literature"

The 1730s and the Rise of a Literary
Public Sphere in Ireland

The decade that followed publication of *A Modest Proposal* and the establishment of a sinking fund for the Debt of the Nation is signifi-cant to the study of Swift's career and the Dublin book trade in two ways. First, it marks a time when Swift, who was growing into more of an Irish nationalist writer than a Tory publicist, was becoming more skeptical of working with London publishers and more inclined to publish his most significant works in Dublin. The Irish book trade's relationship with Lon-don's, meanwhile, was becoming less one of concurrence and cooperation and more one of competition. Second, Swift's choice to work more often with Dublin printers, changes in press licensing, and the development of a broader market for Irish-themed works were enabling the rise of the category of the "literary" in Ireland. Though political economy contin-ued to shape the Irish political public sphere—albeit one, as I explained in Chapters 4 and 5, in which the "public" was limited to the members of the *Monti*—literary work in Ireland, which depended on that genre for its distinction as a national brand identity, was emerging as its own class of print. The literary sphere, consequently, arose from the national symbolism generated by overtly economic works such as the *Drapier's Letters*. As Clive Probyn has written, Swift's persona as the drapier, as the unifying symbol governing the Dublin book market, soon became disseminated enough to support an entire semiotic system for Ireland that went beyond direct political engagement. Swift was becoming "an allegorical figure in the public sphere," and many taverns, coffeehouses, and clubs "adopted the 'Drapier's Head' as their icon." The drapier, as a figure for the bookseller, was featured in street theatre and parades. In general, Dubliners were celebrating the book as the material means by which the *Letters* had expressed Ireland's sovereignty; the Guild of St. Luke's float for a 1728 parade featured a printing press as the "symbol of secular, political, and nationalistic enfranchisement."[1] The semiotic system generated by the *Letters* was the foundation for a larger edifice of culture expressed most visibly in Anglo-Irish literature, which appropriated the style, but not necessarily the substance, of serious political controversy.

The formation of a more strictly literary public sphere was therefore, like Swift's satire itself, to some extent parasitical on political economy as a host text, yet it also functioned to underwrite the goal of that text, the establishment of Ireland as a sovereign economic community. The history of the Irish book in this period thereby problematizes Habermas's chronology of the development of the types of public spheres. If we, for a moment, accept the argument that an apolitical "literary precursor of the public sphere in the political domain" emerges as a "training ground" for political writing in this period, the Dublin book trade, by developing its identity in political economy first, seemingly inverts that genealogy.[2] Though Swift himself may have rehearsed for his later political engagement by writing literary works in England, it does not follow that national print cultures as a whole are shaped in literature first. Unlike the early-twentieth-century Irish Renaissance, an era in which "the cultural revival preceded and in many ways enabled the political revolution," Swift's writings of the 1720s and 1730s show that political economy formed the culture and readership upon which Anglo-Irish literature could thrive.[3]

Swift was not alone in contending that the encouragement of a more strictly literary book market in Ireland would serve to complement the political market that his writings of the 1720s had formed. George Berkeley, the colleague of Swift's who applied the term *Monti* to the fund for the Debt of the Nation, recognized the potential that this literary market held for nation building. His book *The Querist*, published in the mid-1730s, questioned the value of various strategies for improving the economy and living conditions of Ireland, among them the potential establishment of a central bank and national paper currency. The printing press and the development of an Irish book market, however, were central to these more economic projects. Berkeley asked whether "it should not seem worthwhile to erect a Mart of Literature in this Kingdom, under wiser Regulations and better Discipline than in any other Part of *Europe*? And whether this would not be an infallible Means of drawing Men and Money into the Kingdom?"[4] As Richard Sher and others have indicated, Dublin did indeed rise, from the mid-eighteenth century onwards, to become second to London in English-language publishing, especially in reprinting literary works like novels, so perhaps Berkeley's question was answered.[5] This chapter concerns how the seeds of this growth were sown in Swift and Berkeley's era. The 1730s, partly because they witnessed the Dublin printing of George Faulkner's edition of Swift's collected works, marked the emergence of a distinct literary branch of the book market in Ireland. As Barbara Benedict has pointed out, one of the cultural consequences of the publication of eighteenth-century anthologies like Swift's was the formation of a set of nationally important works; and it is clear that Swift, by virtue of this process, became the first figure in a distinctly Anglo-Irish canon.[6]

One of the factors that enabled this transformation of the Irish book market was the specifications of the patent for the printing monopoly belonging to the king's stationer. The patent obtained by George and Constantia Grierson in 1729 and assumed by them in 1732 after the death of Andrew Crooke II was far more limited in scope than that held by previous patentees. This particular license is important because it legally liberated other publishers from regulation of what they could print and because for the first time carried a woman's name. Both of these changes made conditions more conducive to the growth of literary publication than they had been.[7] Though there was "little or no restraint on the printing of such privileged books as almanacs, primers, and school books" before the 1732 patent, rival printers and booksellers had, in all practical senses, the right to compete with the king's printer.[8] The new patent, by giving only a very restricted monopoly to the Griersons, made official what had been the practice, and their press began to publish official documents and Bibles to the exclusion of other genres.[9] The effect of this official change was that other printers felt freer to publish other forms, literary works among them. When the king chartered the Incorporated Society for Protestant Schools in 1733, for which Grierson was the official, though not exclusive, printer, there were "further incentives for publishers to supply schoolbooks and edifying digests."[10] Like

Bibles, textbooks provided the kind of capital to the printing industry that would enable them to publish other varieties of writing, and the literate audience that would be produced by schools would form a broader market. Significantly, the book trade recognized that what was emerging was a uniquely Anglo-Irish form of cultural capital. In their 1735 satire *The Humble Petition of George Faulkner and George Grierson*, these publishers promoted books written and printed in Ireland as valuable for the "honour and luster" of the Dublin trade, suggesting that Irish textual production had begun to acquire a distinct brand identity.[11]

This chapter examines the migration of ideas of Irish national identity from the discipline of political economy to the genres of literature—a migration that mirrors movements in Swift's personal career. First, it documents Swift's further engagements with Ireland's economic issues, showing that he continued to perform the nationalist role of the drapier, though in a much less robust way, through the 1730s. Second, it discusses how Swift's poetry of this period—what some have termed his "anti-poetry"—reflects his increasingly skeptical outlook on the British book trade.[12] Poems of the 1730s such as an *Epistle to a Lady* and *On Poetry: A Rapsody*, I argue, mark his transition to working more exclusively with Dublin printers. They were heavily edited by his London correspondents and they were not well received by the authorities, suggesting that his satire was becoming an embarrassment for the Tory cause as it moved from critique of the Whigs to an outright condemnation of the British government, including the king and his court. This development, I argue, transformed Swift from an opposition publicist into a writer disenchanted with British politics altogether who increasingly embraced a more openly Irish patriotic position that transcended partisanship. Third, it discusses the role of anthologies in forming national literary canons, by showing how this transformation is reflected in Swift's disappointment with *Miscellanies in Prose and Verse*, which he had published in London with Motte, and in his choice to publish his multivolume collected works with Faulkner in Dublin.

I

It has been argued that, after *A Modest Proposal*, Swift's contributions to Anglo-Irish political economy were of little consequence.[13] He had written to Pope that he was growing tired of writing in the genre and that he often threw away his drafts because he felt that they would not make much of a difference (12:xxiv). He also said that he was going to refrain from causing "his Majesty's government any further embarrassment by writing about the condition of Ireland" (12:xxxv). Most of his political prose from the 1730s that does survive was not published during his lifetime; it was used as new material in later editions of his complete works and other productions of the Swift culture industry after his death. Further, those pieces that he did write were on themes that he had discussed before. Nonetheless, they are evidence that he continued to be concerned about the politics and economy of Ireland even as his poetry came closer to actualizing the idea that the best way to improve the country was the development of the book trade. For the most part, Swift's publications on political economy in the 1730s were on coinage and the national debt, on Dublin city politics, on the state of the weavers and the woolen trade, and on Church of Ireland matters such as tithes, appointments to clerical office, and charity.

An Infallible Scheme to Pay the Public Debt of this Nation in Six Months, A Proposal for an Act of Parliament to Pay Off the Debt of the Nation, A Letter on the Fishery, and the *Speech on Lowering the Coin* are Swift's central contributions to political economy in the 1730s, though not all of them were published in his lifetime. The first, often misattributed because its title page says it was written by "D--n S---t," was probably a production of his protégé Matthew Pilkington (12:xxxii). Intervening in the parliamentary controversy of 1731 over renewing the 1729 compromise over funding the national debt, *An Infallible Scheme,* as Kirsten Sundell has argued, appropriates Swift's indictment of the luxury and extravagance of the Anglo-Irish landed class.[14] The pamphlet, printed in Dublin in 1731, contends that by imposing a tax upon *"Perjury, Fornication, Drunkenness, Swearing, Slander, Infidelity, Fraud, Blasphemy,"* and other vices, Parliament would no longer be troubled with the need to pass a secondary supply bill to pay the interest on the debt.[15] Again, however, this satire should be taken as commenting on the role of the printing trade in creating a national economy. More like *Swearer's Bank,* which I discussed in Chapter 2, than like *A Modest Proposal, An Infallible Scheme* recommends a system of fines resembling what Joseph Moxon identified as the "Solaces" of the "Chappel," or printing house.[16] The total revenue to be collected from these vices was predicted to be £477,750 in six months, much more than the approximate debt of £300,000.[17] This pamphlet, perhaps more than any other, shows how Swift's linkage of print culture to finance was being received and understood as such by other Dublin writers.

A Proposal for an Act of Parliament to Pay Off the Debt of the Nation, printed in Dublin in 1732 and almost definitely written by Swift, revisits the actuarial logic of *A Modest Proposal* and *An Infallible Scheme* by recommending that the money that Church of Ireland bishops owned or collected on their land be redistributed towards the Irish Treasury. It announces its non-serious, satirical intent from the outset, claiming that *"The Reader will perceive the following Treatise to be altogether Ironical"* (12:207), yet it contains important information regarding the expenses that government borrowing had been funding. The first cost was national security: "The Debts contracted some Years past, for the Service and Safety of the Nation, are grown so great, that under our present distressed Condition, by the Want of Trade . . . [and] Regiments serving abroad . . . the Kingdom seems altogether unable to discharge them by the common Methods of Payment" (12:207). Whether taken at face value or as an element of the satire that follows it, this statement suggests that the support of the *Monti* was still on Swift's mind in the 1730s, that serious economic proposals were continuing to circulate in this period, and that Swift was still committed to parodying them. He proposes selling bishops' lands for a profit, using half of the money raised, £1,214,400, to pay off the debt and using the other half to store in the Treasury for emergencies.

A Letter on the Fishery was not published until 1729 (in London), four years after Swift's death; it was one of several unfinished items that his publishers used to pad new collections of his works. It shows that Swift was still interested in the problem of Ireland's trade, yet not as invested in printing pieces about it as he was in publishing his poetry. It complains that the Dutch are monopolizing fishing in the British Isles with the tacit support of the English government, and it expresses disappointment with the "lazy" habits of the native Irish and their "Knavery" (13:113). This letter is more important, however, because it offers insight into the motives of his earlier work. In it he writes of the *Drapier's Letters*, claiming the letters as his own, describing the risks he took in the

Wood's halfpence controversy, and saying "What I did for this Country was from perfect Hatred of Tyranny and Oppression" (12:112). The letter is related to *Reasons why We Should not Lower the Coins now Current in this Kingdom*, which was published in 1736 in Dublin (13:xxxvii). This work attempted to arouse the emotions of the earlier controversy, using a new currency problem to revive memory of Swift's contribution. The short speech had been delivered before several merchants on 24 April 1736, when Swift once again asserted the right of the "Irish interest" in Dublin against the "English interest," which was attempting to reset the value of Irish coins because the gold guinea had already dropped in value due to the decrease of silver circulating in Ireland. Swift believed that if this lower value were made official, the average shopkeeper would lose profits while the English appointees in church and state employment would lose nothing. The *Speech* therefore falls into the tradition of his defense of Dublin merchants.

Swift's writings on the city of Dublin and its politics and those on the textile trade reflect his general disappointment with Irish political and economic affairs, but they also show his continuing interest in advocating on behalf of the Irish. *The Substance of What was Said by the Dean of St. Patrick's to the Lord Mayor and Some of the Aldermen, when his Lordship came to Present the said Dean with his Freedom in a Gold Box* (written, but not published, in 1730), Swift's report on how he was honored by the city for his patriotism, takes steps to chastise the sloppy works and administration of Dublin. *An Examination of Certain Abuses, Corruptions, and Enormities, in the City of Dublin*, a pamphlet published in 1732, furthers themes addressed in earlier pamphlets by satirizing paranoia about "*Jacobites* and *Papists*." It illustrates how just about any cry that a hawker of goods might make in Dublin's streets could be interpreted as deliberate political sedition (12:220). *Some Considerations Humbly Offered to the Right Honourable the Lord-Mayor, The Court of Aldermen, and Common Council of the Honourable City of Dublin, in the Choice of a Recorder* (1732) and *Advice to the Free-Men of the City of Dublin in the choice of a Member to Represent them in Parliament* (1733) both concern Dublin elections. These works indicate the importance of the City of Dublin in opposing Ireland's executive branch (the lord lieutenant and his officers). Swift's printers benefited from this opposition because they were judged by city juries, which tended to be packed with sympathetic Dubliners, not representatives of the executive branch. *Advice to the Free-Men* follows a similar line of argument in advocating for a new city of Dublin representative in Parliament. *Observations Occasioned by Reading a Paper Entitled The Case of the Woollen Manufacturers of Dublin*, written, but not published, in December of 1733, revisits Swift's familiar arguments on behalf of the Irish weavers. It is more difficult to read it as an example of the text/textile homology seen in his earlier works on cloth, because it was published later in the eighteenth century (1789) from a manuscript that did not have italics and other typographical devices to signal supplemental meaning. In short, these essays reflect Swift's movement away from direct political engagement with issues in Anglo-Irish political economy.

The vast majority of Swift's prose works in this decade, however, concern religion and the business of the Church of Ireland. These works can be classified generally as short pieces on patronage and appointments of clergymen to parishes, benefices, and other offices, on the sacramental test, and on the income and economic status of the clergy. *A Vindication of his Excellency, the Lord C—t from the Charge of Favouring None but Tories, High-Churchmen and Jacobites* (1730) satirizes Dr. Patrick Delany, a friend of Swift's, for his attempts to gain further patronage from the lord lieutenant of Ireland, John Carteret, who had already, with Swift's intervention, appointed Delany to the chancellorship of St. Patrick's Cathedral. Delany had begun this controversy with a poem, *An Epistle to his Excellency John Lord Carteret Lord Lieutenant of Ireland*, which was "bluntly asserting further preferment."[18] Swift satirized this request in the poems *An Epistle upon an Epistle from a Certain Doctor to a Certain Great Lord, Being a Christmas Box for D. D—ny* (1729) and *A Libel on D— D— and a Certain Great Lord* (1729).[19] The latter was "one of his most violent political verse satires" on "the rottenness of political patronage," leading to more accusations that Swift was a Jacobite disenchanted with the governments of Britain and Ireland (12:xxiv–xxv). *A Vindication* responds to these accusations by showing that the lord lieutenant had appointed far more Whigs than Tories to offices in church and state, proving that neither he nor office holders of the Tory persuasion like Delany, Thomas Sheridan, Arthur Acheson, and Swift himself were guilty of any kind of treason (12:167–169).

Swift's writings on the question of repealing a certain religious test for state and church employees are implicitly about the problems surrounding patronage and government appointments. Mainly, they were concerned with what the right of Dissenters to occupy such offices—especially teaching positions at schools and universities—meant for Ireland's Anglican subjects. *The Advantages Proposed by Repealing the Sacramental Test* (1731), *Queries Relating to the Sacramental Test* (1732), *The Presbyterians Plea of Merit* (1733), *Reasons Humbly Offered to the Parliament of Ireland for Repealing the Sacramental Test, In Favour of the Catholicks* (1733), and *Some Few Thoughts Concerning the Repeal of the Test* (1733) dwell on the controversy over repealing the Sacramental Test for Dissenting Protestants, a debate that was raging in the early 1730s. They underline that the salaried appointments in church and state are what was really at stake in these religious conversations, and they claim those jobs for Irish Anglicans.

On the Bill for the Clergy's Residence on their Livings (1731), *Considerations upon Two Bills* (1731), *Some Reasons Against the Bill for Settling the Tythe of Hemp by a Modus* (1734), *A Character, Panegyric, and Description of the Legion Club* (1736), *Concerning that Universal Hatred, which Prevails against the Clergy* (1736), and *A Proposal for Giving Badges to Beggars* (1737) expand upon this patronage theme. Beginning in the Tudor era, the Church of Ireland had been accumulating "enormous incomes derived from tithes and rents."[20] Legislation regarding the distribution of these funds had been a favorite topic of Swift's since the first decade of the century, when he had been a lobbyist charged with protecting them from appropriation by the crown and British Parliament. Swift himself had been appointed to two parishes in addition to his deanery and was thereby familiar with both rural and urban church business. As a clergyman, he had a stake in the outcome of various governmental and legislative initiatives affecting the survival and prosperity of Anglican churchmen, who, as functionaries of a state church, were the traditional intellectual defenders of the state. Moreover, as a dean unlikely to be promoted to bishop, Swift questioned whether bishops should have the power to dramatically affect the income of the lower-ranked clergy.

For the most part, Swift's prose works of the 1730s repeat themes and arguments that he had been making throughout his life in his British and Irish works. None of them, however, rivaled in popularity and political effectiveness productions such as the *Drapier's Letters* and *A Modest Proposal*. Though a few of them discuss current issues in the Irish Parliament, such as the legislation regarding the repeal of the Sacramental Test for Dissenters, almost none of the later works that were published in his lifetime directly engage with the economic problems associated with the *Monti*. Instead, because Swift was "fully occupied at this time in writing verse," his efforts were targeted at both the production of literature and the vending of it in the Irish literary book market that he was helping to develop (12:xxxii–xxxiii).

II

Swift's migration towards working more often with Irish booksellers than with British ones stems from a series of disappointments that he experienced with the London trade in the late 1720s and early 1730s. As James McLaverty has explained, Lawton Gilliver and Benjamin Motte were working to publish in London a series of volumes under the title *Miscellanies in Prose and Verse*, which appeared from 1727 to 1732, that would reprint many of Pope's and Swift's works. The inspiration for this volume, in part, was that Edmund Curll had brought out an edition of Swift's works (*Miscellanea*) in 1726; and Motte, whose firm had originally published Swift's *Miscellanies* in 1711, may have been seeking to renew his copyright on that work.[21] Pope, the major player pushing the new project, was seeking to publish some of his own works with Swift's, and he was acting as Swift's agent in England. The volumes did not sell well, and Swift felt that Pope was to blame, because he had withheld *The Dunciad* from the collection and published it separately: "The *Miscellanies* had become a repository for Pope's least impressive pieces, but a collection of some of Swift's most impressive works."[22] Swift, in short, felt cheated by the way Pope was editing his writings because it was clear that instead of the monument to their friendship and canonization together, the *Miscellanies* was turning into anthology of pieces that Swift would otherwise have published elsewhere. Pope, meanwhile, was working to preserve his legacy on his own in other works. Swift was becoming less easy in his relationships with his Scriblerian friends in London and less invested in arguing that Tory authors represented higher-quality writing, writing above the fray of the Grub Street popular literature that he had previously associated with the Whigs. The poems *An Epistle to a Lady* and *On Poetry: A Rapsody*, I argue, express this ambivalence and document his transformation from a writer for the Tory opposition into one more invested in the Dublin book trade and Irish nationalism. They signal Swift's alienation from both London publishers and the Tory cause in English politics, as does his choice to publish his *Collected Works* with Dublin bookseller George Faulkner to identify himself more as an Irish writer than an English one. The anti-London orientation of these two poems supports Edward Said's claim that in the 1730s Ireland's culture "began to provide the stabler framework in which he wished the future to regard him."[23]

An Epistle to a Lady and *On Poetry: A Rapsody*, first published in London in 1733, though claiming to be reprints of Dublin editions, reflect Swift's comprehension of how writers' parasitism on major authors was formative of literary public spheres in both London and Dublin.[24] Though they are like Pope's *Dunciad* of a few years earlier in that they target Robert Walpole's culture industry and propaganda machine in London, Swift's observations on how both Whig and Tory writers there were competing for the same Grub Street crown with similar writings are evidence of his growing abandonment of partisan politics in favor of national politics. Especially in *On Poetry: A Rapsody*, Swift displayed a feeling that no change of administration from Whig to Tory would create political conditions more favorable to Ireland, as the kingdom would continue to be raided for its resources by either party. Accordingly, their publication also marks a moment when Swift implicitly announced that, after these London-published poems, he would be making a transition from publishing his more important works with London printers to working with Dublin printers. Though there continued to be cooperation between his publishers in both cities, the Irish book market was beginning to be more profitable for him, and greater control over the editing and content of his works there made it possible for him to better shape his legacy.

An Epistle to a Lady, though addressed to Lady Acheson of Market Hill in Ireland, ventriloquizes her to make a case concerning the political effects of his own satirical works. It is presented in the form of a dialogue between Swift and the lady in which the latter is begging him not to make her the subject of his satire.[25] She asks Swift to praise her, not to smear her in a misogynist manner, as he has done with other female subjects. In making this request, however, she is also asking him to extend those good manners to the treatment of the "Publick," suggesting, essentially, that he change the topic of the poem containing her ventriloquized voice. Accordingly, at line 133, he transitions to a metacommentary on his own political satire that simultaneously issues further challenges, not only to Walpole, his Whig party, and their publicists, but to the king himself. The last six lines of this passage were the most controversial of the poem, comparing the king himself, not just his courtiers, to a "Monkey" and "Baboon" (lines 149–154). Though these lines could be taken as targeting Colley Cibber, the poet laureate, who wore a crown of laurels, they were the object of a prosecution begun only after the much more damaging poem, *On Poetry: A Rapsody*, was published in December. Faulkner, who in the same year was negotiating with Swift to print his collected works, was so wary of these six lines that he printed asterisks for them when he finally reprinted this poem in 1746.[26]

In *An Epistle*, Swift reiterates his long-standing excoriation of Whig literary figures who were composing art in support of the state—figures whom he calls "the Nation's Representers"—in a manner that infers that Tory writers and politicians would be better at statecraft (line 156). He argues that these "Representers . . . enrich themselves" with the "Freight" of the ship of state, which has been "split on Shelves," or built upon books that Whigs write (lines 161–162). He suggests that he is retiring from the Tory opposition, by saying that, though he is trying to fill a "Nitch" in the book market, he will leave the governing of the state to opposition figures such as Henry St. John (Bolingbroke) (lines 171–180). Via the voice of Lady Acheson, he declares that he ought to emulate her detachment from politics and "laugh at Whig and Tory" instead of contemplating "Machinations brewing, / To compleat the Publick Ruin" (lines 193, 189–190). In short, though this poem contains a controversial indictment of the British court, Whig ministry, and Whig publicists, it signals that he may be departing from Tory partisanship into an outright condemnation of a British system of government that has no interest in improving Ireland.

This change of position—from an anti-Whig writer into an anti-British one—is manifest to a greater degree in *On Poetry: A Rapsody*. The poem registers this sentiment by revisiting the homology between literature and money to signal its irony, conveying to the reader the notion that all of the writers, publishers, and booksellers that he discusses in the poem are not worthy of the name "poet." The word "Rapsody" in the poem's title is a "slangy double pun upon "a rap," or spurious, counterfeit coin, and a "rap, or knock on the head," indicating that Swift is aiming to injure British literary culture, which he regards as the source of a counterfeit writing that demeans cultural value.[27] By using the term "rap" he is also referencing the continuing scarcity of small coinage in Ireland; Archbishop Boulter wrote in 1731 that Irish tradesmen were "forced to take raps or counterfeit halfpence."[28] *On Poetry* can thus be taken as a satire that plays on the homology between currency and literature to assert that Ireland gets neither from England. The poem advises the amateur poet to praise statesmen but implies that such flattery is false wit, and it does so in a manner that plays upon this homology:

> Your Poem in its modish Dress,
> Correctly fitted for the Press,
> Convey by Penny-Post to *Lintot*,
> But let no Friend alive look into't.
> If *Lintot* thinks 'twill quit the Cost,
> You need not fear your Labour lost:
> And, how agreeably surpriz'd
> Are you to see it advertiz'd!
> The Hawker shews you one in Print,
> As fresh as Farthings from the Mint:
> The Product of your Toil and Sweating;
> A Bastard of your own begetting.[29]

Here, Swift repeats the familiar claim that a printing press is like a mint, but that comparison is used ironically to invert the value of the writer and the publisher. The term "bastard" connotes not only illegitimate off-spring and texts, but also a kind of cloth, a size of paper, and a counterfeit coin (*OED*), all of which were homologous in Swift's lexicon. This motif is given a more specifically Irish and Swiftian dimension in the poem's comparison of the printed text in question to farthings, which recalls the drapier's discourse on the debased copper coins that William Wood was trying to introduce into Ireland. This stanza thereby revisits the division of the Irish from the British political public sphere that the *Drapier's*

Letters helped bring into being. *On Poetry: A Rapsody* is an Irish text critiquing the British culture industry. Because it implicitly satirizes Pope by reference to his use of the bookseller Lintot, it further reflects the growing distance between Swift and the British Tories.

The poem begins, like much Scriblerian satire, by attempting to create a distinction between high and low art and discussing how to distinguish "which is which, / The poet's Vein, or scribbling Itch?" (lines 73–74). It speaks of the rarity of good verse, asking, "Say *Britain*, cou'd you ever boast, ----- / Three *Poets* in an Age at most?" (lines 5–6). In its address to a young poet seeking advice, it contrasts true poets with Colley Cibber, the poet laureate appointed by Walpole, arguing that most Whig writers who hold positions given to them by Walpole are mercenaries linked to Grub Street (lines 43–60). By comparing a young "true poet" to Cibber, however, these lines actually ironize the pretenses of both, making the poet laureate the "Monarch" of "*Grubstreet*" (line 58), as useless as a novice because he cannot produce art for party or state. *On Poetry* thereby continues in the vein of Scriblerian works that claim that their art would better support the state than that of the Whigs. Indeed, the poem has been referred to by some critics as Swift's version of Pope's *Dunciad* in that it satirizes major Whig writers as residents of Grub Street.[30]

Swift, however, departs from the standard Scriblerian line by saying that both the Whigs and the Tories have their true poets as well as their Grub Street counterfeits. As Michael Conlon has observed, the poem is not trying to establish a hierarchy of British poets so much as lamenting "the liabilities of being any kind of poet—hack or genius—in George II's England."[31] Swift establishes the lack of difference between the poets of these parties by writing, "Two bordering Wits contend for Glory; / And one is *Whig*, and one is *Tory*. / And this, for Epicks claims the Bays, / And that, for Elegiack Lays" (lines 293–296). These writers accuse each other of amateurism and bad writing; they "Lay *Grubstreet* at each others Doors: / Extol the *Greek* and *Roman* Masters, / And curse our modern Poetasters" (lines 346–348). Despite their complaints, hacks and poets who think they have better taste and wit all live in the metonymic neighborhood of Grub Street: "*O, Grubstreet!* how do I bemoan thee, / Whose graceless Children scorn to own thee! / Their filial Piety forgot, / Deny their Country like a SCOT" (lines 357–359). Yet Swift's irony potentially implicates himself in a Grub Street form of production. As Donald Mell observes, "In his alienation from Grub Street Swift is simultaneously both like the dunces and different from them." He is drawing attention to the "close proximity, perhaps the indistinguishable nature, of the true and false, the spurious and genuine, the constructive and destructive, good poetry and bad. And he reveals an awareness of his own mixed motives . . . as a poet desirous of fame in the real world."[32] He had already called for the establishment of a Dublin Grub Street, explaining that he was not necessarily averse to the production of popular literature, or "trash," yet in *On Poetry: A Rapsody* he implies that British writers produce nothing but trash and that he may be capable of better. His reference to a Scot's denying his country, I would argue, is there to make the case that Scottish writers had sold out to England and that Irish writers could make use of the Dublin press's potential to create a form of Irish national feeling superior to Scotland's. By literalizing the metonymy of Grub Street to discuss the real geographical location of Scotland, Swift affiliates English and Scottish writers to suggest that the latter have surrendered their national pride in favor of a larger "Britishness." This abandonment creates space for Ireland as an alternative site of patriotic pride where Irish writers, though working in Grub Street, have more potential to produce great art than do their British counterparts.

On Poetry: A Rapsody follows the *Dunciad's* logic of accusing some writers of prostituting themselves to the popular fiction that produces the culture amenable to the Whig ministry, but *On Poetry* expands the accusation to encompass British Tories. Revisiting the homology of writing and money, Swift accuses the writers of both political parties of being publicists, not practitioners of higher literature. He compares Pope and Gay to Cibber by saying that both Tory and Whig wits are "Jobbers," or writers seeking patronage at court (lines 305–314). The phrase "Jobbers in the Poet's Art" (line 312), referring to all of the writers, Whig and Tory, treats British writing pejoratively as "stock jobbing," once again linking the world of publishing to finance. Earlier in the poem he refers to "A publick, or a private *Robber*; / A *Statesman*, or a South-Sea *Jobber*" as the social figures that readers will assume are the ones that the poet intended to target; and, by connecting them to these poets, he suggests that the South Sea Bubble was as much the work of British writers as it was of financiers and politicians (lines 161–162).

Though Pope and Gay were no longer in favor at court, and indeed disdained Walpole's administration to the extent that they criticized it in their work of the period, they still valued the court as a center of patronage to be regained if the Tories should come back into power. Swift's radicalism in *On Poetry: A Rapsody*, however, lies in how it gives up on regaining the court as an objective, giving the impression that Swift no longer acknowledged the monarchy, or Britain itself, as the center of value:

> Then *Poet*, if you mean to thrive,
> Employ your Muse on Kings alive;
> With Prudence gath'ring up a Cluster
> Of all the Virtues you can muster:
> Which form'd into a Garland sweet,
> Lay humbly at your Monarch's Feet;
> Who, as the Odours reach his Throne,
> Will smile, and think 'em all his own:
> For *Law* and *Gospel* both determine
> All Virtues lodge in royal Ermine.
> (I mean the Oracles of Both,
> Who shall depose it upon Oath.)
> Your Garland in the following Reign,
> Change but their Names will do again. (lines 219–232)

The scatology of this stanza, by comparing poetic lines to "Odours" or farts that the monarch likes so much that he claims them as his own, deconstructs not only poetic claims to authority but also political ones. It ridicules the taste of the monarch and says that he is so open to flattery that he does not recognize that poets use the same lines ("garlands") with each new reign—they change the names of the monarchs and other powerful figures and simply reissue the same poems. These lines, and some of the more controversial ones that were not published in the early editions of the poem, compounded the offenses of an *Epistle to a Lady*, published a few months earlier, to the extent that they led to the arrest of those involved. John Wilford, the London printer, Matthew Pilkington and Mary Barber, friends of Swift who had conveyed the manuscript to London, and Lawton Gilliver and Benjamin Motte, London publishers, were taken into custody. It is said that Walpole "swore out (until later dissuaded) a warrant for the arrest of Swift himself," which would indicate that his authorship was recognized behind the persona of the narrator.[33]

On Poetry: A Rapsody is a pivotal text marking Swift's transition from his preference for publishing his important literary works in London towards his full embrace of Dublin publishers because it indicates that Swift no longer saw a great difference between British Whig and Tory writers, that he thinks a change towards Tory rule would be of little help to Britain or Ireland. This transition can be mapped by examining the changes in his relationship with Pope, who often handled the publication of his work in London, on matters of style, trust, and ideology. As Philip Harth has explained, as early as 1725 Swift was commenting on the differences in satirical style between himself and Pope, saying in letters written on 29 September and 26 November of that year that he was not ready to embrace the sort of retiring, philosophical stance nor a withdrawal from political satire into entertainment that Pope was proposing. Stressing his principal difference from Pope, he writes that "the chief end I propose to myself in all my labors is to vex the world rather than divert it," in lines announcing that he will not soften his critique of corrupt power or the writers and texts that serve it.[34]

Further evidence of a growing gap between Swift and Pope relates to the level of trust between them, especially regarding the handling and editing of Swift's London publications, and indicates the growing difference in their ideological orientations. This difference is most manifest in Pope's excising of lines from poems that Swift sent him to publish with London printers. For example, Pope, without consulting Swift, excluded *A Libel on Dr. Delany* from publication in the final, 1732 volume of their joint *Miscellanies in Prose and Verse*. In that poem, Swift praised Pope as an independent writer—one who made money on his works by subscription, not by direct government patronage—and this was objectionable to Pope on three counts. First, it distanced him from many London writers by saying that Pope did not need the form of patronage that Gay, for instance, had to pursue out of financial necessity, effectively indicating that Pope's claim for the virtue of his work was based on financial independence, not literary merit. Second, praising his independence alienated him from the court "at a time when Pope was hoping . . . to reach some kind of accommodation with the Government," and the poem's lines "claiming that he had avoided the Court and refused a visit from the Queen while scorning to make any overtures to a rascal statesman" undermined that effort. Third, Pope was afraid that his opinions would be associated with Swift's, and *A Libel on Dr. Delany*, like other satires that Swift was publishing during this period, risked running afoul of libel laws. Pope, now more risk-averse, no longer wished to be prosecuted for his works, because such prosecutions would be not only costly but also dangerous to his reputation, just at the moment he was seeking reconciliation with the Walpole government. For such reasons, Pope, in editing *Verses on the Death of Dr. Swift* for a London edition of 1739, also excised, without Swift's approval, sixty-four subversive lines that might have offended the government—lines that were about Ireland.[35]

Swift's ever more fervent Irish patriotism, as Philip Harth has argued, was the reason for this growing distance between the ideologies of Swift and Pope. Swift now believed that "no change of kings, no alteration of the ministry would significantly improve the condition of Ireland. As long as she remained a subordinate and dependent kingdom, subject to a British crown, ministry, and parliament in whose sole interest every viceroy and other resident official must continue to act, it mattered little who was in power in Westminster." Swift's poems of this period, accordingly, "are not Opposition poems in any sense of the word but radically subversive satires" that "implicitly reject the constitutional system itself responsible for Ireland's enslavement."[36] By using the London press to publish these sentiments, which Swift often did in conjunction with Dublin publication, he was taking the battle over Ireland's sovereignty to the empire's home turf. His friends' and printers' censorship of them upon arrival justifies Swift's apparent feeling that Dublin was a more amendable location for these productions, and perhaps that is why he chose to have his complete works published by George Faulkner, a Dublin bookseller.

III

The competition between the Motte-Gilliver *Miscellanies* and Faulkner's emerging *Collected Works* was not only one about intellectual property; it was also about the shaping of a national canon and Swift's place in it. At the same time, because anthologies contribute to the formation of a canon "by continually stealing from each other," this rivalry to anthologize his writing was enhancing his potential canonical status.[37] By working with both anthologists, Swift may have been attempting, however inadvertently, to canonize himself in both the English tradition and the developing Anglo-Irish one. By the time the *Miscellanies* began production in 1727, his reputation in England had already been solidified by such works as *A Tale of a Tub*, *Gulliver's Travels*, the 1711 *Miscellanies*, and various pirated collections. Consolidating his reputation as an Irish writer, however, required the new Faulkner effort. Because "anthologies help to mold both the reader's subjectivity—his or her imaginative interaction with the text—and the literary values that lead to a canon," this project was formative of a modern Irish identity for both the readers and the author.[38] Swift's more strictly literary identity was built upon, yet functioned to support, the political subjectivity that emerged from earlier works such as the *Drapier's Letters*.

When Swift began working with Faulkner on his *Collected Works*, the two men had already known and worked with each other for many years. One of Faulkner's first published pamphlets was *A Defense of the Conduct of the People of Ireland in their . . . Refusal of Mr. Wood's Copper-Money* (1724), a work related to the *Drapier's Letters*, though Swift and Faulkner did not meet until 1726, in London, ironically. In 1725, he printed the *Drapier's Letters* together in *Fraud Detected*, doing so without consulting Swift and sharing the copy with his London partner, William Bowyer, who produced his own edition in 1730 and imported it to Ireland via Faulkner. Faulkner also published *An Answer to the Ballyspellin Ballad* (1728) via an intermediary, John Worrall, whom Swift had asked to help him find an Irish publisher. Faulkner was working "in earnest" as Swift's printer by 1729 or 1730 when he printed *A Vindication of Lord Carteret*. In 1731 he was indicted for printing Swift's *Queries* related to parliamentary bills regarding the clergy in his *Dublin Journal;* he was pardoned in 1733. Swift may have opted to work with him on his complete works as early as 1732, and the first four volumes were produced in late 1734. Faulkner continued to publish Swift manuscripts, printing political works in his *Dublin Journal*, such as Swift's comments on a new scheme for copper halfpence in 1737 and *Directions to Servants* in 1745.[39] Swift's choice to work with Faulkner at this late stage in his life and career reflected a recognition that "his patriotic service to Ireland was the likeliest basis for an enduring reputation."[40] In short, Swift became the founding author of modern Anglo-Irish literature because his selection of a Dublin printer who continued to reprint his work well into the latter half of the eighteenth century helped guarantee his lasting reputation as an Irish author.

Swift's reasons for publishing his *Collected Works* with Faulkner seem to have stemmed from Pope's poor editing and a concern about payment for his contributions to the *Miscellanies*. He may also have chosen this path because British copyright laws did not apply to Ireland, making it possible for him to proceed without payments and delays associated with gaining these rights from booksellers and other copyholders, and because he could have more control over content by working in person with a Dublin printer. His complaints about the publication of the *Miscellanies* mainly concerned which texts the volumes used; Pope had been a poor editor of his prepublication manuscripts, he felt, and, as mentioned, had failed to include *A Libel on Dr. Delany* in the *Miscellanies* because Pope feared alienation from the court, from which he was seeking support.[41] In December 1732, Swift had written to Motte saying, "I am not at all satisfied with the last miscellany" and that he had "no advantage by any one of the four volumes"—no payment for them. He hints at the possibility that, because booksellers in Ireland had "no property" or copyright on what they published, Dublin printers might produce collections of his work that he would "neither encourage or oppose."[42] As McLaverty has written, Swift had already assigned the copyright of eighteen pieces to William Bowyer, Faulkner's London partner, between the years 1729 and 1733 even as he was corresponding with Motte and Pope about giving copyrights to them. In addition, Matthew Pilkington, who had been given the rights to several of Swift's writings, had begun to sell them to Bowyer and Faulkner. In fact, the Faulkner edition of Swift's complete works seems to have been well under way before Swift's 1732 letter to Motte, for *Miscellanies the Fifth*, published by Bowyer to rival the four volumes of *Miscellanies* published by Motte and Gilliver, made use of prepublication sheets from Faulkner's *Works*.[43] It was clear that a conflict was beginning to arise between the Bowyer-Faulkner partnership and the Motte-Gilliver one, though it is unclear whether Swift asserted any agency in fomenting it or whether he was at the mercy of various stakeholders in his works and reputation.

It was not long after Swift's *Collected Works* appeared in Dublin as a native manufacture and in London as an import that Motte brought a lawsuit against Faulkner for piracy against his copyright. The concern about piracy by Dublin printers over the previous decade had not been directed at Irish reprints that were sold in Ireland but at the sale of such reprints in England. In 1735, Motte won the lawsuit against Faulkner when the court issued an injunction stopping the sale of the *Works* in England. To clarify the law concerning this matter, a 1739 amendment to the 1709 English Copyright Act was passed that forbade the import of any book that was a reprint of a title originally published in England.[44] This law, though it may have dampened the Irish reprint business's profits from export to England, did not prevent Dublin printers from selling reprints in North America and other places in the British empire. Nor did it affect their domestic sales; not technically pirated, because of the lack of an Irish copyright law, Dublin reprints of English books continued to form the basis for a thriving home market.[45]

Swift's reaction to Motte's copyright case was an angry one that stands as documentation of the Irish book trade's reaction to this new twist in the copyright problem. It is significant in that it lists some of the reasons why Swift chose to publish his *Collected Works* in Ireland and because its emotion provides insight into Swift's split with London's trade and embrace of Ireland's. In the tradition of the textile/texts homology used in *A Proposal for the Universal Use of Irish Manufacture*, it compares the book trade to the wool trade by saying that both suffer from British oppression:

> [O]nly one thing I know, that the cruel Oppressions of this King-
> dom by England are not to be borne. You send what Books you
> please hither, and the Booksellers here can send nothing to you
> that is written here. As this is absolute Oppression, if I were a
> Bookseller in this Town, I would use all the safe Means to reprint
> *London* Books, and run them to any Town, in *England* that I
> could, because, whoever neither offends the Laws of God, or the
> Country he liveth in, committeth no Sin. It was the Fault of you
> and other Booksellers, who printed any Thing supposed to be
> mine, that you did not agree with each other to print them to-
> gether, if you thought they would sell to any Advantage. I believe
> I told you long ago that Mr. *Faulkner* came to me, and told me
> his intention to print every Thing that my Friends told him they

thought to be mine. . . . But I am so incensed against the Oppressions from *England*, and have so little Regard to the Laws they make, that I do as a Clergyman encourage the Merchants both to export Wool and Woollen Manufactures to any Country in *Europe*, or any where else. . . . And, so I would encourage our Booksellers here to sell your Authors Books printed here, and send them to all the Towns in *England*, if I could do it with Safety and Profit.[46]

This letter reads like a declaration of war against the London publishing industry, articulating why Swift was disappointed with it and why he should not be blamed for its failure to organize a project for his complete writings. The blame, he argues, lies not only with London booksellers, but with a British legal and political system that continually deprives Irish industries like the wool trade and the printing trade of the right to compete with their English counterparts. This letter, referred to by Irvin Ehrenpreis as "Swift's patriotic defence of Dublin booksellers," is evidence of resistance to a colonialism of a particularly culturally imperialistic kind.[47] Anglo-Irish print capitalism, in the context of this mid-1730s copyright dispute, seemed to unite the self-interest of the commercial enterprise with argumentation about political and economic sovereignty in a manner that consolidated the previous decades' efforts to build an Irish imagined community.

The *Collected Works* is thus testament to "the power of anthologists to shape national identity."[48] Through this collection and others to follow over the course of the eighteenth century, Faulkner took charge of a Swift culture industry that he had helped to create. He managed Swift's reputation as a patriot writer in a manner that located his Irish works as the ur-texts of an emergent Irish national canon. As Robert Mahony has argued, "Swift's own claim upon Irish memory" was established as a monument to his patriotism both by the anthology and by the marble bust of him for which Faulkner collected contributions from Dubliners of all classes.[49] In fact, Swift's Irish identity may have come to serve as a model for later patriot writers, themselves in search of an authorial identity and an imagined community for their writings.

Part of creating a national canon via an anthology is converting readers into writers and critics in their own right. Not only is literature turned into a commodity for readers in this anthologizing process, but the anthologies themselves "disseminate literary culture as purchasable elitism" or cultural capital to be used by them.[50] Swift's work retained a general audience, who began to take Anglo-Irish literature as a status symbol and as a proper object of criticism, and it attracted specialized readers involved in cultural production themselves. His Anglo-Irish coterie— people like Patrick and Mary Delany, Matthew and Laetitia Pilkington, Mary Barber, and Constantia Grierson—enhanced his reputation by publishing imitations and parodies of his work. These protégés thereby contributed to the canonization that his *Collected Works* intimated. Their work helped to constitute Anglo-Irish literature as a distinct category of the market in Irish books. By doing so, it participated in the delineation of academic disciplines, a phenomenon that emerged in the eighteenth century from a rapidly expanding print culture in need of a classification system.

The involvement of women, in particular, was crucial in the canonization of Swift, because they played such a large role in the marketing of anthologies and were beginning to be hailed as the main audience for literary works.[51] The rise of Anglo-Irish female writers clearly signifies a move towards a gendered sphere of letters. Constantia Grierson, Barber, and Laetitia Pilkington began to participate in Anglo-Irish cultural production. Whereas Barber and Laetitia Pilkington are usually considered imitators of Swift's style in their poetry and verse, Constantia Grierson tends to be regarded as a writer of a higher caliber. She brought literary imagination and technical ability to her work and was a noted editor and press corrector for the family business. These women modeled the performance of Swift appreciation, informing other women about his work but also enhancing their own reputations.

The 1730s were significant to this gendering process because the sphere of the literary began then to separate from the sphere of the political. Reflecting the broader English and Continental model of classifying literature as a private and domestic category—and therefore the province of women—the Irish book trade contributed to the segregation of a masculinized public sphere of political economy from a feminized private sphere of literary production and consumption.[52] There had begun to be some demand for domestic Anglo-Irish literature that, because it was frequently reprinted outside of its immediate political context, had come to serve more as fashion than as political instrument. These transformations in print culture are significant in that they are evidence of increasing literacy and a taste for the new distinctly Irish art. The splitting of the literary away from the overtly political textuality in eighteenth-century Ireland is an early instance of how niche markets for literatures depend on the conditioning of audiences by an initial, if not continuous, strategy of political exhortation and mobilization.

There is, as well, a more postmodern case to be made for the emergence of an autonomous literary sphere during the 1720s and 1730s. When Swift deployed satire in the 1720s, it had been generally for the purposes of political critique, in which case it could be taken as a parasite on actual events. When imitators began to parody his style, however, their works were becoming parasites on texts, undermining the power of the latter's polemic by mocking its seriousness. What was reified in this act of parody was style, not substance. What began to circulate in the 1730s was a purified form evacuated of serious political content; what was emerging was a taste for an Anglo-Irish literary style, not *realpolitick*.

Epilogue

A Brand Identity Crisis in a National Literature?

Explaining Jonathan Swift's role in the history of the Irish book is telling the story of a nation and its literature in the making. As the concept of imagined communities explains, modern nations are first created in the press, suggesting that the identity and sovereignty of the polity are inextricably bound to the success of their mediation in print. In Ireland's case, the print media, as Declan Kiberd has argued, invented the Irish nation before it had a state.[1] Swift was among the earliest major Anglo-Irish literary figures to participate in this invention, and he did so by exploiting the political potential of his country's book craftsmen. He understood the relationship of a nationalist press to state formation; as Kiberd reminds us, he "assumed the existence of a patriotic entity named 'Ireland' in order to prove a constitutional and economic one."[2] The ideology that arose from this process formed an Irish identity that continues to be the basis of ideas of national sovereignty. What Swift and contemporary Irish publishers brought into being was a national brand of print culture that made a proprietary claim to a distinct media market and enabled the formation of a public that eventually could be recognized as the state itself. On the first count, Anglo-Irish literature, a category of that new market, enhanced the prestige and value of Irish books; it promoted "the medium-as-brand," helping Irish publishing houses obtain a reputation.[3] On the second count, Dublin booksellers and their London affiliates were also selling Irishness as an identity signifying the nation. Swift's contribution to the invention of Ireland was staging it via a continuous branding event that helped constitute a national press and a political entity.

This "cultural branding," the building of a brand, turned Anglo-Irish literature into a cultural icon, an object of secular veneration digested and reproduced by consumers and citizens. As Douglas Holt has explained, some brands move beyond their significance in the marketplace to become synonymous with the nation. In his view, products that are very successful provide an "identity myth," a story that, like national narrative itself, works as a salve for "contradictions in the nation's culture." They evolve into "identity brands, the brands that have spun such compelling myths that they have become cultural icons." To again work within Swift's textile metaphor for national narrative, these identity myths are "useful fabrications" that repair "tears in the cultural fabric of the nation."[4] As Donald Keough, a major philanthropist to Irish studies organizations, has written, some commercial power brands, like Coca-Cola, become linked to political ideas such as "freedom, democracy, equality, and a new beginning" to the extent that they become identical to political ideology.[5] Anglo-Irish literature, a medium traditionally supplying Irish identity myths, is an iconic brand that maintains and revises the Irish nation's narrative of its origins and future. It is thus partially synonymous with the nation to the extent that "Ireland" could not be understood without it.

A problem has arisen, however, in the brand's management: globalization. Criticism and education have hitherto constituted the main means by which the brand of Anglo-Irish literature has been administered, and they have continually made it relevant in new historical circumstances. This cultivation of the brand is significant because it is related to the constitution of the sovereignty myth necessary for the state's maintenance of political and economic control. It is possible that the brand, however, is currently in a state of crisis as the process of globalization hybridizes and homogenizes identity, and with it the very concept of national sovereignty. "Ireland" itself—like "America," "India," and other national identities—has signified feelings, associations, and images characteristic of the era of the nation-state. Ireland's identity as a sovereign nation has been linked to its history of struggle with imperialism, colonialism, and other forms of military and cultural violence. The story of its overcoming of these obstacles has been typical of postcolonial countries' self-constitution as independent entities. As those countries have reconnected to or strengthened their connections with the outside world through the process of globalization, a gap has grown between the brand identity of the nation-state and its cultural brands. In Ireland, there has been an attenuation of the link between political sovereignty and cultural production, as cultural outlets have increasingly advertised global brands and their associative identity effects to the extent that consumers now identify less with national politics and more with what they are consuming. In general, there seems to have been a decline in the Irish national iconic brands that have helped bind national narrative to national consumption. In these circumstances, it is hard to make the case for Anglo-Irish literature's current political relevance within the country, although its creation and preparation for export does contribute to the building of the national identity globally in a manner that aids the tourism industry.

The recent meltdown in the global credit markets suggests that we may be moving into a new era in which nations must again consider the connections between their financial situation, issues of sovereignty, and the state of their national cultures. The history of an impoverished colony's understanding of those links and its remedies for its problems may inform our contemporary thinking about globalization and its effect on national cultural identity. Factions that included writers encouraged the rise of an Irish national culture industry that could form a public amenable to the political solutions they considered necessary to improve its condition, developments which may be instructive in the future. As globalization changes the environment in which national cultural brands exist, the question that we must ask is, "will we see another Swift?"

Abbreviations

BL   British Library
NLI   National Library of Ireland
PRO   Public Record Office (National Archives)
PRONI   Public Record Office of Northern Ireland
SP   State Papers Ireland
TCD   Trinity College Dublin

Introduction

1. Brewer, *The Sinews of Power*, xvii.
2. Colley, *Britons*, 71.
3. Hardt and Negri, *Empire*, 87.
4. Ehrenpreis, *Swift: The Man*, 3:616.
5. Sher, *Enlightenment and the Book*, 443.
6. McGrath, *The Making of the Eighteenth-Century Irish Constitution*, 25–26.
7. Ibid., 35–36.
8. Poovey, *A History of the Modern Fact*, 92–143.
9. Eccleshall, "Anglican Political Thought," 37.
10. Roncaglia, *Petty*, 5.
11. T. J. Kiernan, *History of the Financial Administration of Ireland*, 144–148.
12. McGrath, "Public Wealth," 177–178.
13. Rowley, *An Answer to a Book*, 40.
14. Berkeley, "Some Thoughts Touching an Irish Bank," Egmont Manuscripts, PRONI MSS T/3315/3/81.
15. King to Blake, Nov. 30, 1725, King Manuscripts, TCD MSS 750/8/59.
16. The evidence of this recruitment, especially for his *Drapier's Letters*, is discussed in James Woolley, "Poor John Harding and Mad Tom," 109; Ferguson, *Jonathan Swift and Ireland*, 96; O'Regan, *Archbishop William King*, 304, 313; and Baltes, *The Pamphlet Controversy about Wood's Halfpence*, 186.
17. Thompson, *Models of Value*, 22.
18. Cullen, "The Value of Contemporary Printed Sources," 150.

19. Cullen, "Problems in the Interpretation," 1.

20. Lecky, *The Leaders of Public Opinion in Ireland*, xviii–xix, 43.

21. McDowell, *Irish Public Opinion*, 30, 32.

22. Abercorn to Perceval, 2 June 1720, Egmont Manuscripts, PRONI MSS T/3315/2/34.

23. Macartny et al. to Perceval, 2 June 1720, Egmont Manuscripts, PRONI MSS T/3315/2/34.

24. *Reflections and Resolutions for the Gentlemen of Ireland*, 6, 20.

25. Siskin, *The Work of Writing*, 43.

26. Ibid., 9.

27. Ibid., 52.

28. Ibid., 38.

29. Ibid., 51.

30. Ibid., 11.

31. Anderson, *Imagined Communities*, 24.

32. Ibid., 15–16.

33. Adorno, *The Culture Industry*, 98–100.

34. Guillory, *Cultural Capital*, 305–306.

35. Brantlinger, *Fictions of State*, 35.

36. Ibid., 20.

37. Thompson, 21–22.

38. Sherman, *Finance and Fictionality*, 1–2.

39. Lynch, *The Economy of Character*, 81.

40. Ibid., 112.

41. Ingrassia, *Authorship, Commerce, and Gender*, 81.

42. Ibid., 16.

43. Nicholson, *Writing and the Rise of Finance*, xii–xiii.

44. Said, *The World, the Text, and the Critic*, 83–84.

45. Phiddian, "Have You Eaten Yet?" 609; Kumar, "World Bank Literature," passim.

46. Hawkes, *Idols of the Marketplace*, 19.

47. Goux, *Symbolic Economies*, 23.

48. Ibid., 45.

49. Parsons, "Money and Sovereignty," 62.

50. Ibid., 61.

51. Thompson, 21.

52. Ibid., 83.

53. Ehrenpreis, *Swift: The Man*, 3:722.

54. Ibid., 3:181.

55. Chakrabarty, *Provincializing Europe*, 62–71.

56. See Chapter 2 for the role of patronage and secret service money in publishing.

57. Price, "Introduction: Reading Matter," 9.

58. Darnton, *The Great Cat Massacre*, 223–224.

59. Johns, *The Nature of the Book*, 2–3; Maruca, *The Work of Print*, 5.

60. Eisenstein, *Printing Press*, 71–88, 113–126, and *Printing Revolution*, 42–88.

61. Darnton, *The Business of Enlightenment*, 3–4; Rose, "The History of Books," 87.

62. Darnton and Roche, *Revolution in Print*, vii–ix.

63. Chartier, *The Cultural Uses of Print*, 7, 11.

64. Zimmerman, *Swift's Narrative Satires*, 48.

65. Ibid., 88.

66. Pollard, *Dublin's Trade in Books*, 165–226.

67. Sher, 469.

68. Ibid., 445.

69. Young, "Satire as a Virus," 51.

70. Bullitt, *Jonathan Swift*, 50, 56–67.

71. Booth, *A Rhetoric of Irony*, 6, 105, 114, 120.

72. Leavis, "The Irony of Swift," 94.

73. Treadwell, "Swift's Relations with the London Book Trade," 17.

74. Booth, 101, 119.

75. Jameson, "Third World Literature," 80.

76. Szeman, "Who's Afraid of National Allegory," 804–805.

77. Jameson, 84.

78. Leyburn, *Satiric Allegory*, 8; Clifford, *The Transformations of Allegory*, 110–111.

79. Quilligan, *The Language of Allegory*, 156.

80. Zimmerman, 14.

81. Ehrenpreis, *Swift: The Man*, 3:701.

82. Zimmerman, 24.

83. Deane, *A Short History of Irish Literature*, 37; McDiarmid, *The Irish Art of Controversy*, passim.

84. Kiberd, *Irish Classics*, 85.

Chapter 1

1. The quotation used in the chapter title is from Jonathan Swift, *A Proposal that All the Ladies and Women of Ireland Should Appear Constantly in*

Irish Manufactures, in *Prose Works*, ed. Davis, 12:123. Hereafter in the text, works from this anthology will be cited parenthetically by the volume and page number.

2. Plummer, *The London Weaver's Company*, 292–314.

3. Probyn, "Jonathan Swift," 237.

4. Lefanu, *Catalogue of Books Belonging to Swift*, 24; Faulkner, *Catalogue of the Library of Dr. Swift*, 9.

5. Sher, *The Enlightenment and the Book*, 476.

6. Arnold, *Cultural Identities*, passim.

7. Branch, "Plain Style," 438; Trivedi, *Clothing Gandhi's Nation*, passim.

8. Baucom, *Out of Place*, 75–100; Webster, *Englishness and Empire*, 92–188.

9. McClintock, *Imperial Leather*, 207–231.

10. Viswanathan, *Masks of Conquest*, 2–3.

11. Mackie, *Market à la Mode*, 3.

12. Moretti, *The Way of the World*, 16.

13. Brewer, *The Sinews of Power*, xx.

14. Hardt and Negri, *Empire*, 87; Festa, *Sentimental Figures of Empire*, 51.

15. Branch, 442.

16. Goux, *Symbolic Economies*, 23.

17. Gibbons, *Edmund Burke and Ireland*, 235–236.

18. For some early modern political thought on the integration of the powers of printing and censorship into the monarch's body, see Bodin, *Six Books of the Commonwealth*, 34, 47, 181–185; and Hobbes, *Leviathan*, 228–239.

19. Berkeley, "Some Thoughts Touching an Irish Bank," Egmont Manuscripts, PRONI MSS T/3315/3/81.

20. Warner, *Licensing Entertainment*, 127, 179.

21. Lawrence, *The Interest of Ireland*, Preface. See Mahony's reference to the Lawrence antecedent to Swift in "Protestant Dependence," 83.

22. Ehrenpreis, *Swift: The Man*, 3:123.

23. Maruca, *The Work of Print*, 28.

24. Dunlevy, *Dress in Ireland*, 175.

25. Burke, *Riotous Performances*, 57.

26. Ibid., 57.

27. Jones and Stallybrass, *Renaissance Clothing*, 100.

28. Maruca, 3, 34.

29. Moxon, *Mechanick Exercises*, 2:227.

30. Ibid., 2:39.

31. Ibid., 2:201, 284–301.

32. Ibid., 2:301–308.

33. R. C., *Minerva*, 7.

34. Ibid., 18.

35. Ibid., 8.

36. Jonathan Swift, *Epilogue to a Play, for the Benefit of the Weavers in Ireland 1721*, in *Miscellanies*, 193.

37. Congreve, *Love For Love*, 12.

38. Jones and Stallybrass, 12.

39. Pocock, *Virtue, Commerce, and History*, 94.

40. Ibid., 94.

41. Bosteels, "The Obscure Subject," 296.

42. Pocock, *Virtue, Commerce, and History*, 94.

43. Johnston-Liik, *History of the Irish Parliament*, 3:194–195.

44. William Grimston, *The Lawyer's Fortune*, Preface.

45. Burke, 77.

46. Glendinning, *Jonathan Swift*, 101.

47. Rowley, *An Answer to a Book*, 37–38.

48. Lock, *Swift's Tory Politics*, 152–153.

49. Higgins, *Swift's Politics*, 8.

50. Ibid., 75.

51. Downie, *Jonathan Swift*, 83–84.

52. Oakleaf, *A Political Biography of Jonathan Swift*, 14–16.

53. Ibid., 12, 17; Moore, "Devouring Posterity," 680–681.

54. Pincus, *1688*, 369.

55. Speck, *Reluctant Revolutionaries*, 33, 57, 65.

56. Pincus, 393.

57. Ibid., 382–393.

58. Brewer, 207.

59. Pincus, 368.

60. Kramnick, *Bolingbroke and His Circle*, passim.

61. Rose, Craig, *England in the 1690s*, 132; Speck, *The Birth of Britain*, 19; Pincus, 30–31.

62. Rose, *England in the 1690s*, 136.

63. Habermas, *Structural Transformation*, 57–67.

64. Cowan, "Mr. Spectator," 346–347.

65. Gillespie, "Print Culture, 1550–1700," 3:29.

66. Said, *Culture and Imperialism*, xxi; Pollard, *Dublin's Trade in Books*, 30–31.

67. Anderson, *Imagined Communities*, 44.

68. Kennedy, *French Books*, 66–128.

69. Pollard, *Dublin's Trade in Books*, 36.

70. Kennedy, 6.

71. Pollard, *Dublin's Trade in Books*, 31.

72. Molyneux, *The Case of Ireland*, 17, 47–49.

73. McGrath, *The Making of the Eighteenth-Century Irish Constitution*, 134–169.

74. O'Regan, *Archbishop William King*, 108.

75. Ibid., 102.

76. McMinn, *Swift's Irish Pamphlets*, 14.

77. Barry, *Colony and Frontier*, passim; Canny, *Kingdom and Colony*, 12–13; V. G. Kiernan, "The Emergence of a Nation," 16–49, 19; Foster, *Modern Ireland*, 42, 45; Clarke, *Prelude to Restoration in Ireland*, 4; Clarke, "Patrick Darcy, 35–55, 36–37; Ohlmeyer, "Introduction," 4–5; Patrick Kelly, "Recasting a Tradition," 83–106, 85; Canny, "Identity Formation in Ireland," 159–212, 159; Canny, *Kingdom and Colony*, 12–13; ibid., 1–3, 5–6, 9, 14, 16–17; Brady, "The Road to the View," 25–45; Canny, *Kingdom and Colony*, 26–28; Canny, *Making Ireland British*, 123–129, 133, 247, 275, 556.

78. Howe, *Ireland and Empire*, 1.

79. Connolly, *Religion, Law, and Power*, 104–105.

80. Ibid., 4.

81. McGrath, *The Making of the Eighteenth-Century Irish Constitution*, 22.

82. Beckett, "Introduction," 4:xxxix.

83. Simms, "The Establishment of Protestant Ascendancy," 4:1.

84. York, *Neither Kingdom nor Nation*, 2.

85. Lloyd, *Ireland After History*, 7.

86. Gibbons, *Edmund Burke and Ireland*, 235–236.

87. Carpenter, "Introduction," xv–xvii.

88. Pollard, *Dublin's Trade in Books*, ix.

89. Ibid., ix–3.

90. Ibid., 37.

91. Ibid., 4–7.

92. Gillespie, "Print Culture," 3:29.

93. Pollard, *Dublin's Trade in Books*, 7–11.

94. Ibid., 31, 67, 71–72.

95. Ibid., 224, 67.

96. Ibid., 2, 17, 19.

97. McGrath, "Public Wealth," 174, 185, 198.

98. Ibid., 177.

99. Ibid.

100. Guha, *Dominance Without Hegemony*, 71–72.

101. Swift, *Correspondence*, 2:342–343; Hayton, "The Stanhope/Sunderland Ministry," 610–636.

102. Connolly, "Precedent and Principle," 130–158; Berman, 123–134.

103. Connolly, *Religion, Law, and Power*, 108.

104. Connolly, "Precedent and Principle," 132.

Chapter 2

1. Irwin, *To the Nobility, Gentry and Commonality of this Kingdom of Ireland*. NLI MSS 2256, Bank of Ireland Manuscripts.

2. NLI MSS 2256/7, Bank of Ireland Manuscripts.

3. Ryder, "The Bank of Ireland, 1721," 560–563.

4. O'Regan, *Archbishop William King*, 292.

5. Victory, "Colonial Nationalism in Ireland," 163.

6. Hall, *History of the Bank of Ireland*, 21–22.

7. Ryder, 558, 581.

8. *A Letter to the Gentlemen of the Landed Interest*, 16.

9. For the controversy over attributing this pamphlet to Swift, see *Prose Works*, ed. Davis, xxiv–xxvi; Ehrenpreis, *Swift: The Man* 3:135–137; and Fussell; Krappe; Matlack; and Weitzman.

10. Maruca, *The Work of Print*, 79–80.

11. Moxon, *Mechanick Exercises*, 13.

12. Coleborne, "The Dublin Grub Street"

13. Ingrassia, *Authorship, Commerce, and Gender*, 82.

14. Downie, "Secret Service Payments to Daniel Defoe," passim.

15. Woolley, "Poor John Harding and Mad Tom," 105; McCormack, "Reflections on Writing and Editing," 263–272.

16. Pocock, *Virtue, Commerce, and History*, 112.

17. Nicholson, *Writing and the Rise of Finance*, 70, 52.

18. Conolly to Grafton, 18 Oct. 1720, Castletown MSS T/2825/A/15, in O'Regan, 291.

19. King to Annesley, 24 Dec. 1720, King Manuscripts, in Ehrenpreis, *Swift: The Man*, 3:155.

20. Pearson to Bonnell, 12 Mar. 1719/20, Smyth of Barbavilla Papers, BL ADD MS 41,580/24.

21. Swift, *The Poems of Jonathan Swift*, ed. Harold Williams, 1:238–241. All quotations of this poem are from this edition.

22. Ibid., 1:248–259. All quotations of this poem are from the Williams edition.

23. Swift, *Complete Poems*, ed. Pat Rogers, 703.

24. Randolph, "Structural Design," 369. For a more thorough discussion of the "satiric norm" in Swift's writing, see Peterson, "The Satiric Norm of Jonathan Swift."

25. Randolph, 382, 13.

26. Rosenheim, *Swift and the Satirist's Art*, 184, 179–180.

27. Ibid., 184–185.

28. "Norms, Moral or Other," 9.

29. Zomchick, "Satire and the Bourgeois Subject," 348.

30. Ibid., 350.

31. de Bolla, *The Discourse of the Sublime*, 136.

32. Pocock, *Virtue, Commerce, and History*, 112.

33. P. G. M. Dickson, *The Financial Revolution*, 164–167.

34. Ibid., 170, 166–167, 178–180.

35. King to Stearne, 4 Oct. 1720, King Manuscripts, TCD MSS 8191/132.

36. King to George, 12 Oct. 1720, King Manuscripts, TCD MSS 8191/139.

37. Stearne to King, 9Oct. 1721, King Manuscripts, TCD MSS 1995–2008/1990.

38. O'Regan, *Archbishop William King*, 297.

39. Sherman, *Finance and Fictionality*, 46–47.

40. Though this piece is anonymous, it is generally authenticated as Swift's by the fact that it was printed by John Harding, the printer who published *Subscribers to the Bank Plac'd According to Their Order and Quality* and other pieces Swift was to write in this controversy.

41. For more on the authorship of this pamphlet, see Swift, *Prose Works*, 9:xix.

42. Moxon, 2:357.

43. All citations from this poem are from Swift, *The Poems of Jonathan Swift*, ed. Williams, 1:286–288.

44. Ryder, 581.

45. Ibid., 60–61.

46. Ibid., Postscript.

47. Ibid., 4–6.

48. For an assessment of the role of private banks, clergymen, and other constituencies in the bank debate, see Moore, "Satiric Norms," 44–54.

49. Misolestes, *Objections Against the General Bank in Ireland*, 2–3.

50. Ibid., 3.

51. Ibid.

52. Ibid.

53. Irwin, *The Phoenix*, 4.

54. Ibid., 5, 12.

55. *A Letter to the Gentlemen of the Landed Interest in Ireland*, 16.

56. Ibid., 16–17.

57. Cullen, "The Value of Contemporary Printed Sources," 150, 153.

Chapter 3

1. Ehrenpreis, *Swift: The Man*, 3:749–750.

2. Treadwell, "Swift's Relations with the London Book Trade," 12–13; Treadwell, "Benjamin Motte, Andrew Tooke and *Gulliver's Travels*," 297.

3. Ehrenpreis, *Swift: The Man*, 3:776–777.

4. Treadwell, "Swift's Relations with the London Book Trade," 14.

5. Ehrenpreis, *Swift: The Man*, 3:828–831.

6. Pollard, *Dictionary of Members of the Dublin Book Trade*, 254.

7. Ibid., 133.

8. Ibid., 571.

9. Treadwell, "Swift's Relations with the London Book Trade," 9–11, 20–27.

10. *Dictionary of National Biography*, "Benjamin Tooke"; Treadwell, "Benjamin Motte," 293–299

11. Pollard, *Dictionary of Members of the Dublin Book Trade*, 304–307.

12. Ibid., 198–205.

13. Sher, *The Enlightenment and the Book*, 2, 14–17.

14. Zimmerman, *Swift's Narrative Satires*, 88.

15. Though the title page of this pamphlet says it was "*Written by Dean SWIFT*," it is considered unlikely to be his work. See Harold Williams's critique of Hermann Teerink's attribution in "Review [untitled]," 370. See also the English Short-Title Catalogue entry for this work.

16. Swift, *A Tale of a Tub and Other Works*, xii–xv.

17. Ibid., 106.

18. Ibid., 104.

19. Saccamano, "Authority and Publication," 258.

20. Swift, *A Tale of a Tub*, 107.

21. Ibid., 115.

22. Ibid., 109.

23. Ibid., 112, 115–117.

24. Treadwell, "Benjamin Motte," 290; Johns, *The Nature of the Book*, 259–262.

25. Treadwell, "Benjamin Motte," 290–291.

26. Ellis, "No Apologies, Dr. Swift," 75.

27. Treadwell, "Swift's Relations with the London Book Trade," 11.

28. Hansard, *Typographia*, 180–182.

29. A. Z., "Memorials of the Family Tooke," 604.

30. Swift, *A Tale of a Tub*, 110–115.

31. Schmitt, *Political Theology*, 36–37.

32. Weinbrot, *Menippean Satire Reconsidered*, 115.

33. Thorne, "Thumbing Our Nose," 533.

34. Ibid., 536–537.

35. McDowell, "Defoe and the Contagion of the Oral," 95.

36. Stallybrass and White, *The Politics and Poetics of Transgression*, 103.

37. Weinbrot, 11.

38. Ibid., 7, 24.

39. Nokes, *Jonathan Swift, A Hypocrite Reversed*, 99.

40. Phiddian, *Swift's Parody*, 140. See also Walsh, "Text, 'Text,' and Swift's *A Tale of a Tub*," 87; Probyn, "'Haranguing Upon Texts,'" 189; and Wyrick, *Jonathan Swift and the Vested Word*, 33.

41. Plato, "Phaedrus," 521.

42. Ibid., 528.

43. Derrida, *Dissemination*, 76.

44. Karian, "Reading the Material Text," 531, 538.

45. Swift, *A Tale of a Tub*, 33.

46. Wyrick, 32.

47. Swift, *A Tale of a Tub*, 39.

48. Ibid., 65.

49. Ibid., 66.

50. Weinbrot, 119–120.

51. Ibid., 67.

52. Walsh, "Swift and Religion," 169.

53. Mueller, "*A Tale of a Tub* and Early Prose," 202.

54. Maruca, *The Work of Print*, 13.

55. Eagleton, *The Ideology of the Aesthetic*, 36; Moretti, *The Way of the World*, 16; Lawrence Klein, *Shaftesbury and the Culture of Politeness*, 197.

56. Johns, *The Nature of the Book*, 28.

57. Siskin, *The Work of Writing*, 52, 21, 26, 88.

58. Lloyd, *Ireland After History*, 35–36.

59. Lloyd, *Anomalous States*, 42.

60. Fabricant, *Swift's Landscape*, 24.

61. *A Paradox. The Best Perfume.*

62. Berman, *Berkeley and Irish Philosophy*, 80–81; Esty, "Excremental Postcolonialism," 26–28; Gibbons, *Edmund Burke and Ireland*, 235–236.

63. Sher, 443.

64. Ashcroft, Griffiths, and Tiffin, *The Empire Writes Back*, 1–4; Armah, *The Beautyful Ones*, 9.

65. Langford, *A Polite and Commercial People*, 1–7.
66. Derrida, "Economimesis," 3.
67. Lloyd, *Anomalous States*, 54.
68. Habermas, *Structural Transformation*, passim.
69. Ashfield and de Bolla, "Introduction," 1.
70. Shaftesbury, *Characteristicks of Men*, 1:59–60.
71. Ibid., 1:55.
72. Ibid., 1:38–39.
73. Ibid., 1:44–45.
74. Ibid., 1:39.
75. Klein, *Shaftesbury and the Culture of Politeness*, 125, 153.
76. Shaftesbury, 1:62.
77. Ayers, "Introduction," xvi.
78. Horkheimer and Adorno, *Dialectic of Enlightenment*, 94.
79. Bond, *The Spectator*, 530, 529.
80. *The Tatler*, 4:140.
81. Ayres, xxvii.
82. Richards, *Rhetoric and Courtliness in Early Modern Literature*, passim.
83. Klein, *Shaftesbury*, 197.
84. Cowan, "Mr. Spectator and the Coffeehouse Public Sphere," 351.
85. Ibid., 4.
86. Nash, *Wild Enlightenment*, 11.
87. Thorne, 536–537.
88. Habermas, passim.
89. Downie, *Robert Harley and the Press*, 1–15; Downie, "Secret Service Payments," 440.
90. Downie, "Public and Private," 74.
91. Regan, "'Pranks Unfit for Naming,'" 53; Stallybrass and White, 94.
92. Anderson, *Imagined Communities*, 24, 28.
93. Ibid., 30.
94. Ingrassia, *Authorship, Commerce, and Gender*, 4.
95. Goux, *Symbolic Economies*, 29.
96. Gee, "The Sewers," 103.
97. Nicholson, *Writing and the Rise of Finance*, 8.
98. Lee, *Swift and Scatological Satire*, 81–82. For psychoanalytic interpretations of Swift's scatology, see Norman Brown; Ehrenpreis, *The Personality of Jonathan Swift*; Manousos; Murray; and Voigt.
99. Lee, 7–9.
100. Ibid., 37–38.
101. Gee, 106.

102. Lee, 39.

103. Braverman, "Satiric Embodiments," 83.

104. Lockwood, "Fielding and the Licensing Act," 379–393.

105. Eagleton, 41.

106. See Mason, "The Quack Has Become God."

107. All of these references are to Jonathan Swift, *Miscellanies*.

108. This translation appears only in the original pamphlet, not the version in the *Miscellanies*. See Don Fartinhando Puffindorst, *The Benefit of Farting Explain'd*, 7.

109. Swift, *Miscellanies*, title page.

110. Ibid., title page, Postscript.

111. Neill, "Broken English and Broken Irish," 3.

112. Carroll, "Barbarous Slaves and Civil Cannibals," 69.

113. Spenser, *A View of the State of Ireland*, 94; Milton, *Works*, 3:303–304.

114. Lee, 71.

115. Esty, 33–35.

116. Blackwell, "The Two Jonathans," 129–149.

117. Gibbons, 172.

118. Thorne, 541.

119. There has been some debate as to whether *Gulliver's Travels* is a specifically Tory opposition text. See Oakleaf, *Political Biography of Jonathan Swift*, 183–201.

120. McLaverty, "The Failure of the Swift-Pope *Miscellanies*," 136. See Chapter 6 for a more detailed discussion of the *Miscellanies* project.

121. McKeon, *Origins of the English Novel*, 351.

122. Hunter, "*Gulliver's Travels* and the Novel," 69.

123. Watt, *The Rise of the Novel*, 28; McKeon, 352.

124. Hunter, 66.

125. Ehrenpreis, *Swift: The Man*, 3:444, Ferguson, *Jonathan Swift and Ireland*, 135.

126. Ehrenpreis, *Swift: The Man*, 3:444.

127. Treadwell, "Benjamin Motte," 296–299.

128. Treadwell, "The Text of *Gulliver's Travels*," 67–68, 75–78.

129. Treadwell, "Observations on the Printing of *Gulliver's Travels*," 174, 171; Pollard, *Dictionary*, 203.

130. Pollard, *Dictionary of Members of the Dublin Book Trade*, 203, 305.

131. Gaonkar, *Alternative Modernities*, 17.

132. Ibid., 8–9.

133. Mahony, "Swift, Postcolonialism, and Irish Studies," 217–235; Boyle, *Swift as Nemesis*, xii.

134. Boyle, 31.

135. Gaonkar, 1–2.

136. Swift, *Gulliver's Travels*, 248.

137. Hawes, *The British Eighteenth Century*, 142, 147.

138. Ibid., 145.

139. Swift, *Gulliver's Travels*, 154.

140. Ibid.

141. Ibid., 155.

142. Ibid.

143. Hawes, *The British Eighteenth Century*, 150.

144. Ibid., 146.

145. Ibid., 146–147.

146. Locke, *An Essay Concerning Human Understanding*, 439.

147. Ibid., 442.

148. Ibid., 407–408.

149. Swift, *Gulliver's Travels*, 157.

150. Louis, *Swift's Anatomy of Misunderstanding*, 22–23.

151. Rodino, "Splendide Mendax," 1062.

152. Swift, *Gulliver's Travels*, 65–66.

153. Ibid., 122.

154. For recent critics who have written about the "Sinon problem," see Castle, "Why the Houyhnhnms Don't Write," 390, 379, 393; Zimmerman, *Swift's Narrative Satires*, 140, 139, 35, 17–18, 13; Rawson, *God, Gulliver, and Genocide*, 45; Passman, "An Allusion to Mandeville," 206, 206–207, 207; and Rodino, 1059–1060, 1063, 1060, 1066.

155. Hunter, 68–69.

156. Ibid., 66.

157. McKeon, 352–353.

158. Swift, *Gulliver's Travels*, 54, 64.

159. Ibid., 74.

160. Ibid., 84–85.

161. Louis, 135.

162. Swift, *Gulliver's Travels*, 123.

163. Ibid., 123, 124–125.

164. Ibid., 125.

165. Ibid., 28–29.

166. Louis, 149–150.

Chapter 4

1. Swift, *Prose Works*, 10:61.

2. Aravamudan, *Tropicopolitans*, 18.

3. Hawkes, *Idols of the Marketplace*, 19.

4. Woolley, "Poor John Harding and Mad Tom," 109; Ferguson, *Jonathan Swift and Ireland*, 96; O'Regan, *Archbishop William King*, 304, 313; Baltes, *The Pamphlet Controversy about Wood's Halfpence*, 186.

5. Maruca, *The Work of Print*, 3, 28.

6. Ibid., 63, 106, 108.

7. Gillespie, "Select Documents XLII," 415.

8. Ibid., 416.

9. Ibid., 415.

10. Ibid., 414.

11. Parsons, "Money and Sovereignty," 61.

12. Fauske, *Jonathan Swift*, 111.

13. Ehrenpreis, *Swift: The Man*, 3:192.

14. Midleton to Abbadis, 21 Sept. 1723, State Papers Ireland, SP63/381/135; King to Hopkins, 11 Dec. 1722, King Manuscripts, TCD MSS 750/7/246; King to Lord King, 19 Jan. 1725, King Manuscripts, TCD MSS 750/8/75; James Kelly, "Harvests and Hardship," 69; Maxwell, *Mr. Maxwell's Second Letter to Mr. Rowley*, 6.

15. A copy of William Wood's royal patent for coining copper halfpence and farthings is at PRO SP63/380/187.

16. Johnston, *Bishop Berkeley's Querist*, 45.

17. King to Southwell, 9 June 1724, King Manuscripts, TCD MSS 2537/110.

18. King to Gorge, 17 Oct., 1724, King Manuscripts, TCD MSS 2537/279; King to Lord King, 6 Dec. 1726, King Manuscripts, TCD MSS 750/8/163; King to Southwell, 9 June 1724, King Manuscripts, TCD MSS 2537/110.

19. Beckett, "Swift and the Anglo-Irish Tradition," 151–165, 158.

20. Connolly, "Swift and Protestant Ireland," 28–46, 40.

21. Baltes, *The Pamphlet Controversy about Wood's Halfpence*, 186, 186n196, 186n197.

22. James Kelly, "Jonathan Swift and the Irish Economy," 7.

23. Rowley, *An Answer to a Book*, 40.

24. Johnston-Liik, *History of the Irish Parliament*, 1:395.

25. Chartier, *The Cultural Origins of the French Revolution*, 37.

26. Gunn, "Public Opinion," 247–265, 251.

27. Baltes, 135.

28. Ann Cline Kelly, "The Birth of Swift," 13–23.

29. Baker, *Inventing the French Revolution*, 86.

30. Crow, *Painters and Public Life*, 5.

31. Mah, "Phantasies of the Public Sphere," 168.

32. Ozouf, "'Public Opinion at the End of the Old Regime," S1–S21.

33. Dean, *Publicity's Secret*, passim.

34. Pocock, *Virtue, Commerce, and History*, 68, 61.

35. Ibid., 97.

36. Pocock, *Virtue, Commerce, and History*, 68, 61, 97.

37. King to Hopkins, 21 July 1722, King Manuscripts, TCD MSS 750/7/166.

38. King to Gorge, 12 Dec. 1724, King Manuscripts, TCD MSS 2537/195.

39. Ehrenpreis, *Swift: The Man*, 3:254–255.

40. Revenue Commissioners to Hopkins, 7 Aug. 1722, PRO SP63/380/110.

41. Midleton to Abbadis, 21 Sept. 1723, PRO SP 63/381/135.

42. King to Grafton, 10 July 1722, King Manuscripts, TCD MSS 750/7/159.

43. PRO SP63/384/19.

44. PRO SP63/383/231.

45. PRO SP63/384/38.

46. King to Molyneux, 6 Apr, 1723, King Manuscripts, TCD MSS 750/7/329.

47. PRO SP63/384/156.

48. PRO SP63/383/209.

49. King to Hopkins, 11 Dec. 1722, King Manuscripts, TCD MSS 750/7/246.

50. PRO SP63/384/141.

51. Newman, *Early Paper Money of America*, 134.

52. Ehrenpreis, *Swift: The Man*, 3:188.

53. Fabricant, "Speaking for the Irish Nation," 352.

54. Boylan and Foley, *Political Economy and Colonial Ireland*, 2.

55. Rashid, "The Irish School of Economic Development," 346.

56. Ibid., 347.

57. Poovey, *A History of the Modern Fact*, 94–95.

58. Ibid., 98–99.

59. Cullen, "Value of Contemporary Printed Sources," 154.

60. Rashid, 347.

61. Cullen, "Value of Contemporary Printed Sources," 147.

62. Thompson, *Models of Value*, 21, 83.

63. Ibid., 44–45.

64. Aravamudan, 274–275.

Chapter 5

1. Smith, "Towards a 'Participatory Rhetoric,'" 136–137.

2. Culler, *On Deconstruction*, 34–35.

3. Phiddian, "Have You Eaten Yet?," 618; Culler, 34.

4. Joyce, *Ulysses*, 187.

5. I would like to thank Professors Sarah Sherman and James Woolley for comments on drafts of this chapter.

6. Mandeville, *A Modest Defence of Public Stews*, 14.

7. Ibid., Preface.

8. Ibid.

9. Barthes, *Image, Music, Text*, 147; Derrida, *Dissemination*, 76; Plato, "Phaedrus," 523; Swift, *A Tale of a Tub*, 34.

10. Mandeville, Preface.

11. Ibid.

12. Mandell, "Bawds and Merchants," 112.

13. Nicholson, *Writing and the Rise of Finance*, 103.

14. Swift, *Correspondence*, 3:278.

15. Nicholson, 3.

16. Downie, "Public and Private," 59.

17. Bacon, *The Essays; or, Councils, Civil and Moral*, 20.

18. Marana, *Eight Volumes of Letters*, 130.

19. Forman, *Second Letter to Walpole*, 38.

20. Bolingbroke, "Vampires."

21. Ingrassia, *Authorship, Commerce, and Gender*, 3.

22. Ibid., 41.

23. Pope, *The Dunciad Variorum*, lines 1–44.

24. Ingrassia, 50.

25. Ibid., 53.

26. Pope, line 7.

27. For a comparison of the use of "melancholy" and the cannibal theme in *A Modest Proposal* and *Cato's Letters*, see Higgins, *Swift's Politics*, 190–192.

28. Rawson, *God, Gulliver, and Genocide*, 240.

29. Nokes, *Jonathan Swift*, 348.

30. Woolley, "Sarah Harding," 165–166.

31. Ibid., 167.

32. Ibid., 168.

33. Higgins, 190.

34. Scriblerus, "Peri Bathos," 10:345.

35. de Bolla, *The Discourse of the Sublime*, 65.

36. Furniss, *Edmund Burke's Aesthetic Ideology*, 235.

37. Scriblerus, 10:345–346.

38. Bell, "'Not Lucre's Madman,'" 53.

39. Scriblerus, 10:345.

40. Ibid., 10:348.

41. Bell, "Not Lucre's Madman," 54.

42. Laura Brown, "Reading Race and Gender," 429.

43. Hawes, "Three Times Round the Globe," 198.

44. Aravamudan, *Tropicopolitans*, 18.

45. Ehrenpreis, *Swift: The Man*, 3:155.

46. James Kelly, "Harvests and Hardship," 72–89.

47. Ferguson, *Jonathan Swift and Ireland*, 170.

48. Swift and Sheridan, *The Intelligencer*, 198.

49. Rawson, 242.

50. Barnard, *A New Anatomy of Ireland*, 323; James Kelly, "Harvests," 102.

51. Legg, "Money and Reputations," 75–76; Johnston-Liik, *History of the Irish Parliament*, 6:114.

52. *Reflections on the National Debt*, 12.

53. James Kelly, "Harvests," 72–89; Coghill to Perceval, 5 Apr. 1729, Southwell Papers, BL ADD MS 47032/107—9, Public Record Office of Northern Ireland copy.

54. King to Grafton, 10 July 1722, King Manuscripts, TCD MSS 750/7/159.

55. King, "Taxation of Ireland," 297–298.

56. Carpenter, "Two Possible Sources," 147–148; Coleborne, "We Flea the People," 132–133.

57. Rawson, 243.

58. Swift, *The Poems of Jonathan Swift*, ed. Harold Williams, 3:772–782, lines 9–22.

59. Coghill to Southwell, 18 June 1728, Southwell Papers, HM 28675, Public Record Office of Northern Ireland copy.

60. Swift, *The Poems of Jonathan Swift*, ed. Williams, 3:772–773.

61. Ibid., 847, 851; Swift and Sheridan, 206; Johnston-Liik, 6:250, 3:53.

62. Mahony, "Protestant Dependence," 94.

63. Swift, *The Poems of Jonathan Swift*, ed. Williams, 3:859–861.

64. Swift, *Correspondence*, 3:341–342.

65. *Journals of the House of Lords*, 86–87.

66. McGrath, "'Public Wealth,'" 182.

67. Ibid., 178–183.

68. Ibid., 181.

69. McGrath, "Central Aspects of the Constitutional Framework," 18.

70. Swift, *Correspondence*, 3:372–373.

71. Coghill to Southwell, 13 Nov. 1729, Southwell Papers, BL ADD MS 21122/95-6, Public Record Office of Northern Ireland copy; Hayton, *The Letters of Marmaduke Coghill*, 78 n260

72. Johnston-Liik, 3:444.

73. Ibid., 1:423.

74. DePorte, "*Vinum Daemonum*," 56–68; Cullen, "Economic Development, 1750–1800," 177; McCracken, "The Political Structure, 1714–60," 46; McDowell, "Ireland in 1800," 673.

75. Johnston-Liik, 1:423.

76. James Kelly, "Jonathan Swift and the Irish Economy," 34.

77. James Kelly, "Swift on Money and Economics," 140.

78. Johnston-Liik, 1:425.

79. Nicholson, 22.

80. Booth, *A Rhetoric of Irony*, 105.

81. Real, *Securing Swift*, 185.

Chapter 6

1. Probyn, "Jonathan Swift at the Sign of the Drapier," 226–228.

2. Habermas, *Structural Transformation*, 29.

3. Kiberd, *Inventing Ireland*, 4.

4. Berkeley, *The Querist*, 21–22.

5. Sher, *The Enlightenment and the Book*, 450.

6. Benedict, *Making the Modern Reader*, 3.

7. Griffith, "Mobilising Office, Education and Gender" 65.

8. Carpenter, "Introduction," ix.

9. Pollard, *Dictionary of Members of the Dublin Book Trade*, ix; Pollard, *Dublin's Trade in Books*, 3–11, 37.

10. Griffith, 65; Barnard, "Print Culture," 53–54.

11. Faulkner, *The Humble Petition*.

12. San Juan, "The Anti-Poetry of Jonathan Swift," 27; Peake, "Swift on Poets and Poetry," 97; Fischer, Mell, and Vieth, *Contemporary Studies of Swift's Poetry*, 13.

13. Ferguson, *Jonathan Swift and Ireland*, 181; Swift, *Prose Works*, 12:xxi.

14. Sundell, "A Savage and Unnatural Taste," 90.

15. Pilkington, *An Infallible Scheme*, 4.

16. Moxon, *Mechanick Exercises*, 356–357.

17. Pilkington, 12–13.

18. Ehrenpreis, *Swift: The Man*, 658; Swift, *The Poems of Jonathan Swift*, ed. Harold Williams, 471.

19. Swift, *The Poems of Jonathan Swift*, ed. Williams, 2:470–486.

20. Brynn, "Repercussions of Union on Church of Ireland," 286.

21. Karian, "Edmund Curll," 121, 127–128: McLaverty, "The Failure of the Swift-Pope *Miscellanies*," 134.

22. McLaverty, 138.

23. Said, *The World, the Text, and the Critic*, 66.

24. Ehrenpreis, *Swift: The Man*, 3:776–777.

25. Swift, *The Poems of Jonathan Swift*, ed. Williams, 2:634, lines 49–56. Further citations from this poem are from this edition, pages 2:628–638.

26. George Mayhew, *Rage or Raillery*, 109.

27. Ibid., 112.

28. Archbishop Hugh Boulter to Duke of Dorset, 21 Apr. 1731. In Woolley, *Swift's Later Poems*, 129.

29. Swift, *The Poems of Jonathan Swift*, ed. Williams, 2:643–644, lines 105–116. Further citations from this poem are from this edition pages 2:639–659.

30. Maurice Johnson, *The Sin of Wit*, 15.

31. Conlon, "Original Swift," 72.

32. Mell, "Irony, Poetry, and Swift," 319, 324.

33. Ehrenpreis, *Swift: The Man*, 3:777; Mayhew, 109–110.

34. Swift to Pope, 26 Nov. 1725, Swift, *Correspondence*, 3:102. Quoted in Harth, "Swift's Self-Image as a Satirist," 115–116.

35. Harth, "Friendship and Politics," 241–247.

36. Ibid., 246.

37. Benedict, 17.

38. Ibid., 6.

39. Pollard, "George Faulkner," 79–96.

40. Mahony, *Jonathan Swift*, 1.

41. McLaverty, 143–144.

42. Swift to Motte, 9 Dec. 1732, Swift, *Correspondence*, 4:89–90.

43. McLaverty, 139–143.

44. Phillips, *Printing and Bookselling in Dublin*, 104–105.

45. Sher, 448, 467.

46. Swift to Motte, 25 May 1736, Swift, *Correspondence*, 4:493–494.

47. Ehrenpreis, *Swift: The Man*, 3:789.

48. Price, *The Anthology and the Rise of the Novel*, 3.

49. Mahony, *Jonathan Swift*, xiii, 11–12.

50. Benedict, 109.

51. Ibid., 111–127.

52. Armstrong, *Desire and Domestic Fiction*, passim.

Epilogue

1. Kiberd, *Inventing Ireland*, 4.
2. Kiberd, *Irish Classics*, 85.
3. Naomi Klein, *No Logo*, 44.
4. Holt, *How Brands Become Icons*, 11, xi, 5, 8.
5. Keough, "The Importance of Brand Power," 18, 26.

Adorno, Theodor W. *The Culture Industry: Selected Essays on Mass Culture.* Edited by J. M. Bernstein. London: Routledge, 1991.

Anderson, Benedict. *Imagined Communities: Reflections on the Origins and Spread of Nationalism.* London: Verso, 1983.

Appleby, Joyce. *Economic Thought and Ideology in Seventeenth-Century England.* Princeton: Princeton University Press, 1978.

———. *Liberalism and Republicanism in the Historical Imagination.* Cambridge: Harvard University Press, 1992.

Aravamudan, Srinivas. *Tropicopolitans: Colonialism and Agency, 1688–1804.* Durham: Duke University Press, 1999.

Armah, Ayi Kwei. *The Beautyful Ones Are Not Yet Born.* Portsmouth, N.H.: Heinemann, 1968.

Armstrong, Nancy. *Desire and Domestic Fiction: A Political History of the Novel.* Oxford: Oxford University Press, 1987.

Arnold, Dana, ed. *Cultural Identities and the Aesthetics of Britishness.* Manchester, England: Manchester University Press, 2004.

Ashcroft, Bill, Gareth Griffiths, and Helen Tiffin. *The Empire Writes Back: Theory and Practice in Post-Colonial Literatures.* London: Routledge, 1989.

Ashfield, Andrew, and Peter de Bolla, eds. "Introduction." In *The Sublime: A Reader in British Eighteenth-Century Aesthetic Theory,* 1–16. Cambridge: Cambridge University Press, 1996.

Ayres, Philip, ed. "Introduction." In *Characteristicks of Men, Manners, Opinions, Times,* by the 3rd Earl of Shaftesbury, xiii–xxxviii. Oxford: Clarendon Press, 1999.

"A.Z." "Memorials of the Family Tooke," *Gentleman's Magazine* (Dec. 1839): 602–606.

Bacon, Francis. *The Essays; or Councils, Civil and Moral.* London, 1701.

Baker, Keith Michael. *Inventing the French Revolution: Essays on French Political Culture in the Eighteenth Century.* Cambridge: Cambridge University Press, 1990.

Baltes, Sabine. *The Pamphlet Controversy about Wood's Halfpence (1722–25) and the Tradition of Irish Constitutional Nationalism.* Frankfurt: Peter Lang, 2003.

Bank of Ireland Manuscripts. National Library of Ireland, Dublin.

Barnard, Toby. *A New Anatomy of Ireland: The Irish Protestants, 1649–1770.* New Haven: Yale University Press, 2003.

———. "Print Culture, 1700–1800." In *The Irish Book in English, 1550–1800,* edited by Raymond Gillespie and Andrew Hadfield, 34–60. Oxford: Oxford University Press, 2006.

Barry, T. B., ed. *Colony and Frontier in Medieval Ireland.* London: Hambledon Press, 1995.

Barthes, Roland. *Image, Music, Text.* Translated by Stephen Heath. New York: Hill & Wang, 1977.

Baucom, Ian. *Out of Place: Englishness, Empire, and the Locations of Identity.* Princeton: Princeton University Press, 1999.

Beckett, J. C. "Introduction: Eighteenth-Century Ireland." In vol. 4 of *A New History of Ireland,* edited by T. W. Moody and W. E. Vaughn, xxxix–lxiv. Oxford: Clarendon Press, 1986.

———. "Swift and the Anglo-Irish Tradition." In *The Character of Swift's Satire: A Revised Focus,* edited by Claude Rawson, 151–165. Newark: University of Delaware Press, 1983.

Bell, Ian. " 'Not Lucre's Madman': Pope, Money, and Independence." In *Alexander Pope: Essays for the Tercentenary,* edited by Colin Nicholson, 53–67. Aberdeen, Scotland: Aberdeen University Press, 1989.

Benedict, Barbara. *Making the Modern Reader: Cultural Mediation in Early Modern Literary Anthologies.* Princeton: Princeton University Press, 1996.

Berkeley, George. *The Querist, Containing Several Queries, Proposed to the Consideration of the Public.* London, 1736.

———. "Some Thoughts Touching an Irish Bank." Egmont Manuscripts, MSS T/3315/3. Public Record Office of Northern Ireland.

———. *The Works of George Berkeley Bishop of Cloyne.* Edited by A. A. Luce and T. E. Jessop. 9 vols. London: Thomas Nelson & Sons Ltd., 1953.

Berman, David. *Berkeley and Irish Philosophy.* London: Continuum, 2005.

———. "The Irish Pragmatist." In *Archbishop William King and the Anglican Irish Context, 1688–1729,* edited by Christopher J. Fauske, 123–134. Dublin: Four Courts Press, 2004.

Black, Stephanie. *Life and Debt.* New York: New Yorker Films, 2001.

Blackwell, Mark R. "The Two Jonathans: Swift, Smedley, and the Outhouse Ethos." In *Locating Swift: Essays from Dublin on the 250th Anniversary of the Death of Jonathan Swift, 1667–1745,* edited by Aileen Douglas, Patrick Kelly, and Ian Campbell Ross, 129–149. Dublin: Four Courts Press, 1998.

Bodin, Jean. *Six Books of the Commonwealth.* Translated by M. J. Tooley. Oxford: Basil Blackwell, 1955.

Bolingbroke, Henry. "Vampires in England." *The Country Journal: Or, the Crafts-man* 307 (May 20, 1732). Reel 940, *English Literary Periodicals of the 17th, 18th, and 19th Centuries*. Ann Arbor, Mich.: University Microfilms International, 1976.

Bond, Donald F., ed. *The Spectator*. Oxford: Clarendon Press, 1965.

Booth, Wayne. *A Rhetoric of Irony*. Chicago: University of Chicago Press, 1974.

Bosteels, Bruno. "The Obscure Subject: Sovereignty and Geopolitics in Carl Schmitt's *The Nomos of the Earth*." *South Atlantic Quarterly* 104.2 (Spring 2005): 295–305.

Bowers, Toni. *The Politics of Motherhood: British Writing and Culture, 1680–1760*. Cambridge: Cambridge University Press, 1996.

Boylan, Thomas A., and Timothy P. Foley. *Political Economy and Colonial Ireland: The Propagation and Ideological Function of Economic Discourse in the Nineteenth Century*. London: Routledge, 1992.

Boyle, Frank. *Swift as Nemesis: Modernity and Its Satirist*. Stanford: Stanford University Press, 2000.

Brady, Ciaran. "The Road to the View: On the Decline of Reform Thought in Tudor Ireland." In *Spenser and Ireland: An Interdisciplinary Perspective*, edited by Patricia Coughlan, 25–45. Cork: Cork University Press, 1989.

Branch, Lori. "Plain Style; or, the High Fashion of Empire: Colonialism, Resistance and Assimilation in Adam Smith's *Lectures on Rhetoric and Belles Lettres*." *Studies in Scottish Literature (SSL)* 33–34 (2004): 435–453.

Brantlinger, Patrick. *Fictions of State: Culture and Credit in Britain, 1694–1994*. Ithaca: Cornell University Press, 1996.

Braverman, Richard. "Satiric Embodiments: Butler, Swift, Sterne." In *Cutting Edges: Postmodern Critical Essays on Eighteenth-Century Satire*, edited by James Gill, 76–93. Knoxville: University of Tennessee Press, 1995.

Brewer, John. *The Sinews of Power: War, Money, and the English State, 1688–1783*. Cambridge: Harvard University Press, 1990.

Brown, Laura. "Reading Race and Gender: Jonathan Swift." *Eighteenth-Century Studies* 23.4 (Summer 1990): 424–443.

Brown, Michael. *Francis Hutcheson in Dublin, 1719–30: The Crucible of His Thought*. Dublin: Four Courts Press, 2002.

Brown, Norman O. *Life Against Death*. Middletown: Wesleyan University Press, 1959.

Brynn, Edward. "Some Repercussions of the Act of Union on the Church of Ireland, 1801–1820." *Church History* 40.3 (Sept. 1971): 284–296.

Bullitt, John M. *Jonathan Swift and the Anatomy of Satire: A Study of Satiric Technique*. Cambridge: Harvard University Press, 1961.

Bum-fodder for the Ladies. A Poem, (upon soft paper). London, 1753.

Burgess, Miranda J. *British Fiction and the Production of Social Order, 1740–1830*. Cambridge: Cambridge University Press, 2000.

Burke, Helen. *Riotous Performances: The Struggle for Hegemony in the Irish Theater, 1712–1784*. Notre Dame: University of Notre Dame Press, 2003.

Canny, Nicholas. "Identity Formation in Ireland: The Emergence of the Anglo-Irish." In *Colonial Identity in the Atlantic World, 1500–1800*, edited by Nicholas Canny and Anthony Pagden, 159–212. Princeton: Princeton University Press, 1987.

———. *Kingdom and Colony: Ireland in the Atlantic World, 1560–1800*. Baltimore: Johns Hopkins University Press, 1988.

———. *Making Ireland British, 1580–1650*. Oxford: Oxford University Press, 2001.

Carpenter, Andrew, ed. "Introduction." In *The Dublin Scuffle*, by John Dunton, vii–xxx. Dublin: Four Courts Press, 2000.

———. "Two Possible Sources for Swift's *A Modest Proposal*." *Irish Booklore* 2 (1972): 147–148.

Carroll, Clare. "Barbarous Slaves and Civil Cannibals: Translating Civility in Early Modern Ireland." In *Ireland and Postcolonial Theory*, edited by Clare Carroll and Patricia King, 63–80. Notre Dame: University of Notre Dame Press, 2003.

Castle, Terry. "Why the Houyhnhnms Don't Write: Swift, Satire, and the Fear of the Text." In *Gulliver's Travels*, edited by Christopher Fox, 379–394. Boston: Bedford, 1995.

Chakrabarty, Dipesh. *Provincializing Europe: Postcolonial Thought and Historical Difference*. Princeton: Princeton University Press, 2000.

Chartier, Roger. *The Cultural Origins of the French Revolution*. Translated by Lydia G. Cochrane. Durham: Duke University Press, 1991.

———. *The Cultural Uses of Print in Early Modern France*. Translated by Lydia G. Cochrane. Princeton: Princeton University Press, 1987.

Clarke, Aidan. "Patrick Darcy and the Constitutional Relationship between Ireland and Britain." In *Political Thought in Seventeenth-Century Ireland: Kingdom or Colony*, edited by Jane Ohlmeyer, 35–55. Cambridge: Cambridge University Press, 2000.

———. *Prelude to Restoration in Ireland: The End of the Commonwealth, 1659–1660*. Cambridge: Cambridge University Press, 1999.

Clements Manuscripts. Historical Manuscripts Commission. National Archives of the United Kingdom, London.

Clifford, Gay. *The Transformations of Allegory*. London: Routledge & Kegan Paul, 1974.

Coleborne, Bryan. "The Dublin Grub Street: The Documentary Evidence in the Case of John Browne." *Swift Studies* 2 (1987): 12–24.

———. "We Flea the People & Sell their Skins." *Scriblerian* 15.2 (Spring 1983): 132–133.

Colley, Linda. *Britons: Forging the Nation, 1707–1837.* New Haven: Yale University Press, 1992.

Congreve, William. *Love For Love, a Comedy. Acted at the Theatre-Royal in Dublin.* Dublin, 1722.

Conlon, Michael J. "Original Swift: Anonymity, Parody, and the Example of *On Poetry: A Rapsody.*" *Swift Studies* 12 (1997): 69–79.

Connolly, S. J. "Precedent and Principle: The Patriots and Their Critics." In *Political Ideas in Eighteenth Century Ireland*, edited by Sean J. Connolly, 130–158. Dublin: Four Courts Press, 2000.

———. *Religion, Law, and Power: The Making of Protestant Ireland.* Oxford: Clarendon Press, 1992.

———. "Swift and Protestant Ireland: Images and Reality." In *Locating Swift: Essays from Dublin on the 250th Anniversary of the Death of Jonathan Swift, 1667–1745*, edited by Aileen Douglas, Patrick Kelly, and Ian Campbell Ross, 28–46. Dublin: Four Courts Press, 1998.

Cooper, Anthony Ashley, 3rd Earl of Shaftesbury. *Characteristicks of Men, Manners, Opinions, Times.* Edited by Philip Ayres. Oxford: Clarendon Press, 1999.

Cowan, Brian. "Mr. Spectator and the Coffeehouse Public Sphere." *Eighteenth Century Studies* 37.3 (Spring 2004): 345–366.

Crawford, Robert. *Devolving English Literature.* Oxford: Clarendon Press, 1992.

Crow, Thomas E. *Painters and Public Life in Eighteenth-Century Paris.* New Haven: Yale University Press, 1985.

Cullen, L. M. "Economic Development, 1750–1800." In vol. 4 of *A New History of Ireland*, edited by T. W. Moody and W. E. Vaughan, 159–194. Oxford: Clarendon Press, 1986.

———. "Problems in the Interpretation and Revision of Eighteenth Century Irish Economic History." *Transactions of the Royal Historical Society* 5:17 (1967): 1–22.

———. "The Value of Contemporary Printed Sources for Irish Economic History in the Eighteenth Century." *Irish Historical Studies* 14.54 (1964): 142–155.

Culler, Jonathan. *On Deconstruction: Theory and Criticism after Structuralism.* Ithaca: Cornell University Press, 1982.

Darnton, Robert. *The Business of Enlightenment: A Publishing History of the*

Encyclopédie 1775–1800. Cambridge: The Belknap Press of Harvard University Press, 1979.

———. *The Great Cat Massacre and Other Episodes in French Cultural History*. New York: Basic Books, 1984.

Darnton, Robert, and Daniel Roche, eds. *Revolution in Print: The Press in France 1775–1800*. Berkeley: University of California Press, 1989.

Daston, Lorraine. "Baconian Facts, Academic Civility, and the Prehistory of Objectivity." *Annals of Scholarship* 8:3–4 (1991): 337–363.

Dean, Jodi. *Publicity's Secret: How Technoculture Capitalizes on Democracy*. Ithaca: Cornell University Press, 2002.

Deane, Seamus. *A Short History of Irish Literature*. London: Hutchinson, 1986.

de Bolla, Peter. *The Discourse of the Sublime*. Cambridge: Cambridge University Press, 1989.

Delany, Patrick. *Observations Upon Lord Orrery's Remarks on the Life and Writings of Dr. Jonathan Swift*. New York: Garland, 1974.

DePorte, Michael. "Vinum Daemonum: Swift and the Grape." *Swift Studies* 12 (1997): 56–68.

Derrida, Jacques. *Dissemination*. Translated by Barbara Johnson. Chicago: University of Chicago Press, 1981.

———. "Economimesis." *Diacritics* 11.2 (June 1981): 3–25.

———. *Given Time. I, Counterfeit Money*. Chicago: University of Chicago Press, 1992.

———. *Of Grammatology*. Baltimore: Johns Hopkins University Press, 1998.

A Dialogue Between Mr. Freeport, a Merchant, and Tom Handy, a Trades Man, Concerning the Bank. Dublin, 1721.

Dickson, P. G. M. *The Financial Revolution in England: A Study in the Development of Public Credit, 1688–1756*. London: Macmillan, 1967.

Downie, J. A. *Jonathan Swift: Political Writer*. London: Routledge, 1984.

———. "Public and Private: The Myth of the Bourgeois Public Sphere." In *A Concise Companion to the Restoration and Eighteenth Century*, edited by Cynthia Wall, 58–79. Oxford: Blackwell, 2005.

———. *Robert Harley and the Press: Propaganda and Public Opinion in the Age of Swift and Defoe*. Cambridge: Cambridge University Press, 1979.

———. "Secret Service Payments to Daniel Defoe, 1710–1714." *Review of English Studies* 30.120 (Nov. 1979): 437–441.

———. "Swift's Politics." In *Proceedings of the First Münster Symposium on Jonathan Swift*, edited by Hermann J. Real and Heinz J. Vienken, 47–58. Munich: Wilhelm Fink Verlag, 1985.

———. *Telling People What to Think: Early Eighteenth Century Periodicals from The Review to The Rambler*. London: Frank Cass, 1993.

Dunlevy, Mairead. *Dress in Ireland*. New York: Holmes & Meier, 1989.

Eagleton, Terry. *The Ideology of the Aesthetic*. Oxford: Blackwell, 1990.

Eccleshall, Robert. "Anglican Political Thought in the Century after the Revolution of 1688." In *Political Thought in Ireland Since the Seventeenth Century*, edited by D. George Boyce, Robert Eccleshall, and Vincent Geoghegan, 36–72. London: Routledge, 1993.

Egmont Papers. Public Record Office of Northern Ireland, Belfast.

Ehrenpreis, Irvin. *The Personality of Jonathan Swift*. Albuquerque: University of New Mexico Press, 1971.

———. *Swift: The Man, His Works, and the Age*. 3 vols. Cambridge: Harvard University Press, 1983.

Eisenstein, Elizabeth. *The Printing Press as an Agent of Change: Communications and Cultural Transformations in Early Modern Europe*. Cambridge: Cambridge University Press, 1979.

———. *The Printing Revolution in Early Modern Europe*. Cambridge: Cambridge University Press, 1983.

Elias, A. C. "The Full Text of Swift's *On Poetry: A Rapsody* (1733)." *Swift Studies* 9 (1994): 17–32.

Ellis, Frank. "No Apologies, Dr. Swift." *Eighteenth-Century Life* 21.3 (Nov. 1997): 71–76.

Esty, Joshua D. "Excremental Postcolonialism." *Contemporary Literature* 40.1 (Spring 1999): 22–59.

Fabricant, Carole. "Speaking for the Irish Nation: The Drapier, the Bishop, and the Problems of Colonial Representation." *ELH* 66 (1999): 337–372.

———. *Swift's Landscape*. Baltimore: Johns Hopkins University Press, 1982.

Faulkner, George. *A Catalogue of Books, the Library of the Late Rev. Dr. Swift, Dean of St. Patrick's, Dublin. To be Sold by Auction*. Dublin: Faulkner, 1745.

Faulkner, George, and George Grierson. *The Humble Petition of George Faulkner and George Grierson*. Dublin, 1735.

Fauske, Christopher. *Jonathan Swift and the Church of Ireland*. Dublin: Irish Academic Press, 2002.

Ferguson, Oliver. *Jonathan Swift and Ireland*. Urbana: University of Illinois Press, 1962.

Festa, Lynn. *Sentimental Figures of Empire in Eighteenth-Century Britain and France*. Baltimore: Johns Hopkins University Press, 2006.

Fischer, John Irwin, Donald C. Mell, Jr., and David M. Vieth, eds. *Contemporary Studies of Swift's Poetry*. Newark: University of Delaware Press, 1981.

Fish, Stanley. *Doing What Comes Naturally: Change, Rhetoric, and the Practice of Theory in Literary and Legal Studies*. Durham: Duke University Press, 1989.

Forman, Charles. *A Second Letter to the Right Honourable Sir Robert Walpole.* London, 1733.

Foster, Roy. *Modern Ireland, 1600–1972.* London: Penguin, 1988.

Foucault, Michel. "What Is an Author?" In *Textual Strategies: Perspectives in Post Structuralist Criticism,* edited and translated by Josue V. Harari, 141–160. Ithaca: Cornell University Press, 1979.

Furniss, Tom. *Edmund Burke's Aesthetic Ideology.* Cambridge: Cambridge University Press, 1993.

Fussell, Paul, Jr. "Speaker and Style in *A Letter of Advice to a Young Poet* (1721), and the Problem of Attribution." *Review of English Studies: A Quarterly Journal of English Literature and the English Language* 10.37 (Feb. 1959): 63–67.

Gaonkar, Dilip. *Alternative Modernities.* Durham: Duke University Press, 2001.

Gee, Sophie. "The Sewers: Ordure, Effluence, and Excess in the Eighteenth Century." In *A Concise Companion to the Restoration and Eighteenth Century,* edited by Cynthia Wall, 101–120. Oxford: Blackwell, 2005.

Gibbons, Luke. *Edmund Burke and Ireland: Aesthetics, Politics, and the Colonial Sublime.* Cambridge: Cambridge University Press, 2003.

Gillespie, Raymond. "Print Culture, 1550–1700." In *The Irish Book in English, 1550–1800,* edited by Raymond Gillespie and Andrew Hadfield, 3:17–33. Oxford: Oxford University Press, 2006.

——. "Select Documents XLII: Peter French's Petition for an Irish Mint, 1619." *Irish Historical Studies* 25.100 (Nov. 1987): 413–420.

Glendinning, Victoria. *Jonathan Swift: A Portrait.* New York: Henry Holt, 1998.

Goux, Jean-Joseph. *Symbolic Economies: After Marx and Freud.* Translated by Jennifer Curtiss Gage. Ithaca: Cornell University Press, 1990.

Griffith, Lisa Marie. "Mobilising Office, Education and Gender in Eighteenth-Century Ireland: the Case of the Griersons." *Eighteenth-Century Ireland* 22 (2007): 64–80.

Grimston, William. *The Lawyer's Fortune: or, Love in a Hollow Tree.* London, 1705.

Guha, Ranajit. *Dominance Without Hegemony: History and Power in Colonial India.* Cambridge: Harvard University Press, 1997.

Guillory, John. *Cultural Capital: The Problem of Literary Canon Formation.* Chicago: University of Chicago Press, 1993.

Gunn, J. A. W. "Public Opinion." In *Political Innovation and Conceptual Change,* edited by Terence Ball, James Farr, and Russell L. Hanson, 247–265. Cambridge: Cambridge University Press, 1989.

Habermas, Jürgen. *The Structural Transformation of the Public Sphere: An In-*

quiry into a Category of Bourgeois Society. Translated by Thomas Burger. Cambridge: MIT Press, 1989.

Hall, F. G. *History of the Bank of Ireland.* Dublin: Hodges, Figgis, 1949.

Hansard, T. C. *Typographia: An Historical Sketch of the Origin and Progress of the Art of Printing.* London: Baldwin, Cradock & Joy, 1825.

Hardt, Michael, and Antonio Negri. *Empire.* Cambridge: Harvard University Press, 2000.

Harth, Phillip. "Friendship and Politics: Swift's Relations with Pope in the Early 1730s." In *Reading Swift: Papers from the Third Münster Symposium on Jonathan Swift,* edited by Herman J. Real and Helgard Stover-Leidig, 239–248. Munich: Wilhelm Fink Verlag, 1998.

———. "Swift's Self-Image as a Satirist." In *Proceedings of the First Münster Symposium on Jonathan Swift,* edited by Herman J. Real and Heinz J. Vienken, 113–121. Munich: Wilhelm Fink Verlag, 1985.

Hawes, Clement. *The British Eighteenth Century and Global Critique.* New York: Palgrave Macmillan, 2005.

———. "Three Times Round the Globe: Gulliver and Colonial Discourse." *Cultural Critique* 18 (Spring 1991): 187–214.

Hawkes, David. *Idols of the Marketplace: Idolatry and Commodity Fetishism in English Literature, 1580–1680.* London: Palgrave, 2001.

Hayton, David, ed. *The Letters of Marmaduke Coghill, 1722–1738.* Dublin: Irish Manuscripts Commission, 2005.

———. "The Stanhope/Sunderland Ministry and the Repudiation of Irish Parliamentary Independence." *English Historical Review* (June 1998): 610–636.

Higgins, Ian. *Swift's Politics: A Study in Disaffection.* Cambridge: Cambridge University Press, 1994.

Hobbes, Thomas. *Leviathan.* Edited by Crawford Brough MacPherson. London: Penguin, 1968.

Holt, Douglas B. *How Brands Become Icons: The Principles of Cultural Branding.* Boston: Harvard Business School Press, 2004.

Horkheimer, Max, and Theodor W. Adorno. *Dialectic of Enlightenment: Philosophical Fragments.* Edited by Gunzelin Schmid Noeer. Translated by Edmund Jephcott. Stanford: Stanford University Press, 2002.

Howe, Stephen. *Ireland and Empire.* Oxford: Oxford University Press, 2000.

Hume, David. "Of Public Credit." In *Political Essays,* edited by Knud Haakonssen, 166–178. Cambridge: Cambridge University Press, 1994.

Hunter, J. Paul. "*Gulliver's Travels* and the Novel." In *The Genres of Gulliver's Travels,* edited by Frederik N. Smith, 56–74. Newark: University of Delaware Press, 1990.

Ingrassia, Catherine. *Authorship, Commerce, and Gender in Early Eighteenth-*

Century England: A Culture of Paper Credit. Cambridge: Cambridge University Press, 1998.

Irwin, John. *The Phoenix: or, a New Scheme for Establishing Credit, Upon the Most Solid and Satisfactory Foundation, and Intirely Free from All Objections Made to the Former Intended Bank.* Dublin, 1721.

Jameson, Fredric. "Third-World Literature in the Era of Multinational Capitalism." *Social Text* 15 (Autumn 1986): 65–88.

Johns, Adrian. *The Nature of the Book: Print and Knowledge in the Making.* Chicago: University of Chicago Press, 1998.

Johnson, A. F. "The King's Printers, 1660–1742." *The Library* s5-III (1) (1948): 33–38.

Johnson, Maurice. *The Sin of Wit: Jonathan Swift as Poet.* Syracuse: Syracuse University Press, 1950.

Johnston, Joseph. *Bishop Berkeley's Querist in Historical Perspective.* Dundalk, Ireland: Dundalgan Press, 1970.

Johnston-Liik, Edith Mary. *History of the Irish Parliament 1692–1800: Commons, Constituencies and Statutes.* 6 vols. Belfast: Ulster Historical Foundation, 2002.

Jones, Ann Rosalind, and Peter Stallybrass. *Renaissance Clothing and the Materials of Memory.* Cambridge: Cambridge University Press, 2000.

The Journals of the House of Commons of the Kingdom of Ireland, from the Eleventh Year of King James the First. 2nd ed. Dublin: Abraham Bradley, 1763.

Journals of the House of Lords. Dublin: William Sleater, 1780.

Joyce, James. *Ulysses.* New York: Vintage, 1990.

Karian, Stephen. "Edmund Curll and the Circulation of Swift's Writings." In *Reading Swift: Papers from the Fifth Münster Symposium on Jonathan Swift,* ed. Hermann J. Real, 99–129. Munich: Wilhelm Fink Verlag, 2008.

———. "Reading the Material Text of Swift's *Verses on the Death.*" *SEL* 41.3 (Summer 2001): 515–544.

Kelly, Ann Cline. "The Birth of Swift." In *Reading Swift: Papers from the Second Münster Symposium on Jonathan Swift,* edited by Richard H. Rodino and Hermann J. Real, 13–23. Munich: Wilhelm Fink Verlag, 1993.

———. *Jonathan Swift and Popular Culture: Myth, Media, and the Man.* New York: Palgrave, 2002.

Kelly, James. "Harvests and Hardship: Famine and Scarcity in Ireland in the Late 1720s." *Studia Hibernica* 26 (1991–1992): 65–105.

———. "Jonathan Swift and the Irish Economy in the 1720s." *Eighteenth Century Ireland* 6 (1991): 7–36.

Kelly, Patrick, ed. *Locke on Money.* 2 vols. Oxford: Clarendon Press, 1991.

———. "Recasting a Tradition: William Molyneux and the Sources of *The Case of Ireland . . . Stated* (1698)." In *Political Thought in Seventeenth-Century Ireland: Kingdom or Colony*, edited by Jane Ohlmeyer, 83–106. Cambridge: Cambridge University Press, 2000.

———. "Swift on Money and Economics." In *The Cambridge Companion to Jonathan Swift*, edited by Christopher Fox, 128–145. Cambridge: Cambridge University Press, 2003.

Kennedy, Maíre. *French Books in Eighteenth-Century Ireland. Studies in Voltaire and the Eighteenth Century (SVEC)* 2001:07. Oxford: Voltaire Foundation, 2001.

Keough, Donald. "The Importance of Brand Power." In *Brand Power*, edited by Paul Stobart, 17–32. New York: New York University Press, 1994.

Kiberd, Declan. *Inventing Ireland*. Cambridge: Harvard University Press, 1996.

———. *Irish Classics*. Cambridge: Harvard University Press, 2001.

Kiernan, T. J. *History of the Financial Administration of Ireland to 1817*. London: King, 1930.

Kiernan, V. G. "The Emergence of a Nation." In *Nationalism and Popular Protest in Ireland*, edited by C. H. E. Philpin, 16–49. Cambridge: Cambridge University Press, 1987.

Kincaid, Jamaica. *A Small Place*. New York: Farrar, Straus, & Giroux, 1988.

King, William. "Taxation of Ireland." In *British Literature 1640-1789: An Anthology*. 2nd ed. Edited by Robert Demaria, Jr., 297–298. Oxford: Blackwell, 2001.

King Manuscripts. Trinity College Dublin.

King, William. "Taxation of Ireland." In *British Literature 1640-1789: An Anthology*. 2nd ed. Edited by Robert Demaria, Jr., 297–298. Oxford: Blackwell Publishing, 2001.

Klein, Lawrence. *Shaftesbury and the Culture of Politeness: Moral Discourse and Cultural Politics in Early Eighteenth-Century England*. Cambridge: Cambridge University Press, 1994.

Klein, Naomi. *No Logo: Taking Aim at the Brand Bullies*. New York: Picador, 1999.

Kosok, Heinz. "Anglo-Irish Literature and Comparative Literary Studies in English." In *Literary Interrelations: Ireland, England, and the World*, edited by Wolfgang Zach and Heinz Kosok, 3–13. Tubingen: Narr, 1987.

Kramnick, Isaac. *Bolingbroke and His Circle: The Politics of Nostalgia in the Age of Walpole*. Cambridge: Harvard University Press, 1968.

Krappe, Edith Smith. "A Lapsus Calami of Jonathan Swift." *Modern Language Notes* 53.2 (Feb. 1938): 116–117.

Kumar, Amitava. "World Bank Literature: A New Name for Post-colonial Studies in the Next Century." *College Literature* 26.3 (Fall 1999): 125–134.

Landa, Louis. "A Modest Proposal and Populousness." *Modern Philology* 40 (1942): 161–170.

———. *Swift and the Church of Ireland.* Oxford: Clarendon Press, 1954.

Langford, Paul. *A Polite and Commercial People: England 1727–1783.* Oxford: Clarendon Press, 1989.

Latouche, Robert. *The Birth of Western Economy: Economic Aspects of the Dark Ages.* London: Methuen, 1961.

Lawrence, Richard. *The Interest of Ireland in its Trade and Wealth Stated.* Dublin, 1682.

Leavis, F. R. "The Irony of Swift." In *Determinations: Critical Essays,* edited by F. R. Leavis, 79–108. London: Chatto & Windus, 1934.

Lecky, W. E. H. *The Leaders of Public Opinion in Ireland.* New York: D. Appleton, 1883.

Lee, Jae Num. *Swift and Scatological Satire.* Albuquerque: University of New Mexico Press, 1971.

Lefanu, William, ed. *A Catalogue of Books Belonging to Dr. Jonathan Swift, Dean of St. Patrick's, Dublin, Aug. 19. 1715.* Cambridge: Cambridge Bibliographical Society, 1988.

Legg, Mary Louise. "Money and Reputations: The Effects of the Banking Crises of 1755 and 1760." *Eighteenth-Century Ireland* 11 (1996): 74–87.

A Letter to a Member of Parliament Touching the Late Intended Bank. Dublin, 1721.

A Letter to Henry Maxwell, Esq; Plainly Shewing the Great Danger that the Kingdom has Escaped, and the Great Inconveniencies, that Must of Necessity have Happen'd, if a Bank had been Establish'd in this Kingdom. Dublin: Thomas Hume, 1721.

A Letter to the Gentlemen of the Landed Interest in Ireland, Relating to a Bank. Dublin: Aaron Rhames, 1721.

Leyburn, Ellen Douglas. *Satiric Allegory: Mirror of Man.* New Haven: Yale University Press, 1956.

Lloyd, David. *Anomalous States: Irish Writing and the Post-Colonial Moment.* Durham: Duke University Press, 1993.

———. *Ireland After History.* Notre Dame: University of Notre Dame Press, 1999.

Lock, F. P. *Swift's Tory Politics.* Newark: University of Delaware Press, 1983.

Locke, John. *An Essay Concerning Human Understanding.* Edited by Peter H. Nidditch. Oxford: Clarendon Press, 1975.

———. *Two Treatises of Government.* Edited by Peter Laslett. Cambridge: Cambridge University Press, 1988.

Lockwood, Thomas. "Fielding and the Licensing Act." *Huntington Library Quarterly* 50.4 (Autumn 1987): 379–393.

Louis, Frances D. *Swift's Anatomy of Misunderstanding: A Study of Swift's Epistemological Imagination in* A Tale of a Tub *and* Gulliver's Travels. Totowa, N.J.: Barnes & Noble, 1981.

Lynch, Deidre. *The Economy of Character: Novels, Market Culture, and the Business of Inner Meaning.* Chicago: University of Chicago Press, 1998.

Mackie, Erin. *Market à la Mode: Fashion, Commodity, and Gender in* The Tatler *and* The Spectator. Baltimore: Johns Hopkins University Press, 1997.

———, ed. *The Commerce of Everyday Life: Selections from* The Tatler *and* The Spectator. Boston: Bedford / St. Martin's, 1998.

Mah, Harold. "Phantasies of the Public Sphere: Rethinking the Habermas of Historians." *Journal of Modern History* 72 (Mar. 2000): 153–182.

Mahony, Robert. *Jonathan Swift: The Irish Identity.* New Haven: Yale University Press, 1995.

———. "Protestant Dependence and Consumption in Swift's Irish Writings." In *Political Ideas in Eighteenth-Century Ireland*, edited by S. J. Connolly, 83–104. Dublin: Four Courts Press, 2000.

———. "Swift, Postcolonialism, and Irish Studies: The Valence of Ambivalence." In *Representations of Swift*, edited by Brian A. Connery, 217–235. Newark: University of Delaware Press, 2002.

Mandell, Laura. "Bawds and Merchants: Engendering Capitalist Desires." *ELH* 59.1 (Spring 1992): 107–123.

Mandeville, Bernard. *A Modest Defence of Public Stews: or, An Essay upon Whoring, as it is Now Practis'd in these Kingdoms.* London: A. Moore, 1724.

Manousos, Anthony. "Swiftian Scatology and Lockean Psychology." *The Gypsy Scholar: A Graduate Forum for Literary Criticism* 7.1 (Winter 1980): 15–25.

Marana, Giovanni Paolo. *The Eight Volumes of Letters Writ by a Turkish Spy.* 8 vols. London, 1702–1703.

Markley, Robert. "Credit Exhausted": Satire and Scarcity in the 1690s." In *Cutting Edges: Postmodern Critical Essays on Eighteenth-Century Satire*, edited by James Gill, 110–126. Knoxville: University of Tennessee Press, 1995.

Maruca, Lisa. *The Work of Print: Authorship and the English Text Trades, 1660–1760.* Seattle: University of Washington Press, 2007.

Mason, Nicholas. "'The Quack Has Become God': Puffery, Print, and the 'Death' of Literature in Romantic-Era Britain." *Nineteenth Century Literature* 60.1 (June 2005): 1–31.

Mather, Cotton. *Some Considerations on the Bills of Credit Now Passing in New England.* Vol. 1, *Colonial Currency Reprints, 1682–1751*, edited by Andrew

McFarland Davis and Joseph Dorfman, 189–196. New York: Augustus M. Kelley, 1964.

Matlack, Cynthia S. "A Statistical Approach to Problems of Attribution: *A Letter of Advice to a Young Poet.*" *College English* 29.8 (May 1968): 627–632.

Maxwell, Henry. *Mr. Maxwell's Second Letter to Mr. Rowley: Wherein the Objections Against the Bank are Answer'd.* Dublin: Aaron Rhames, 1721.

———. *Reasons Offer'd for Erecting a Bank in Ireland; in a Letter to Hercules Rowley, Esq,* 2nd ed. Dublin: Aaron Rhames, 1721.

Mayhew, George P. *Rage or Raillery: The Swift Manuscripts at the Huntington Library.* San Marino, Calif.: Huntington Library, 1967.

Mayhew, Nicholas. *Sterling: The History of a Currency.* New York: John Wiley & Sons, 2000.

McClintock, Anne. *Imperial Leather: Race, Gender, and Sexuality in the Colonial Contest.* New York: Routledge, 1995.

McCormack, W. J. "Reflections on Writing and Editing with Reference to National Archives (UK), Co 904/1-3 & HO 161/1-5." In *That Woman! Studies in Irish Bibliography: A Festschrift for Mary 'Paul' Pollard,* edited by Charles Benson and Siobhan Fitzpatrick, 258–285. Dublin: Lilliput Press / Library Association of Ireland Rare Books Group, 2005.

McCracken, J. L. "The Political Structure, 1714–60." In vol. 4 of *A New History of Ireland,* edited by T. W. Moody and W. E. Vaughan, 57–82. Oxford: Clarendon Press, 1986.

McDiarmid, Lucy. *The Irish Art of Controversy.* Ithaca: Cornell University Press, 2005.

McDowell, Paula. "Defoe and the Contagion of the Oral: Modeling Media Shift in *A Journal of the Plague Year.*" *PMLA* 121.1 (Jan. 2006), 87–106.

McDowell, R. B. "Ireland in 1800." In vol. 4 of *A New History of Ireland,* edited by T. W. Moody and W. E. Vaughan, 657–711. Oxford: Clarendon Press, 1986.

———. *Irish Public Opinion 1750–1800.* Westport: Greenwood Press, 1975.

McGrath, Charles Ivar. "Central Aspects of the Eighteenth-Century Constitutional Framework in Ireland: The Government Supply Bill and Biennial Parliamentary Sessions, 1715–82." *Eighteenth-Century Ireland* 16 (2001): 9–34.

———. *The Making of the Eighteenth-Century Irish Constitution: Government, Parliament and the Revenue, 1692–1714.* Dublin: Four Courts Press, 2000.

———. "'The Public Wealth is the Sinew, the Life, of every Public Measure': The Creation and Maintenance of a National Debt in Ireland, 1715–1745." In *The Empire of Credit: The Financial Revolution in the British Atlantic World,* edited by Dan Carey and Christopher Finlay, 174–203. Dublin: Irish Academic Press, 2010.

McKeon, Michael. *The Origins of the English Novel, 1600–1740.* Baltimore: Johns Hopkins University Press, 1987.

McLaverty, James. "The Failure of the Swift-Pope *Miscellanies* (1727–32) and the Life and Genuine Character of Doctor Swift." In *Reading Swift: Papers from the Fifth Münster Symposium on Jonathan Swift,* edited by Hermann J. Real, 131–148. Munich: Wilhelm Fink Verlag, 2008.

McMinn, Joseph, ed. *Swift's Irish Pamphlets: An Introductory Selection.* Savage, Md.: Barnes & Noble, 1991.

Mell, Donald C., Jr., "Irony, Poetry, and Swift: Entrapment in 'On Poetry: A Rapsody.'" *Papers on Language and Literature: A Journal for Scholars and Critics of Language and Literature* 18:3 (Summer 1982): 310–324.

Metscher, Thomas. "The Radicalism of Swift: *Gulliver's Travels* and the Irish Point of View." In *Studies in Anglo-Irish Literature,* edited by Heinz Kosok, 13–22. Bonn: Bouvier Verlag Herbert Gundmann, 1982.

Michaels, Walter Benn, *The Gold Standard and the Logic of Naturalism.* Berkeley: University of California Press, 1987.

Miller, John. *The Glorious Revolution.* 2nd ed. New York: Longman, 1997.

Milton, John. *The Works of John Milton.* 18 vols. Edited by Frank Allen Patterson. New York: Columbia University Press, 1931–1938.

Misolestes, Patriophilus. *Objections Against the General Bank in Ireland as It Stands Now Circumstantiated, Whether it Do's or Do's not Receive a Parliamentary Sanction, in Answer to a Letter sent from a Gentleman in the City to his Friend in the Country.* Dublin: C. Carter, 1721.

Molyneux, William. *The Case of Ireland Being Bound by Acts of Parliament in England, Stated.* Dublin, 1698.

Moody, T. W., and W. E. Vaughn, eds. *A New History of Ireland.* 10 vols. Oxford: Clarendon Press, 1986.

Moore, Sean. "Devouring Posterity: *A Modest Proposal,* Empire, and Ireland's 'Debt of the Nation.'" *PMLA* 122.3 (May 2007): 679–695.

———. "Satiric Norms, Swift's Financial Satires, and the Bank of Ireland Controversy of 1720–1721." *Eighteenth-Century Ireland* 17 (2002): 26–56.

Moretti, Franco. *The Way of the World: The Bildungsroman in European Culture.* Translated by Albert Sbragia. London: Verso, 1987.

Mowry, Melissa M. *The Bawdy Politic in Stuart England, 1660–1714: Political Pornography and Prostitution.* Aldershot, England: Ashgate, 2004.

Moxon, Joseph. *Mechanick Exercises on the Whole Art of Printing.* Vol. 2 of *Mechanick Exercises, or, The Doctrine of Handy-works.* 2 vols. London: Moxon, 1677–1683.

Mueller, Judith. "*A Tale of a Tub* and Early Prose." In *The Cambridge Companion* to *Jonathan Swift*, edited by Christopher Fox, 202–215. Cambridge: Cambridge University Press, 2003.

Murray, John Middleton. *Jonathan Swift: A Critical Biography*. New York: Farrar, Straus, & Giroux, 1955.

Nash, Richard. *Wild Enlightenment: The Borders of Human Identity in the Eighteenth Century*. Charlottesville: University Press of Virginia, 2003.

Neill, Michael. "Broken English and Broken Irish: Nation, Language, and the Optic of Power in Shakespeare's Histories." *Shakespeare Quarterly* 45.1 (Spring 1994): 1–32.

Newman, Eric. *The Early Paper Money of America*. Racine: Western Publishing, 1976.

Nicholson, Colin. *Writing and the Rise of Finance: Capital Satires of the Early Eighteenth Century*. Cambridge: Cambridge University Press, 1994.

Nokes, David. *Jonathan Swift, A Hypocrite Reversed: A Critical Biography*. Oxford: Oxford University Press, 1985.

"Norms, Moral or Other, in Satire: A Symposium." *Satire Newsletter* (Fall 1964): 2–25.

Oakleaf, David. *A Political Biography of Jonathan Swift*. London: Pickering & Chatto, 2008.

Ohlmeyer, Jane. "Introduction: for God, King, or Country? Political Thought and Culture in Seventeenth-Century Ireland." In *Political Thought in Seventeenth-Century Ireland: Kingdom or Colony*, edited by Jane Ohlmeyer, 1–31. Cambridge: Cambridge University Press, 2000.

O'Regan, Philip. *Archbishop William King of Dublin (1650–1729) and the Constitution in Church and State*. Dublin: Four Courts Press, 2000.

Ozouf, Mona. "'Public Opinion' at the End of the Old Regime." *Journal of Modern History* 60 Supplement (1988): S1–S21.

A Paradox: The Best Perfume; or, a Paradox in Praise of Farting. Dublin: 1723.

Parsons, Jotham. "Money and Sovereignty in Early Modern France." *Journal of the History of Ideas* 62.1 (Jan. 2001): 59–79.

Passman, Dirk. "An Allusion to Mandeville in *Gulliver's Travels*: 'The Air of Truth' Polluted." *Notes and Queries* 230.2 (June 1985): 205–207.

Peake, Charles H. "Swift on Poets and Poetry." In *Swift and His Contexts*, edited by John Irwin Fischer, Hermann J. Real, and James Woolley, 97–114. New York: AMS Press, 1989.

Peterson, Leland. "The Satiric Norm of Jonathan Swift." Ph.D. diss., University of Minnesota, 1962.

Petty, William. *The Economic Writings of Sir William Petty*. Vol. 1, edited by C. H. Hull. New York: Augustus M. Kelley, 1963.

Phiddian, Robert. "Have You Eaten Yet? The Reader in *A Modest Proposal*." *SEL* 36.3 (Summer 1996): 603–621.

———. *Swift's Parody*. Cambridge: Cambridge University Press, 1995.

Phillips, James W. *Printing and Bookselling in Dublin, 1670–1800: A Bibliographical Enquiry*. Dublin: Irish Academic Press, 1998.

Pilkington, Matthew. *An Infallible Scheme to Pay the Publick Debt of this Nation in Six Months. Humbly Offered to the Consideration of the Present P—t*. Dublin, 1731.

Pincus, Steve. *1688: The First Modern Revolution*. New Haven: Yale University Press, 2009.

Plato. "Phaedrus." In *The Collected Dialogues of Plato*, edited by Edith Hamilton and Huntington Cairns, 475–525. Princeton: Princeton University Press, 1961.

Plummer, Alfred. *The London Weaver's Company, 1600–1970*. London: Routledge, 1972.

Pocock, J. G. A. *The Discovery of Islands: Essays in British History*. Cambridge: Cambridge University Press, 2005.

———. *The Machiavellian Moment*. Cambridge: Cambridge University Press, 1975.

———. *Virtue, Commerce, and History: Essays on Political Thought and History, Chiefly in the Eighteenth Century*. Cambridge: Cambridge University Press, 1985.

Pollard, Mary. *A Dictionary of Members of the Dublin Book Trade, 1550–1800*. London: Bibliographical Society, 2000.

———. *Dublin's Trade in Books, 1550–1800*. Oxford: Clarendon Press, 1989.

———. "George Faulkner." *Swift Studies* 7 (1992): 79–96.

Poovey, Mary. *A History of the Modern Fact: Problems of Knowledge in the Sciences of Wealth and Society*. Chicago: Chicago University Press, 1998.

Pope, Alexander. *The Dunciad Variorum*. Menston, England: Scolar Press, 1968.

Price, Leah. "Introduction: Reading Matter." *PMLA* 121.1 (Jan. 2006): 9–15.

———. *The Anthology and the Rise of the Novel: From Richardson to George Eliot*. Cambridge: Cambridge University Press, 2000.

Probyn, Clive T. "'Haranguing Upon Texts': Swift and the Idea of the Book." In *Proceedings of the First Münster Symposium on Jonathan Swift*, edited by Hermann J. Real and Heinz J. Vienken, 187–197. Munich: Wilhelm Fink Verlag, 1985.

———. "Jonathan Swift at the Sign of the Drapier." In *Proceedings of the Third Münster Symposium on Jonathan Swift*, edited by Hermann J. Real and Helgard Stover-Leidig, 225–237. Munich: Wilhelm Fink Verlag, 1998.

Puffindorst, Don Fartinhando. *The Benefit of Farting Explain'd*. London, 1722.

Quilligan, Maureen. *The Language of Allegory: Defining the Genre*. Ithaca: Cornell University Press, 1979.

Randolph, Mary Clare. "The Structural Design of the Formal Verse Satire." *Philological Quarterly* 21 (1942): 368–384.

Rashid, Salim. "The Irish School of Economic Development: 1720–1750." *The Manchester School* 56:4 (Dec. 1988): 358–362.

Rawson, Claude. *God, Gulliver, and Genocide: Barbarism and the European Imagination, 1492–1945*. Oxford: Oxford University Press, 2001.

R. C. *Minerva, or, the Art of Weaving Containing the Antiquity, Utility and Excellency of Weaving: Written in Verse and Divided into Three Parts*. London: Moxon, 1677.

Real, Hermann. *Securing Swift: Selected Essays*. Dublin: Maunsel, 2001.

Reflections and Resolutions for the Gentlemen of Ireland. Dublin, 1738.

Reflections on the National Debt; with Reasons for Reducing the Legal Interest; and Against a Public Loan. With Some Advice to the Electors of Members of Parliament. Dublin, 1731.

Regan, Shaun. "'Pranks Unfit for Naming': Pope, Curll, and the 'Satirical Grotesque.'" *The Eighteenth Century* 46.1 (Spring 2005): 37–57.

Richards, Jennifer. *Rhetoric and Courtliness in Early Modern Literature*. Cambridge: Cambridge University Press, 2003.

Richardson, John. "Still to Seek: Politics, Irony, Swift." *Essays in Criticism* 49.4 (Oct. 1999): 300–318.

Rodino, Richard. "'Splendide Mendax': Authors, Characters, and Readers in Gulliver's Travels." *PMLA* 106:5 (Oct. 1991): 1054–1070.

Roncaglia, Alessandro. *Petty: The Origins of Political Economy*. Translated by Isabella Cherubini. Armonk, N.Y.: M. E. Sharp, 1985.

Rose, Craig. *England in the 1690s: Revolution, Religion, and War*. Oxford: Blackwell, 1999.

Rose, Jonathan. "The History of Books: Revised and Enlarged." *Studies on Voltaire and the Eighteenth Century* 359 (1998): 83–104.

Rosenheim, Edward W., Jr., *Swift and the Satirist's Art*. Chicago: University of Chicago Press, 1963.

Roseveare, Henry. *The Treasury: The Evolution of a British Institution*. New York: Columbia University Press, 1969.

Rowley, Hercules. *An Answer to a Book, Intitl'd, Reasons Offer'd for Erecting a Bank in Ireland. In a Letter to Henry Maxwell, Esq*. Dublin: Geo. Grierson, 1721.

Ryder, Michael. "The Bank of Ireland, 1721: Land, Credit, and Dependency." *Historical Journal* 25.3 (1982): 557–582.

Saccamano, Neil. "Authority and Publication: The Works of 'Swift.'" *The Eighteenth Century: Theory and Interpretation* 25.3 (Fall 1984): 241–262.

Said, Edward. *Culture and Imperialism*. New York: Vintage, 1994.

———. *The World, the Text, and the Critic*. Cambridge: Harvard University Press, 1983.

San Juan, E. "The Anti-Poetry of Jonathan Swift." In *Essential Articles for the Study of Jonathan Swift's Poetry*, edited by David M. Vieth, 21–32. Hamden, Conn.: Archon Books, 1984.

Schmitt, Carl. *Political Theology: Four Chapters on the Concept of Sovereignty*. Translated by George Schwab. Cambridge: MIT Press, 1985.

Schwoerer, Lois. *The Ingenious Mr. Henry Care, Restoration Publicist*. Baltimore: Johns Hopkins University Press, 2001.

Scriblerus, Martin. "Peri Bathos, or, The Art of Sinking in Poetry." In vol. 10 of *The Works of Alexander Pope*, edited by John W. Croker, Whitwell Elwin and William J. Courthope, 344–409. London: J. Murray, 1871–1889.

Shaftesbury, Anthony Ashley Cooper. *Characteristicks of Men, Manners, Opinions, Times*. Edited by Philip Ayres. 2 vols. Oxford: Clarendon Press, 1999.

Sharpe, Kevin. *Reading Revolutions: The Politics of Reading in Early Modern England*. New Haven: Yale University Press, 2000.

Sher, Richard. *The Enlightenment and the Book: Scottish Authors and Their Publishers in Eighteenth-Century Britain, Ireland, and America*. Chicago: University of Chicago Press, 2006.

Sherman, Sandra. *Finance and Fictionality in the Early Eighteenth Century: Accounting for Defoe*. Cambridge: Cambridge University Press, 1996.

Simms, J. G. "The Establishment of Protestant Ascendancy." In vol. 4 of *A New History of Ireland*, edited by T. W. Moody and W. E. Vaughn, 1–30. Oxford: Clarendon Press, 1986.

Siskin, Clifford. *The Work of Writing: Literature and Social Change in Britain, 1700–1830*. Baltimore: Johns Hopkins University Press, 1998.

Smith, Charles K. "Towards a 'Participatory Rhetoric': Teaching Swift's *Modest Proposal*." *College English* 30.2 (Nov. 1968): 135–149.

Smyth of Barbavilla Papers. British Library. London. This book references copies of these papers at the National Library of Ireland, Dublin.

Southwell Papers. British Library. London. This book references copies of the papers at the Public Record Office of Northern Ireland, Belfast, and the Huntington Library, San Marino, Calif.

Speck, W. A. *The Birth of Britain: A New Nation, 1700–1710*. Oxford: Blackwell, 1994.

———. *Reluctant Revolutionaries: Englishmen and the Revolution of 1688*. Oxford: Oxford University Press, 1988.

Spenser, Edmund. *A View of the State of Ireland, Written Dialogue-Wise, Betweene Eudoxus and Irenaeus.* In *Ancient Irish Histories: The Works of Spencer, Campion, Hanmer, and Marleburrough,* edited by James Ware, 1–266. Dublin: Hibernia Press, 1809.

Spivak, Gayatri. *Outside in the Teaching Machine.* New York: Routledge, 1993.

Stallybrass, Peter, and Allon White. *The Politics and Poetics of Transgression.* Ithaca: Cornell University Press, 1989.

State Papers Ireland. Public Record Office, London. This book references the copies of these papers at the National Library of Ireland, Dublin.

Sundell, Kirsten. "'A Savage and Unnatural Taste': Anglo-Irish Imitations of *A Modest Proposal.*" *Swift Studies* 18 (2003): 80–98.

Sussman, Charlotte. "The Colonial Afterlife of Political Arithmetic: Swift, Demography, and Mobile Populations." *Cultural Critique* 56 (Winter 2004): 96–126.

———. *Consuming Anxieties: Consumer Protest, Gender, and British Slavery, 1713–1833.* Stanford: Stanford University Press, 2000.

Swift, Jonathan. *The Correspondence of Jonathan Swift.* Edited by Harold Williams. 5 vols. Oxford: Clarendon Press, 1963–1965.

———. *Gulliver's Travels.* Edited by Albert Rivero. New York: Norton, 2002.

———. *Jonathan Swift: The Complete Poems.* Edited by Pat Rogers. New Haven: Yale University Press, 1983.

———. *Journal to Stella.* Edited by Harold Williams. Oxford: Clarendon Press, 1948.

———. *Miscellanies.* 4th ed. London, 1722.

———. *The Poems of Jonathan Swift.* Edited by Harold Williams. 3 vols. Oxford: Clarendon Press, 1937.

———. *Swift: Poetical Works.* Edited by Herbert Davis. London: Oxford University Press, 1967.

———. *The Prose Works of Jonathan Swift.* Edited by Herbert Davis. 14 vols. Oxford: Blackwell, 1939–1968.

———. *A Tale of a Tub and Other Works.* Edited by Angus Ross and David Woolley. Oxford: Oxford University Press, 1986.

Swift, Jonathan, and Thomas Sheridan. *The Intelligencer.* Edited James Woolley. Oxford: Oxford University Press, 1992.

Szeman, Imre. "Who's Afraid of National Allegory." *South Atlantic Quarterly* 100.3 (Summer 2001): 803–827.

The Tatler; or, Lucubrations of Isaac Bickerstaff, Esq. 4 vols. London: Tonson, 1764.

Thompson, James. *Models of Value: Eighteenth-Century Political Economy and the Novel.* Durham: Duke University Press, 1996.

Thorne, Christian. "Thumbing Our Nose at the Public Sphere: Satire, the Market, and the Invention of Literature." *PMLA* 116:3 (May 2001): 531–544.

Treadwell, Michael. "Benjamin Motte, Andrew Tooke, and *Gulliver's Travels*." In *Proceedings of the First Münster Symposium on Jonathan Swift*, edited by Hermann J. Real and Heinz J. Vienken, 287–304. Munich: Wilhelm Fink Verlag, 1985.

———. "Observations on the Printing of Motte's Octavo Editions of *Gulliver's Travels*." In *Reading Swift: Papers from the Third Münster Symposium on Jonathan Swift*, edited by Hermann J. Real and Helgard Stöver-Leidig, 157–177. Munich: Wilhelm Fink Verlag, 1998.

———. "Swift's Relations with the London Book Trade to 1714." In *Author/Publisher Relations During the Eighteenth and Nineteenth Centuries*. Edited by Robin Myers and Michael Harris, 1–36. Oxford: Oxford Polytechnic Press, 1983.

———. "The Text of *Gulliver's Travels*, Again." *Swift Studies* 10 (1995): 62–79.

Trivedi, Lisa. *Clothing Gandhi's Nation: Homespun and Modern India*. Indianapolis: Indiana University Press, 2007.

The True Picture of an Ancient Tory, in a Dialogue between Vassal a Tory, and Freeman a Whig. London, 1702.

Victory, Isolde Louise. "Colonial Nationalism in Ireland, 1692–1725: From Common Law to Natural Right." Ph.D. diss., Trinity College Dublin, 1984.

Viswanathan, Gauri. *Masks of Conquest: Literary Study and British Rule in India*. New York: Columbia University Press, 1989.

Voigt, Milton. *Swift and the Twentieth Century*. Detroit: Wayne State University Press, 1964.

Walsh, Marcus. "Swift and Religion." In *The Cambridge Companion to Jonathan Swift*, edited by Christopher Fox, 161–176. Cambridge: Cambridge University Press, 2003.

———. "Text, 'Text,' and Swift's *A Tale of a Tub*." In *Jonathan Swift: A Collection of Critical Essays*, edited by Claude Rawson, 290–303. Englewood Cliffs, N.J.: Prentice Hall, 1995.

Ward, Edward. *The Auction, or the Poet Turn'd Painter. By the Author of The Step to the Bath*. London, 1703.

Warner, Michael. *The Letters of the Republic: Publication and the Public Sphere in Eighteenth Century America*. Cambridge: Harvard University Press, 1990.

———. *Licensing Entertainment: The Elevation of Novel Reading in Britain, 1684–1750*. Berkeley: University of California Press, 1998.

Watt, Ian. *The Rise of the Novel: Studies in Defoe, Richardson and Fielding*. London: Chatto & Windus, 1957.

Webster, Wendy. *Englishness and Empire, 1939-1965*. Oxford: Oxford University Press, 2005.

Weinbrot, Howard D. *Menippean Satire Reconsidered: From Antiquity to the Eighteenth Century*. Baltimore: Johns Hopkins University Press, 2005.

Weitzman, Arthur J. "A Spider's Poison: Wit in Swift's 'Letter of Advice to a Young Poet.'" *Ariel: A Review of International English Literature* 4.1 (1973): 24–34.

Williams, Harold. "Review." *Review of English Studies* 13.51 (July 1937): 366–373.

Wittkowsky, George. "Swift's Modest Proposal: The Biography of an Early Georgian Pamphlet." *Journal of the History of Ideas* 4.1 (Jan. 1943): 81–101.

Woolley, James. "Poor John Harding and Mad Tom: 'Harding's Resurrection' (1724)." In *That Woman! Studies in Irish Bibliography: A Festschrift for Mary 'Paul' Pollard*, edited by Charles Benson and Siobhan Fitzpatrick, 102–121. Dublin: Lilliput Press / Library Association of Ireland Rare Books Group, 2005.

———. "Sarah Harding as Swift's Printer." In *Walking Naboth's Vineyard: New Studies of Swift*, edited by Christopher Fox, 164–177. Notre Dame: University of Notre Dame Press, 1995.

———. *Swift's Later Poems: Studies in Circumstances and Texts*. New York: Garland, 1988.

Wyrick, Deborah Baker. *Jonathan Swift and the Vested Word*. Chapel Hill: University of North Carolina Press, 1988.

York, Neil Longley. *Neither Kingdom nor Nation: The Irish Quest for Constitutional Rights, 1698-1800*. Washington, D.C.: Catholic University Press, 1994.

Young, Heather. "Satire as a Virus: Generic Inhabitation and Transformation in Swift's *Tale*." *Swift Studies* 21 (2006): 48–55.

Zimbardo, Rose. "The Semiotics of Restoration Satire." In *Cutting Edges: Postmodern Critical Essays on Eighteenth-Century Satire*, edited by James Gill, 23–42. Knoxville: University of Tennessee Press, 1995.

Zimmerman, Everett. *Swift's Narrative Satires: Author and Authority*. Ithaca: Cornell University Press, 1983.

Zomchick, John. "Satire and the Bourgeois Subject in Frances Burney's *Evelina*." In *Cutting Edges: Postmodern Critical Essays on Eighteenth-Century Satire*, edited by James Gill, 347–366. Knoxville: University of Tennessee Press, 1995.

58, 60, 68–72, 80–83, 85, 88, 115–116,
118, 130–167, 174, 178, 191–192, 194,
196, 202; and American colonies,
161; and epistemology, 162–167; and
identity, 58, 135–137, 152, 162–167. *See
also* minting

custom. *See* memory, social

Darnton, Robert, 17
Davenant, Charles, 81
Davies, John, 36–37
Davis, Herbert, 63, 185
Dean, Jodi, 155
Deane, Seamus, 24
de Bolla, Peter, 178
Debt of the Nation (Ireland), 4–6, 23,
37–39, 54–55, 59, 62, 135, 137, 149,
168–170, 174, 180–181, 184–188, 190–
191, 194–195
Declaratory Act, 4, 6, 29, 37, 56–59,
61–62, 66, 70, 83–87, 93, 119–120,
150, 181–182
decolonization, 28, 107, 109, 111. *See also*
colonialism; postcolonial theory
Defoe, Daniel, 26, 67–68, 78, 102, 113,
126, 129
Delany, Mary, 212
Delany, Patrick, 197, 212
Derrida, Jacques, 104
Dickson, P. G. M., 75
Dissenters, 23, 42, 85, 104, 154, 198–
199. *See also* Presbyterianism
Downie, J. A., 41
Dryden, John, 66, 173
Dunlevy, Mairead, 32
Dutch Republic, 44–45, 85, 195

East India Company, 26, 42, 45, 75
economics. *See* political economy
Egmont, 1st Earl of (John Perceval)
Ehrenpreis, Irvin, 23, 151, 161, 211
Elizabeth I, Queen, 47, 118
"English interest," 182–183, 196
Enlightenment, British, 9, 15–17, 92–93,
106–134, 155, 167
Enlightenment, Irish, 92–93, 108, 122,
124, 134
epistemology, 121–133, 136, 162–167
Exclusion Crisis, 42

famine, 170, 180, 184.
Faulkner, George. *See under* booksellers,
bookselling, and printers (Irish)
Fauske, Christopher, 150
feminist criticism. *See* gender criticism
Ferguson, Oliver, 180
financial revolution, English, 1, 11–13,
15, 28, 40, 43, 106, 108, 115, 117, 120,
124, 170, 178, 188. *See also* financial
revolution, Irish
financial revolution, Irish, 3–4, 15, 29,
58. *See also* Debt of the Nation; *Monti*
fiscal-military state, 1–2, 10, 12–14, 16,
22, 24, 28–29, 40, 42–43, 55, 71, 101–
103, 107–109, 111, 116, 119, 123–127,
133, 170–171, 179
Ford, Charles, 31, 122
Forman, Charles, 173
Foster, Roy, 49
France, 44, 47, 78–79, 81, 155, 168, 177,
184

Gay, John, 67, 101, 113, 172–173, 186,
204, 206
Gee, Sophie, 115
gender criticism, 10–11, 170–171, 173–
174, 179, 212–213
George I, King, 85, 146, 148, 151, 159
George II, King, 203
Gillespie, Raymond, 46
Glendinning, Victoria, 40
globalization, 215–216
Glorious Revolution, 40–43, 55, 101,
110–111, 113, 177, 181
Godolphin, Sidney, 45
Goux, Jean-Joseph, 14
Grand Alliance of the League of Augsburg, 44
Great Britain
—currency of (sterling), 1, 48, 69, 135–
136, 151–152, 156–162, 165–167
—financial system of: Exchequer, 143,
Treasury, 40, 55, 178. *See also* Bank of
England
—military of, 40, 159–160 (*see also*
fiscal-military state)
—national debt of, 1, 3–4, 40, 43, 172–
173, 178–179, 183, 186
—nationalism in, 9–10

Great Britain (*continued*)
—national security in, 41, 163 (*see also* fiscal-military state)
—political institutions in: crown, the, 9–10, 144, 150, 181–182, 193–194, 198, 201, 205; Parliament, 29, 37, 47–50, 57, 59, 75, 85–86, 144, 148, 158, 165, 181, 198; prime minister, 181, 183–184 (*see also* Walpole, Robert); Privy Council, 159
—religion of, 103–106, 111. *See also* Church of England; Dissenters; Presbyterianism; Roman Catholicism
—revenue and taxation in, 1, 40, 43–45, 47–49, 124, 173, 178–179
Gresham's Law, 151, 157–158, 160
Grierson, George and Constantia *See under* booksellers, bookselling, and printers (Irish)
Grimston, William Luckyn, 38–39, 94
Grub Street, 66–67, 173–174, 199–200, 203–204
Gunn, J. A. W., 154

Habermas, Jürgen, 45, 113, 172, 191
Hall, F. G., 61
Harth, Philip, 206–207
Hawes, Clement, 124–126, 179
Hayton, David, 187
Haywood, Eliza, 174
Higgins, Ian, 41, 177
historical bibliography. *See* history of the book
history of the book: and *The Battle of the Books*, 90, 93, 95–101; and *A Defence of English Commodities*, 93–95, 101; and English publishing, 18, 45–47, 90–133; and *Gulliver's Travels*, 90–93, 121–133; and Irish publishing, 2, 6, 18–19, 25, 51–56, 58–59, 62–68, 90–93, 108, 117–118, 121, 133, 138–142, 146–150, 162–167, 169–171, 174–176, 179–180, 190–197, 199–201, 206–211, 214; and *A Modest Proposal*, 168–189; and *A Proposal for the Universal Use of Irish Manufacture*, 26–40, 55–56, 62, 94–95, 101; scatology

and, 106–120; and *A Tale of a Tub*, 90, 93, 99–106; theory of, 17–19
Hobbes, Thomas, 41, 106, 220n18
Holland. *See* Dutch Republic
Holt, Douglas, 215

identity: Anglo-Irish, 4, 15, 23, 38, 54, 57, 94, 135, 152, 162, 166–167, 169–170; British, 9–14, 27–28, 53, 94, 114, 136, 152, 162, 166–167, 178, 204; Irish, 2, 6, 15, 23–24, 28, 58, 59, 68, 89, 135–136, 152, 193, 211, 214–216; Scots-Irish (Ulster Scots), 52. *See also* Protestant interest, Irish; *Monti*
imagined communities, 9–10, 12, 16, 19, 28, 32, 58, 62–63, 83, 100, 115, 136, 139, 170, 211, 214
imperialism. *See* colonialism; Great Britain; postcolonial theory
Importation Act of 1739, 53, 92, 210
India, 26–27
Ingrassia, Catherine, 10–11, 67, 115
ink production, 97–98
Ireland
—banks, private, in, 70–71, 82, 151
—culture in. *See under* identity
—currency of, 60, 68, 70, 82, 134–167, 174, 191, 194, 196. *See also* Swift, Jonathan, works by: *The Drapier's Letters*
—economic development in, 29–31, 61, 169–170, 174–177
—educational institutions in: Incorporated Society for Protestant Schools, 192; Trinity College Dublin, 47, 67
—financial system of, 159, 171–172, 180–188; Exchequer, 143, 184; Treasury, 54–56, 62, 158, 180–182, 195; *See also* Bank of Ireland; Debt of the Nation; *Monti*
—military in, 137, 159–160
—national debt of. *See* Debt of the Nation
—national security in, 3, 6, 163, 195. *See also Monti*
—political institutions in: Commissioners of the Revenue, 150–151, 158–159, 160, 187; crown, the, 150, 158, 181–182, 185, 193–194; Lord Lieuten-

minting, 135, 144–146, 150; homology of, with printing, 135–136, 138–142, 149, 201–202, 204; and Irish mint, 135, 142–143, 145, 149

Mississippi Company, 60, 79, 180

modernity and modernization, 24–25, 122–125, 129, 136, 156, 170, 208

Molesworth, Robert, 146–148

Molyneux, William, 39, 47, 50–51, 57, 61, 89, 91

money. *See* currency

money bill dispute of 1753, 5

moneyed interest, 40, 42–45, 60–62, 69, 71, 73, 81–82, 84, 87, 154, 173

Monti, 5–8, 15, 17, 22–24, 29, 45, 49, 54–56, 58–59, 61–62, 66, 68–70, 73–74, 76–77, 79, 82–85, 108, 120, 124, 133–137, 149, 152, 156, 158, 167–170, 176, 190–191, 195, 199

Moor, Roger, 145

Moxon, James, 34, 36

Moxon, Joseph, 27, 33–34, 66, 194

national debt, 1, 3–6, 10–11, 13–14, 40, 43–45, 169, 172–174, 178–179, 183–184, 186–188. *See also* Debt of the Nation

Netherlands. *See* Dutch Republic

new criticism, 72

new economic criticism, 10–16, 67, 78, 115, 180

New England, 83–84, 161

Nicholson, Colin, 10–13

Nicolson, William (bishop of Londonderry), 31

nomos, 37, 41, 120

novel, 93, 121–122, 126–127, 129–130, 133, 191

Oakleaf, David, 42, 228n119

Ohlmeyer, Jane, 49

O'Regan, Philip, 61

Ovid, 32–33, 36, 95

Oxford, 1st Earl of (Robert Harley), 43

paper credit, 1, 10–12, 31, 68–74, 77–78, 81–82, 84–85, 88, 115, 118, 120

papermaking, 32, 36, 97–98, 175

papists. *See* Jacobites; James II, King; Roman Catholicism

parody, 19, 64, 78, 93, 102, 106, 110, 114, 121, 133, 169, 175, 177, 189, 195, 212–213

Parsons, Jotham, 14, 144

Partition Treaty, 44

patriot discourse: British, 40; Irish, 2, 6–8, 10, 17, 19, 21, 24, 29–30, 32, 37, 39, 46, 54, 58, 61, 83, 87, 121, 135–136, 140, 146, 148–149, 174, 186, 193, 196, 204, 207–208, 211, 214

penal laws, Irish, 3, 153–154

Petty, William, 3, 81

Phiddian, Robert, 13, 103

Pilkington, Laetitia, 212

Pilkington, Matthew, 123, 194, 205, 209, 212

Pincus, Steven, 42

Plato, 103–104, 171

Pocock, J. G. A., 36–37, 155–156

politeness, ideology of, 93, 106–107, 109–118, 121, 139

political economy, 6–9, 15, 23, 29–31, 42, 58, 64, 81, 89, 135, 137, 162–167, 169–170, 174–177, 190–191, 193–199

political theology, 101, 127

political thought: British, 1–2, 36–37, 40–45, 73, 111; Irish, 1–8, 14–15, 46–51, 56–57, 61–62, 83–89, 139–162, 168–170, 180–188, 193–199

Pollard, Mary, 19, 46

Poovey, Mary, 164

Pope, Alexander, 67, 100–101, 113, 121, 172–174, 184–186, 194, 199–200, 203–204, 206–207, 209

postcolonial theory, 13–15, 17, 21–23, 29, 46, 72, 110–111, 124–126, 166–167, 179–180, 214–216

Presbyterianism, 3, 52, 104, 154

pretender. *See* Jacobites; James II

Price, Leah, 17

print capitalism, 9–10, 16

print culture: British, 18, 186, 191; Irish, 2, 6–10, 12–13, 15–19, 21–25, 150, 162–167, 169–170, 174–176, 191, 194–195, 213–214. *See also* booksellers, bookselling, and printers (English);

booksellers, bookselling, and printers (Irish); history of the book

printing, history of, 34, 98–99

Probyn, Clive, 26, 190

Protestant interest, Irish, 3–4, 29, 47–48, 50, 55, 61–62, 67, 85, 95, 135, 150, 152, 154, 172, 174, 177, 180, 184. *See also* identity: Anglo-Irish; *Monti*

public credit, 10, 12

public opinion, 6–8, 14, 18–19, 23, 26, 29, 38–39, 45–46, 51, 54–57, 60, 62, 84, 102, 111, 126, 133–134, 136, 146, 148–149, 150, 153–155, 159, 170

public sphere, British, 10, 45, 101–102, 106, 110–121, 126, 133, 142, 169–170, 172, 191, 200, 202–203

public sphere, Irish, 7, 24, 54, 56, 62, 64, 67–68, 77, 83, 87, 89, 118, 120, 134–136, 148–151, 153–155, 169–170, 176, 190–191, 200, 202–203, 213–214, 216. *See also* Habermas, Jürgen

publishing. *See* booksellers, bookselling, and printers (English); booksellers, bookselling, and printers (Irish); history of the book; print capitalism; print culture; printing, history of

Quakers, 153

Quilligan, Maureen, 22

Rashid, Salim, 163

Rawson, Claude, 180

realism, 120, 122, 126, 128–130, 133

Reformation, Protestant, 2–3

republics and republicanism, 3–4, 24, 44, 55, 116, 156, 177–178

rhetoric, 37–38, 57, 62, 64, 89, 108, 113, 116, 170, 173, 175, 179, 188

Rodino, Richard, 129

Rogers, Pat, 72

Roman Catholicism, 2–4, 23, 49, 80–81, 85, 104–105, 141, 152–154, 157, 159–160, 177, 183

Rowley, Hercules, 84, 86–88, 153–154

Royal Africa Company, 42

Royal Society, 125, 127

"rump, the," 116, 118

Ryder, Michael, 61–62, 82

Sacramental Test for Dissenting Protestants, 198–199. *See also* Dissenters

Said, Edward, 13, 46, 200

satire, 12–13, 19–24, 68–74, 82, 92–94, 99–103, 106–133, 138, 154–155, 168–172, 194–196, 200, 202; financial, 12–13, 68–74, 82, 108, 120, 206–207; Horatian, 72; Juvenalian, 72; Menippean, 102–103, 124–125; scatological, 18, 36, 78, 93–94, 100, 106–121, 205; Scriblerian, 72, 101–102, 113–116, 172–174, 177, 187, 200–201, 203. *See also* allegory; irony; parody

scientific revolution, 22, 123–125, 127, 132

Scotland, 27, 50, 54–55, 203–204

Scriblerians (Scriblerus Club), 72, 101–102, 113–116, 172–174, 177–179, 182, 186–188, 199, 200–201, 203. *See also* Gay, John; Pope, Alexander

secret service. *See* Concordatum

Seven Years War, 168

Shaftesbury, 3rd Earl of (Anthony Ashley Cooper), 110–114

Sher, Richard, 92, 192

Sheridan, Thomas, 197

Sherman, Sandra, 10–11, 78

Simms, J. G., 50

Simpson, Ralph, 99

Siskin, Clifford, 8–9, 107

South Sea Act, 56, 70

South Sea Bubble, 4, 6, 16, 59–60, 63, 65, 68–77, 79, 83, 89, 93, 108, 116, 120, 134, 172, 180–181, 204

South Sea Company, 44, 56, 58, 60, 70–71, 73–77, 82, 85, 109, 171–172, 204

Southwell, Edward, 187

sovereignty, 2, 6, 9–10, 50–51, 57, 104, 125–127, 214–216; and American colonies, 50–51, 168; and bookselling/printing prerogative, 6, 14, 16, 29, 40, 45, 52, 108, 125–126, 131, 133–135, 139, 142, 150, 211–212, 191; and Britain, 36–37, 43–45, 74, 87, 95, 111; and currency/minting, 15–16, 58, 131–132, 135–136, 139–140, 142–144, 149, 150, 156, 162–163, 165, 167; and Jacques Derrida, 104; and epistemology,

sovereignty (*continued*)
125–127, 131–134, 162–163, 165, 167;
and Ireland, 23, 26, 28–29, 36–37,
39–40, 47, 50–51, 57–58, 61, 68, 74,
84, 86–87, 95, 108, 110, 120, 133,
135–136, 146, 168–169, 171, 181, 187,
189, 191, 207, 211, 214–216; and postcolonial theory, 13–15, 28–29, 51, 111,
125–127

Spain, 44, 168

Speck, W. A., 42

Spenser, Edmund, 49, 118

Sprat, Thomas, 128

Stamp Act, 53

Stationer's Company of London, 33,
51–52, 96

Stearne, John (bishop of Clogher), 75,
76

Steele, Richard, 45, 111–112, 114

"stuff(s)," 17, 32, 35, 139, 147–148. *See
also* papermaking; textiles; weavers
and weaving

Sundell, Kirsten, 194

Sunderland, Duke of, 45

Swift, Jonathan, works by: *An Account
of the Short Life, Sudden Death, and
Pompous Funeral of Michy Windy-
bank, & c.*, 119; *The Advantages Pro-
posed by Repealing the Sacramental
Test*, 198; *Advice to the Free-Men of
the City of Dublin in the Choice of a
Member to Represent Them in Parliament*, 196–197; *An Answer to the
Ballyspellin Ballad*, 208; *The Bank
Thrown Down, To an Excellent New
Tune*, 78, 81–82; *The Battle of the
Books*, 18, 32, 90, 93, 95–101, 121,
128–129; *The Bubble*, 63, 69–72; *A
Character, Panegyric, and Description of the Legion Club*, 198; *Collected
Works*, 200, 207–212; *Concerning
that Universal Hatred, which Prevails
against the Clergy*, 198; *The Conduct
of the Allies*, 40, 44–45; *Considerations upon Two Bills*, 198; *Directions
to Servants*, 208; *A Discourse of the
Contests and Dissensions Between
the Nobles and Commons in Athens
and Rome*, 99; *The Drapier's Letters*,
23–24, 120, 132, 134–167, 169, 176,
190–191, 195–196, 199, 202–203, 208
(*see also individual letter titles in this
list*); *Epistle to a Lady*, 193, 200–201,
205; *An Essay upon an Epistle from
a Certain Doctor to a Certain Great
Lord, Being a Christmas Box for D.
D—ny*, 197; *An Examination of Certain Abuses, Corruptions, and Enormities, in the City of Dublin*, 196; *The
Examiner*, 40, 43–44, 173; *Gulliver's
Travels (Travels into Several Remote
Nations of the World . . .)*, 18, 22–23,
43, 63, 90–93, 99, 121–133, 172, 182,
186, 208; *Hints Towards an Essay
on Conversation*, 114; *An Humble
Address to Both Houses of Parliament*, 146, 149–150, 156; *An Infallible
Scheme to Pay the Public Debt of this
Nation in Six Months*, 194–195; *Intelligencer*, 180, 182; *Lady A-S-N Weary
of the Dean*, 184; *A Letter from a Lady
in Town to her Friend in the Country,
Concerning the Bank, Or, the List of
the Subscribers Farther Explain'd*,
80–81; *A Letter on the Fishery*,
194–196; *A Letter to Mr. Harding
the Printer*, 140–141, 147; *A Letter to
the Archbishop of Dublin, Concerning the Weavers*, 174; *A Letter to the
King at Arms*, 79; *A Letter to the Lord
Chancellor Middleton*, 146, 148–149;
*A Letter to the Right Honourable the
Lord Viscount Molesworth*, 146–148;
*A Letter to the Shop-Keepers, Trades-
men, Farmers, and Common-People
of Ireland*, 139–140, 147, 157; *A Letter to the Whole People of Ireland*,
140–142, 146–147, 152–154; *A Libel
on D— D— and a Certain Great Lord*,
197, 206–207, 209; *Mad Mullinix
and Timothy*, 182–183; *Maxims
Controlled in Ireland*, 57–58; *The
Mechanical Operation of the Spirit*,
93, 99; *Miscellanies in Prose and
Verse*, 121, 193, 199, 206, 208–209;
A Modest Proposal, 20–21, 64, 120,
167–190, 193–195, 199; *Observations
Occasioned by Reading a Paper En-*

War of the Spanish Succession, 43–45

weavers and weaving, 22, 26–27, 30, 32–36, 142, 174, 194, 197; guild of, 27; as metaphors for writing and printing, 22, 26–27, 29, 32–36, 139, 142, 147, 175, 197, 210; and social memory, 36–37. *See also* print culture; textiles

Weinbrot, Howard, 105

Wharton, 1st Earl of (Thomas Wharton), 118

Whigs, 40–45, 69, 101–102, 106, 110–116, 118, 129, 137, 169–170, 172–175, 177–179, 182–184, 188, 193, 197, 200–201, 203–204, 206

Whitshed, William (Lord Chief Justice of Ireland), 150

William III, King, 3, 43–44, 144

Williams, Harold, 225n15

Wood, William, 134, 138, 140, 141–142, 145–146, 149, 151–152, 159, 161, 202

Wood's halfpence, 134, 136–139, 141–142, 144–145, 147–152, 157–159, 166, 196. *See also* currency; Swift, Jonathan, works by: *The Drapier's Letters*; Wood, William

wool, 21, 30–34, 37, 39, 47, 94–95, 143, 147–149, 194, 197, 210–211. *See also* textiles

Wool Act, 30, 33, 37, 39, 47. *See also* textiles

Woolley, James, 180

"World Bank literature," 13. *See also* postcolonial theory

Worrall, John, 208

Wotton, William, 96, 98–99

Wyrick, Deborah Baker, 104

Zimmerman, Everett, 18